Moving Dhamma

Volume 1

Bhante Vimalaraṁsi

Copyright © Bhante Vimalaraṁsi
All rights reserved.
ISBN-13: 978-1478373063, ISBN-10: 1478373067
1st print: December 1, 2012

Other books by Bhante Vimalaramsi:

*The Anapanasati Sutta:
A Practical Guide to Mindfulness of Breathing and
Tranquil Wisdom*
(2006)

Breath of Love
(2012)

Dhamma Sukha Meditation Center
8218 County Road 204, Annapolis, MO 63620 USA
www.dhammasukha.org
info@dhammasukha.org
Phone: +1 (573) 546-1214

Dedication

For all present and future students of the Buddha and his teachings.
"Strive on with Diligence."
The Buddha

Table of Contents

Dedication v
Table of Contents vii
Preface ix
Acknowledgements xi
Introduction xiii
Mindfulness and the Six R's xv
Orientation From Joshua Tree #5 Retreat 1
MN-20: The Removal of Distracting Thoughts
    (Vitakkasaṇṭhāna Sutta) 25
MN-10: The Foundations of Mindfulness
    (Satipaṭṭhāna Sutta) 53
MN-111: One By One As They Occurred
    (Anupada Sutta) 113
MN-38: The Greater Discourse on the Destruction of
    Craving (Mahātaṇhāsankhaya Sutta) 145
MN-135: The Shorter Discourse of Action
    (Cūḷakammavibhanga Sutta) 183
MN-95: With Cankī (Cankī Sutta) 209
MN-148: The Six Sets of Six (Chachakka Sutta) 237
MN-21: The Simile of the Saw (Kakacūpama Sutta) 261
About the Author 295
Index of Suttas 297
Glossary – Frequent Substitutions 299

Preface

This book of Dhamma Talks is an explanation of the earliest Buddhist Suttas available. By reading them and having practiced what is written there, I explain their meaning as it affects the meditation practice.

My life as a monk has been trying to find the earliest teachings that the Buddha gave to his Disciples and his Saṅgha of Monks 2600 years ago. I have spent the last 37 years of my life doing just this. I did many practices during that time, but it was in 1995 that I decided to drop all other practices and just use the Majjhima Nikāya, which had just been translated and published by Bhikkhu Bodhi through Wisdom Publications, and to actually practice the meditation using only those as a guide and nothing else.

In a sense it was like remembering the experience of sitting under the rose apple tree after having been through 6 years of severe ascetic practice. I want to go back to what the Buddha was supposed to have said.

Amazingly, I found all of the Buddha's teachings contained right there. And by that I mean the entire meditation instructions, the progress of insight, and the final goal and how that is attained.

You need nothing else but the Majjhima Nikāya and the Saṃyutta Nikāya; however, but you do need a guide to help explain these if you have not been down this path before.

I have changed some words in the translations to other words with definitions that I think are closer to the original meaning of the Pāli and what I believe the Buddha really meant. For example, I use "Collectedness" vs. "Concentration." Also in some places of the Sutta I have put back in the older translation of the Sutta that was left out so that you may understand the meaning better.

The reader, if using an electronic file reader like a Kindle or an iPad, may wish to turn on the "text to speech" function to listen to these talks. This is the way they were given. They will have a more personal style than the reader may be used to in a book. They have been left unedited so the student may go to the Dhamma Sukha web site and listen to the audio if he/she wishes.

The teachings of the Buddha are right here. I hope you find these teachings as interesting as I have.

Bhante Vimalaraṁsi
Abbot of the Dhamma Sukha Meditation Center
UIBDS United International Buddha Dhamma Society
July 15, 2012

Acknowledgements

David Johnson compiled and edited these talks and organized all of this material, while Christopher Farrant in Australia, our proofreader and editor, would sometimes spend sleepless nights, working around the clock on perfecting the rough transcripts.

Sukha Sisso, the Dhamma Sukha webmaster in Texas, originally gathered all of the transcripts together with the audios, and did most of the early audio and transcript editing work. An additional mention may be made of the few people who did a couple of transcripts from home and submitted those to our webmaster.

Many thanks to Jens Tröger, who went through this manuscript and who spent many days transcribing it into eBooks of different formats; and who contributed the cover art. Also to Doug Kraft who helped us get this into a format that would be accepted by the publisher.

And of course to the Students who kept asking good questions so that many issues could be raised and answered.

An additional book will be available later with more talks.

Sutta translation © Bhikkhu Bodhi 1995, 2001. Reprinted from The Middle Length Discourses of the Buddha: A Translation of the Majjhima Nikāya; and The Connected Discourses of the Buddha: A Translation of the Saṃyutta Nikāya. With permission of Wisdom Publications, 199 Elm Street, Somerville, MA 02144 U.S.A., www.wisdompubs.org

I share the merit of this book with all my students, past and present, the editors and collaborators of this book, Bhikkhu Bodhi and Wisdom Publications, and with my parents who supported and raised me.

Introduction

Bhante Vimalaraṁsi is an American Buddhist Monk of over 25 years. He started when he was 28 years old practicing meditation in California in the Burmese style of Vipassanā. Gradually he gave up the material world and got on a plane for Thailand where he became a monk in 1986. He then went on to practice meditation intensively doing thirty days, three months retreats, and even a two years retreat in Burma under Sayadaw U Janaka.

At the end of this two years retreat his Burmese meditation teacher told him they had nothing left to teach him; he was now ready to go and teach on his own. Even with these high remarks a feeling that there was something more to learn kept nagging at him.

He went on to Malaysia and instead of Vipassanā taught Mettā (Loving-Kindness) Meditation.

In Sri Lanka Bhante took the advice of a monk to use only the suttas, and he obtained a copy of Bhikkhu Bodhi's translation of the Majjhima Nikāya and headed off for a cave in Thailand where he spent three months practicing with the Suttas as a guide and a cobra for company!

He started doing just what the Suttas stated. He found out that in the Suttas there was another step that appears to have been left out by later day teachers. The idea of "Tranquilizing the bodily formations" (sankhāra) was included in the Satipaṭṭhāna Sutta yet had never been mentioned by other teachers Bhante studied with. (Check the chapter on MN-10, the Satipaṭṭhāna Sutta, in this book.)

When he added this Relaxing step, the practice took on a completely new tone. The jhānas, as discussed in the Suttas, became very real but with a slightly different flavor which Bhante calls a "Tranquil Aware jhāna." When he added the relax step the meditation completely changed and progress was very fast.

This book is the first book of a set of talks that Bhante gives on his 10 day retreats, many of which may be watched directly on the Internet. Unlike many other teachers he actually reads from the Sutta itself and then provides a commentary that explains what the Buddha meant. Every night the student hears a Sutta that is geared to where they are in their daily progress on the retreat. Also, unlike other teachers, he invites questions from the audience and wants to make sure that everyone has understood the text as it is written.

Bhante uses and prefers the translations that are done by Bhikkhu Bodhi vs. other translations that exist. He also will replace certain words as he reads from the book with his own interpretation of what the word should really be. For example, whenever the word "concentration" is written in the Suttas, Bhante will say "collectedness" which he believes is a better translation. So the reader should be aware that Bhante will, at times, substitute his own translation as he reads along so that the text may not fully agree with the printed book by Wisdom Publications.

The book is made up of transcripts of Bhante's talks. Some of the talks have introductions that were written by Phra Khantiphalo, the editor of A Treasury of the Buddha's Words: Discourses From the Middle Collection, translated by Nyanamoli and edited by Phra Khantipalo, with notes by Phra Khantipalo. Then Bhante reads the Sutta and comments on them. The actual Sutta is **bolded** in the text of this book. Students ask questions periodically and he answers them, and then continues.

Bhante Vimalaraṁsi continues to give talks and retreats at his meditation center in Missouri, U.S.A and elsewhere around the world. You may see his web site at www.dhammasukha.org.

Mindfulness and the Six R's

Taken from the book "The Breath of Love" by Venerable Bhante Vimalaraṁsi

Mindfulness (sati) is "remembering to observe how mind's attention moves moment-to-moment and remembering what to do with any arising phenomena!" Successful meditation needs a highly developed skill of mindfulness. The 6R's training taught at Dhamma Sukha Meditation Center is a reclaimed ancient guidance system which develops this skill.

The first R is to Recognize but before we do it, the meditator must remember to use their observation power (mindfulness) for the meditation cycle to start running. Mindfulness is the fuel. It's just like gas for an engine. Without mindfulness, everything stops!

Being persistent with this practice will relieve suffering of all kinds.

To begin this cycle smoothly you must start the engine and have lots of gas (mindfulness) in the tank!

Meditation (bhāvanā) helps you to let go of such difficult delusional states in life as fear, anger, tension, stress, anxiety, depression, sadness, sorrow, fatigue, condemnation, feelings of helplessness, or whatever the "catch (attachment) of the day" happens to be. Delusional means here, taking things that arise personally and identifying with them to be "I," "Me," "Mine" or "atta" in Pāli. These states result in suffering that we cause ourselves. This suffering comes from a lack of understanding in how things actually occur.

The 6R's are steps which evolve into one fluid motion becoming a new wholesome habitual tendency that relieves any dis-ease in mind and body. This cycle begins when mindfulness remembers the 6R's which are:

1. Recognize
2. Release
3. Relax
4. Re-Smile
5. Return
6. Repeat

Development of mindfulness (your observation power) observes each step of the practice cycle. Once you understand what the purpose of mindfulness is, keeping it going all the time is no longer a problem, and this makes the meditation easier to understand, plus, it is much more fun to practice. It becomes a part of happy living and this brings up a smile. Remembering the 6R's leads you to having a wholesome uplifted mind.

This remembering by mindfulness is very important. Before practicing the 6R's you have to remember to start the cycle! That's the trick! You have to remember to gas-up the engine, so it can run smoothly!

Then we begin to:

Recognize: Mindfulness remembers how you can recognize and observe any movement of mind's attention from one thing to another. This observation notices any movement of mind's attention away from an object of meditation, such as the breath, sending out mettā, or doing a task in daily life. You will notice a slight tightness or tension sensation as mind's attention barely begins to move toward any arising phenomena.

Pleasant or painful feeling can occur at any one of the six sense doors. Any sight, sound, odor, taste, touch, or thought can cause this pulling sensation to begin. With careful non-judgmental observation, the meditator will notice a slight tightening sensation. Recognizing early movement is vital to successful meditation. You then continue on to:

Release: When a feeling or thought arises, you release it, let it be there without giving anymore attention to it. The content of the distraction is not important at all, but the mechanics of "how" it arose are important! Just let go of any tightness around it; let it be there without placing attention on it. Without attention, the tightness passes away. Mindfulness then reminds you to:

Relax: After releasing the feeling or sensation and allowing it to be there without trying to control it, there is a subtle, barely noticeable tension within mind/body. This is why the Relax step ("Tranquilization" step as stated in the suttas) is being pointed out by the Buddha in his meditation instructions. Please, don't skip this step! It would be like not putting oil in a car so the motor can run smoothly. The important Pāli word here is "pas'sambaya." This word specifically means "to tranquilize" and appears as "an action verb to be performed" as described in the suttas, and is not "a general kind of relaxing" that is included within other release steps found in other kinds of meditation. This point is sometimes misunderstood in translation, which then changes the end result!

Without performing this step of relaxing every time in the cycle, the meditator will not experience a close-up view of the ceasing of the tension caused by craving or the feeling of relief as the tightness is relaxed. Note that craving always first manifests as a tightness or tension in both one's mind and body. You have a momentary opportunity to see and experience the true nature and relief of cessation of tightness and suffering while performing the Release/Relax steps.

Mindfulness moves on by remembering to:

Re-Smile: If you have listened to the Dhamma talks at dhammasukha.org you might remember hearing about how smiling is an important aspect for the meditation. Learning to smile with mind and raising slightly the corners of the mouth helps mind to be observant, alert, and agile. Getting serious, tensing up, or frowning causes mind to become heavy and your mindfulness becomes dull and slow. Your insights become more difficult to see, thus slowing down your understanding of Dhamma.

Imagine for a moment the Bodhisatta resting under the rose apple tree as a young boy. He was not serious and tense when he attained a pleasant abiding (jhāna) and had deep insights with a light mind. Want to see clearly? It's easy!

Just lighten up, have fun exploring, and smile! Smiling leads us to a happier and more interesting practice. If the meditator forgets to Release/Relax, rather than punishing or criticizing yourself, be kind, Re-smile and start again. Keeping up your humor, sense of fun exploration, and recycling is important.

After Re-smiling, mindfulness recalls the next step.

Return or *Re-Direct*: Gently re-direct mind's attention back to the object of meditation (that is the breath and relaxing, or mettā and relaxing) continuing with a gentle collected mind and use that object as a "home base." In daily life, having been pulled off task, this is where you return your attention back to releasing, relaxing, and re-smiling into the task.

Sometimes people say this practice cycle is simpler than expected! In history, simple things can become a mystery through small changes and omissions! Doing this practice develops better focus on daily tasks with less tension and tightness. Mind becomes more naturally balanced and happy. You become more efficient at whatever you do in life and, actually, you have more fun doing all of the things that used to be drudgery. Nearing the end of the cycle.

Mindfulness helps with the final remembering to:

Repeat: Repeat your meditation on your object and keep it going as long as you can, and then repeat this entire practice cycle as needed to attain the results the Buddha said could be reached in this lifetime!

Repeating the "6R's cycle" over and over again will eventually replace old habitual suffering as we see clearly for ourselves what suffering actually is; notice the cause of it and how we become involved with the tension and tightness of it; experience how to reach a cessation of that suffering by releasing and relaxing; and discover how we can exercise the direct path to that same cessation of suffering. We achieve this cessation each time we Release an arising feeling, Relax, and Re-Smile. Notice the Relief!

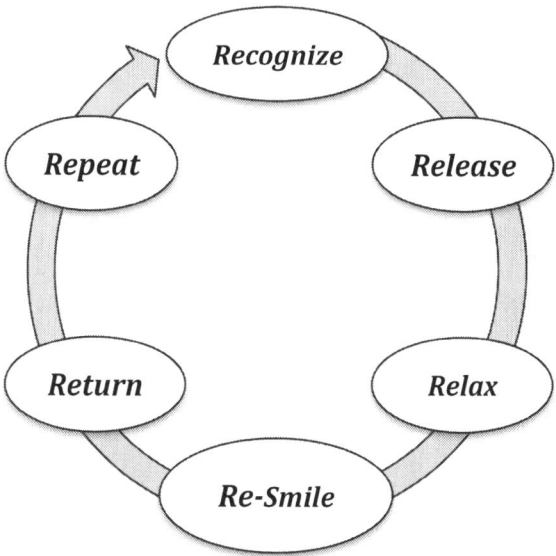

In summary, mindfulness (sati) is very relevant to Buddhist meditation and daily life. Sharpening your skill of mindfulness is the key to simple and smooth meditation. The process of remembering keeps the six steps of the practice moving. Practicing this meditation as close to the instructions (found in the suttas) as possible will lighten life's experience. A very similar practice was taught to people in the time of the Buddha. It was taught as Right Effort. Within the 6R's we have added a couple more steps to make things a little easier to understand.

The remarkable results of doing the meditation in this way are "immediately effective" for anyone who diligently and ardently embraces these instructions. When you have an attachment arise this practice will eventually dissolve the hindrance, but it does take persistent use of the 6R's to have this happen.

When you practice in this way, because it is found to be so relevant in daily life, it changes your perspective and leads you to a more successful, happy, and peaceful experience. As mindfulness develops, knowledge and wisdom grow naturally as you see "how" things work by witnessing the impersonal process of Dependent Origination.

This leads to a form of happiness the Buddha called "Contentment." Contentment is the by-product of living the Buddhist practice. This meditation leads to balance, equanimity, and the dissolution of fear and other dis-ease. With less fear and dread you find new confidence. Then Loving-Kindness, Compassion, Joy, and Equanimity can grow in our lives.

Your degree of success is directly proportional to how well you understand mindfulness, follow the precise instructions, and use the 6R's in both your sitting practice and daily life. This is the way to the end of suffering. It's interesting and fun to practice this way, and certainly it helps you smile while changing the world around you in a positive way.

When you are practicing TWIM, or Tranquil Wisdom Insight Meditation, you do not suppress anything. Suppression means we would push down or push away or not allow certain types of experience. This would temporarily stop hindrances from arising. Instead, when a hindrance arises, you must work to open your mind by seeing clearly anicca (impermanence, it wasn't there and now it is), dukkha (suffering or unsatisfactoriness, you see that when these distractions arise they are painful), and anattā (not taking it personally, seeing the hindrances in the true way as being an impersonal process that you have no control over and not taking these hindrances as "I am that").

You then let go of this obstruction, relax the tightness in the head, calm mind and finally, redirect your craving-free attention back to the practice of "Mindfulness of Breathing."

As a result, you begin to see clearly how mind works and this leads to the development of wisdom. Instead of identifying with them, when you allow them and relax, these hindrances will naturally fade away. Mind becomes more clear and bright. Every time you let go of the ego attachment of "I am that," mind naturally becomes more expanded, alert, and mindful.

Thus, one of the main reasons for this book is to show that whenever you suppress anything, you are not purifying mind or experiencing things as they truly are. At the time of suppression, you are pushing away or not allowing part of your experience. Thus, mind is contracted and pulls the tension even tighter instead of expanding and opening. As a result, this is not purifying mind of ignorance and craving. You are actually stopping the purification of mind!

It is impossible to experience the unconditioned state of the supra-mundane Nibbāna when one does not let go of everything that arises, and in that way purifies mind of the ego belief of "I am that."

The Buddha never taught suppression of any experience nor did he teach a meditation that causes mind to fix on or become absorbed into the meditation object. Remember, he rejected every form of "concentration meditation" as not being the correct way. Actually, any kinds of pain, emotional upset, physical discomfort, and even death must be accepted with equanimity, full awareness and strong attention without identifying with these states or taking them personally.

Real personality change occurs when you open and expand your mind and let go of any kinds of hindrances, pain, suffering, and tension even in your daily life. This means that you open and expand your awareness so that you can observe everything with a silent mind free from tightness and all ego-attachment. You gradually lead a happy and calm life without a lot of mind chatter, especially during your daily activities.

When you practice "concentration meditation," you will feel very comfortable and happy while in the deep meditation. But, when you get out of these exalted stages, your personality remains the same. Old anger, fears, or anxiety remain. This means when the hindrances attack you, you do not recognize them and open your mind and allow the hindrance to be there without taking it personally. Thus, you contract your mind and become even more attached! You might even become prideful and critical! This is because whenever a hindrance arises during the meditation, you let it go and immediately go back to the object of meditation again. You do this without calming and relaxing the tightness caused by the distraction. While in meditation, your mind tends to close or contract and tighten around that experience until mind becomes more deeply "concentrated."

As a result, although this suppresses the hindrance, you have not completely let go of the ego-attachment to that distraction. Your mind is also tight and tense because you are not seeing clearly. You are not opening and allowing, but instead you are closing and fighting with that distraction.

This explains why nowadays meditators complain that they have huge amounts of tension in their head. Actually, if you truly let go of any distraction, there will not ever be any tension in the head. It is as a result of this suppression that there is no real purifying of mind, and thus, personality change does not occur.

The 6R's is a simple technique for the student to use when mind's attention wanders off from the object of meditation. They are a key to cultivating mindfulness, turning hindrances into friends, exploring the Four Noble Truths, living into the Three Characteristics, and more. Getting comfortable and finally mastering this technique fulfills the requirements of the four Right Efforts and takes you quickly to the goal of staying with your object of meditation and letting go of any of the five hindrances when they arise.

Orientation From Joshua Tree #5 Retreat

Presented by Ven Bhante Vimalaraṁsi on 6th March 2010 at Dhamma Dena Vipassanā Center, Joshua Tree, California

BV: So, I'm happy to see all of you. And one of the things that I want to stress with this retreat is that you have fun doing it. I want you to practice smiling all the time. I don't care what you're doing, I don't care if you're going to the bathroom or taking a shower, I want you to smile. I've been called a sneaky monk because I don't really tell people why I want you to smile very often. And I want you to smile for a couple of reasons. The more you smile the better your mindfulness becomes. Okay?

Now the whole thing with the Buddha's teaching is to have an uplifted mind all the time. And that's what the Buddha was really interested in. The more you smile and have fun and laugh with yourself for being serious about things, the easier it is to have the perspective so that you don't get caught by the hindrances for as long a period of time.

Now, the hindrances, there's five of them:

1. Greedy mind - I like it. I want it.
2. Aversion mind - I don't like it. I don't want it.
3. Sleepiness-Dullness.
4. Restlessness-Anxiety.
5. Doubt.

Now, when I start talking about hindrances, quite often I don't tell you which hindrances I'm talking about. I just say that it's a distraction. Anything that distracts your mind away from your object of meditation, is the reason that you have to learn how to practice 6R's:

- Recognize that your mind is distracted.
- Release the distraction. That means don't keep your attention on whatever has pulled your mind away. Now…
- Relax tightness and tension in your mind. And when you relax tension in your mind, you relax tension in your body. Now you…
- Re-smile because you've lost your smile when you get caught up in things. Then you…
- Return to your object of meditation. And you…
- Repeat staying with your object of meditation.

Simple, right? It's simple but sometimes not easy. Yeah?

ST: What is an object of meditation?

BV: I'll get to that in just a moment.

Now, what I generally have people do is practice Loving-Kindness Meditation rather than the breathing meditation. And I have people practicing the Loving-Kindness Meditation because almost everybody starts with the breathing meditation, and they have bad habits, and it's hard to break those habits. So, the easiest way to do that is to change your meditation so that you're starting out right at the ground floor, and that is with the Loving-Kindness Meditation. The Loving-Kindness Meditation is actually more than just loving-kindness. Eventually, it starts working into all of the Brahma Vihāras. That is: compassion, joy, and equanimity along with the loving-kindness.

So, we start out by practicing loving-kindness. The first ten minutes of every sitting, you radiate loving-kindness to yourself. Now, what I'm going to be teaching you is - it might be a little bit different if you've been practicing loving-kindness with other methods - because what I want you to do is: make a wish for yourself and feel the wish. Now, you could make a wish for yourself to be happy. What does it feel like to be happy? Do you know? You make a wish that you feel peaceful and calm. You make a wish that you feel very clear and bright. You can make up your wish; make it wholesome, but feel the wish and take that feeling and put it into your heart, and surround yourself with that feeling.

Now, you're going to have a lot of distracting thoughts at first. Your mind is not going to be very settled. That's okay, doesn't matter. I know that there are some traditions that they talk about: "Well, just clear your mind." Well, I know some people that have worked for two years to clear their mind, so they don't have any thoughts coming in, but thoughts are not your enemy. Thoughts are just thoughts, and it's okay to have thoughts. But you want to recognize that your mind is thinking: let that thought go, that means don't keep your attention on it. Relax, smile, come back to your object of meditation, and stay with your object of meditation for as long as you can.

Now, if your mind wanders thirty times or fifty times in your sitting period, and you notice it - and you let it be, and you relax, and you smile, and comeback to your object of meditation - that is a good sitting. A not good sitting is noticing that you're thinking of something, and it's so important that you have to keep thinking it over and over again. Now you're not really meditating anymore. Keep it light; don't force the meditation; don't snap your mind around; just simply notice it: "Ah, there it goes again. Okay." Let it be, relax, smile, come back; that's all. Every time you do that, your mindfulness improves a little bit. It's just like putting coins in a bank. After a while the bank starts getting filled up with the coins.

Don't fight anything, don't resist anything, allow everything to be there. When something arises, I don't care if it's a pain in your knee, or a pain in your back, or it's a persistent thought; allow it to be there. The truth is, when it arises, it's there. That's the truth, that's the Dhamma of the present moment, and that means it has to be alright because that's the truth; it's there. Now, you allow it to be there, you relax, smile, come back to your object of meditation.

So, the first ten minutes of every sitting, I want you to just send loving and kind thoughts to yourself. Feel that happy feeling, feel joy, feel clarity, feel peace and calm. Whatever wish you make for yourself, feel that. Put that feeling in your heart and radiate that feeling to yourself. After ten minutes, then you start sending loving and kind thoughts to a spiritual friend, and I'll get into that in a little bit.

Now, while you're sitting, I want you to sit with your back nicely straight, not rigid, but nicely straight, so it doesn't cause pain when you sit. Don't move: don't move your toes, don't move your fingers, don't scratch, don't rub, don't change your posture, don't rock back and forth; sit still. And while you're doing that, you can feel… sometimes there'll be an itch, or a want to cough, or sneeze, or just thoughts keep running through; that's fine. Sometimes pain can arise. Don't move, sit very still. You can move as much as he (points at the Buddha image) does. Okay? That's why he's here to remind you how much you can move.

Now, what happens when you get a sensation that arises in the body, like a want to cough, the first thing that happens is you start to think about all the reasons why you don't want that feeling to be there: "I wish it would stop. I wish it would go away. Why does it have to bother me now?" Now, the first thing you want to do is recognize that you're thinking, and let go of that thought, and relax a little bit. Now you notice there's a tight mental fist wrapped around that feeling: "I don't want to cough. I don't want to disturb anybody else." Notice the tight muscles in your throat, and relax. Then notice the tight muscle in your head.

Around your brain there is a membrane called the meninges, and every time your mind gets distracted, it contracts a little bit, and there's tension and tightness in your head. So, after you let go of the tight muscles here, relax the tension and tightness in your head. It's not an easy thing to recognize at first, but as you start to go a little bit deeper, you'll be able to recognize it fairly easily. When you let it go, you'll feel like an expansion happens in your head. It's like the tension just lets go and it feels more open. And you'll notice right after you do that, that there's no thoughts, there's no distraction: your mind is clear, your mind is bright, your mind is pure. Now you bring that mind back to your object of meditation. And then your mind gets distracted by this "want to cough" again. So, you do the same thing again. Now, if you're going to cough, don't fight it. Let your body be on automatic; doesn't matter.

A sound is only a sound. So, if your mind gets distracted by a sound, you treat it in the same way. You let it be there, you relax, you smile, you come back. It doesn't matter how many times your mind gets distracted. Every time your mind gets distracted, you treat it in the same way. You use the 6R's. The 6R's are one of the keys to the meditation. And at first you'll feel like repeating those 6R's in your head, but actually the 6R's are a kind of flow: it's recognizing... releasing... relaxing... smiling... coming back. And you do it that way. Make it a flow. You don't have to stop after each step. Okay?

And the more you smile during your meditation, the faster you'll understand what I'm talking about. That's why I said: "I want you to have fun on this retreat." Why? When you have fun, you learn fast. When you have fun doing something, like when you were in school and you had a subject that you really liked, you learned it very quickly because you were having fun learning it. Have fun with this meditation. Don't get serious. Smile into everything, and when your mind is being really heavy, and it decides that there's something that you should really be serious about, then you laugh with yourself. Just kind of chuckle and go: "Boy, my mind's really crazy right now!" You know it's okay to be crazy? We're all crazy, and it's okay, it's fun! Have fun with it! How does your mind feel now? See?

Anytime you have repeat thoughts, you have an attachment. An attachment is not good, bad, or indifferent, it's just an attachment. How do you let go of the attachment? You: recognize... release... relax... smile... come back, stay with your object of meditation as long as you can remember to.

The function of mindfulness is to remember. To remember what? To remember to smile and have fun. So, anytime you see you're getting serious about something, well, what do we need to do with that?

Now, the relax step is very, very important because the relax step is how to let go of craving. Craving always manifests as tension and tightness in your mind and in your body. That's how you can recognize it. When you relax, then your mind becomes pure. Why? Because you're not identifying with those thoughts and feelings, you're seeing them the way they are, they're just thoughts and feelings; no biggie. So, it's really important that you use the relax step, but sometimes people get over enthusiastic and they want to relax... relax... relax... relax... relax, because the tension didn't go away the first time. Now, just relax one time. Follow all of the 6R's every time you're distracted. So, there's some tension still. Okay, fine. Your mind will go back to that distraction - do it again... and do it again... and do it again... and do it again... and do it again, until it finally lets go. This is how you purify your mind, by letting go of craving.

Now, this is something that's quite unusual in the Buddhist world, to have somebody come up and tell you: "This is how you recognize craving. This is what craving is." And you don't have to fight with the craving, you don't have to control it, you just have to let it be - and relax. The craving will fade away by itself. As it fades away then you start going deeper in your meditation, and you start staying with your object of meditation for longer periods of time.

Mindfulness is your observation power, it's not your controlling power, it's only your observation; being able to recognize when your mind gets distracted. As you begin to stay with your object of meditation for a little longer period of time, you'll start noticing more quickly when your mind gets distracted, and you'll let go a little bit more easily. This is a very natural process of unfolding, and you are your own teachers. I'm not your teacher, I'm a guide. I'll keep you on the path, but you're teaching yourself. And this is something that's quite unusual because most people think that you come to a retreat to have the teacher tell you what to do. I'll tell you what to do, practice your 6R's. Stay with that.

Now, a spiritual friend is a person of the same sex. They are alive, and don't use a member of your family to start off with. A spiritual friend is someone, when you think of them and their good qualities, you really like them. You have a lot of respect for that person. You sincerely do wish them well. So, you pick a spiritual friend and you stay with that same spiritual friend all the time. Now, when you're practicing sending loving and kind thoughts to your spiritual friend, you want to picture them in your mind's eye. Some people can picture them like they were a photograph, and they can see that person very easily. Other people, they're not visual like that. You can feel them smiling. You want to see them smiling and happy. If you visualize, sometimes it's like it's a long ways away, sometimes it's cloudy, sometimes it's fuzzy, sometimes it just won't come up. That's okay.

The most important part of the meditation is the radiation of the loving-kindness. The next most important part of the meditation is making a wish, feeling that wish, taking your spiritual friend, putting them in your heart, and surrounding them with that feeling. When you see your spiritual friend in your mind's eye, you want to see them smiling and happy, and that can help remind you to be smiling and happy.

This is a smiling meditation. You've already heard me say that. She (Sister Khema) says I'll repeat things three times, that's not true. I repeat them hundreds of times, sometimes all on the same talk. Ha Ha! When you smile, you want to smile with your mind. You want to smile with your eyes, even though your eyes are closed. You'll find out that there's tension and tightness, and you smile with your eyes, and that lets go of tension. You want to put a little Buddha smile on your lips, and a smile in your heart. Okay?

So, when you're meditating and you're staying with your spiritual friend, the first day or so you're going to start noticing that you're kind of slipping off your spiritual friend a little bit, and your mind starts ho-humming around. And then it gets a little bit dreamy, and then it gets real dreamy, and then your posture starts to slump, and before long you are dozing… Why does that happen? Now, that's called sloth and torpor if you've wondered about that. That happens because you're not being sincere enough with staying with your spiritual friend. Take more interest in your spiritual friend, and that will help overcome the "sleepies."

Also, when you get sloth and torpor, what happens is you'll notice that you've been like this for a little while, and you go: "Okay! Now I'm going to stay with the object… May they be happy… may they be happy… may they be happy… Oh, I wonder how long this is going to last. Oh, I am starting to sleep again." It's too much energy at one time, too much effort, trying to force it, and this is not a forced meditation. So, if you see that you're a little bit sleepy and you're having trouble staying with your spiritual friend, I want you to sit for thirty minutes; that's the minimum. Okay? Now, after thirty minutes, if you're sleepy, you can get up and you can do your walking meditation, which I'll get into in just a minute. Or, when you're sitting, sit just a little bit straighter, not enough to cause you pain, but a little bit straighter. And then when your back starts slumping like that, you'll notice it and then you can use the 6R's and come back to your spiritual friend much more easily. Okay?

Now, your biggest hindrance is going to be restlessness. That means every thought that distracts your mind away from what you're doing. So, you better get to be friendly with this guy because he's around until you become an arahat. Now, the Buddha said very clearly in the Satipaṭṭhāna Sutta that in seven days you can become an arahat. So, you never know when it's going to happen. Okay?

It's always kind of comical when I give an interview to somebody, they'll come in, I say: "Well, how's your meditation going?" "Oh, my meditation is horrible. My mind is running all over the place. I just, oh, it's so active and I'm thinking about this and I'm thinking about that." And my next question is: "Are you able to notice it? Are you able to recognize it? Are you able to practice your 6R's with it?" "Well, yeah." Excellent meditation! But then sometimes you'll come in and you'll be all mellowed out because you had some candy. You had some good meditation. "Oh, I just stayed on the object of meditation and that was just great." And I go: "Oh, okay, go on. Everything's fine." Isn't that right? Ha ha.

See, your active meditation - and you're using the 6R's - is your working meditation. That's when you're rolling up your sleeves and you're really doing the work. And you're improving your mindfulness, and you're starting to see how this process works more easily. Now, a lot of people, if you ask them when they go to a retreat: "Why are you doing the meditation? What's the point?" "Well, so I can become peaceful and calm." That's not the point of the Buddha's meditation. The point of the Buddha's meditation is, so that you can learn to see how mind's attention moves from one thing to another. And you see that as a process that's impersonal. And before long you'll start to see how this process works. And you'll be teaching yourself this process.

So meditation is - it's great to be peaceful and calm - but I want your understanding of how this process works. I don't care if you're sitting, or you're walking, or you're eating, or you're taking a shower, or you're going to the toilet; keep your meditation going. Keep watching how mind's attention moves away. Let it be, use your 6R's, come back. That way you're teaching yourself what this is all about. And you are teaching yourself - as I said: "I can't teach you."

Now, a lot of people have an idea that the hindrances are the enemy and you're supposed to fight with them, and some people fight with them a lot, and they cause themselves a lot of suffering. "I don't want this to be here. I don't like this. I want it to stop." Who wants it to be different than it is? "Well, I do." Who has an attachment? "Well, maybe I do." Oh, so you're causing your own pain? Is that what we're getting to here? Do you see? You cause your own pain, you cause your own suffering because of that attachment. So, what do we do with attachments? We 6R the attachments.

Now, when a real big hindrance comes up, and the first time it comes up and you get caught for a period of time; it might be a minute, two minutes, three minutes, five minutes, whatever. But as soon as you recognize: "Oh, there I am. I'm caught by this one," you can't criticize yourself. All you do is use the 6R's and come back. Now, the next time your mind goes away because of that attachment, you'll start to be more familiar with how the process is working. And after you become familiar with this distraction for a while, then you'll see: "Right before my mind got really taken away, there was this little thing that happened." So, you 6R and you come back, and you get distracted again, but this time you notice that little thing and you 6R right then. You're teaching yourself how this process works. As you become familiar with that, then the period of time that you're distracted starts to become less and less, and you start staying on your object of meditation for longer periods of time.

The hindrances are a very necessary part of this practice. They're very necessary because the hindrances are showing you where your attachments are. That's why they're hindrances because: "This is 'mine'. This is who 'I' am. This is 'my' concept. This is 'my' idea. This is the way 'I' think things should be. I... I... I... I... I." But the truth is, everything that arises - you didn't ask sadness to arise, you didn't say: "You know, I haven't had any sadness for a long time. I might as well have some now." It comes up because conditions are right for that to come up. You don't have any control over it. You allow it to be, you relax, you smile, you come back to your object of meditation. You might bounce back and forth for a whole sitting with the same hindrance; it doesn't matter. You can't criticize yourself when you forget. Start over again. This is a process of - what was that, Woody Allen: "Play it again, Sam." This is a process of play it again. Do it again, do it again. You'll start to see where your attachments are and how easily you can let go of these things that have been causing you pain. Allow, don't resist anything, don't push anything. Just soften your mind, allow it to be there, and smile.

So, what I want you to do is... when your sitting is good and you can stay with your object of meditation fairly well, sit longer. Okay? You'll want to sit longer. You know the half an hour is up and you go: "Oh no, I don't want to get up now. I want to stay here." Okay, fine, stay there, but don't sit any less than thirty minutes. Okay? And sometimes that thirty minutes can seem like it's three or four hours when your mind is really active, and there's resisting things, and you're all caught up. Other times it'll seem like it's five minutes and you go, "I don't want to stop now. I want to keep going." Fine, do that. And then you get up when you feel like it's time to get up, and you go out and do your walking meditation.

Now, when you're doing your walking meditation, walk at a normal pace. (This means the pace you use during your daily life.) You're using your walking meditation for exercise. Sometimes, I tell people I want them to walk fast, especially if they've been sitting for a longer period of time. Sometimes people sit for two hours or three hours. They need to get the circulation going again. So, you walk a little bit faster, but you stay with your spiritual friend all the time. Okay? Now, the walking is going to be somewhat difficult to start off with because you're not used to walking around staying with the spiritual friend, and your mind likes to think about this and that. You can't criticize; you don't get angry because your mind isn't doing what you want it to. You just go, "Okay, we'll 6R that and come back to my spiritual friend again." That's all. Now, walk no less than fifteen minutes. When you're walking, walk with your eyes down, not looking around. If you're walking with your eyes looking around, there goes your mind, and you can be lost for a long period of time without even recognizing. So, keep your eyes down and stay with your spiritual friend as much as you can, and just recognize that the walking is going to be a little bit more difficult. But, after you get used to it, you'll feel like walking more than fifteen minutes; fine. Walk more than fifteen minutes. Walk up to 45 minutes.

Now, one of the things that you can do that will help the sleepiness - the sloth and torpor that I was talking about. Pick a spot where you walk about thirty feet and then stop. Don't turn around. Walk backwards, and then stop… and then walk forward, and then stop… and then walk backwards, staying with your spiritual friend all the time. This helps pick up your energy, so that your next sitting will be easier. You won't have the sloth and torpor quite so much. It's amazing how well this works.

So, after walking, don't expect the next sitting to be like the one that you just got up from. "Oh, I had a great sitting. It was an hour and a half and everything, my mind was so peaceful and calm. I'll do that again." And then what happens? It doesn't happen that way to start off with, and then you start thinking: "Well, maybe if I put a little bit more effort into it, maybe if I put a little bit more energy into it, I'll be able to get back to that place that I was before." And your mind starts to get more restless and more active. Why? Because you're putting in too much effort, you're putting in too much energy, you're trying to make things happen the way you want them to happen. Things are going to happen the way they happen. Don't try to force anything, don't try to push, don't try to make your meditation be better. If you have an active meditation when you sit, fine… 6R, smile, come back, have fun with it. "Well, it's not as good as it was." Okay, so? Who said it was supposed to be? Right? "Well, I want it... oh, there I go again."

So, this meditation is about allowing whatever is going to happen in the present moment to be there by itself; 6R, come back to your object of meditation. It's never going to be the same. It's always going to be changing, it's always going to be different, and you can't control it. You can't make it be the way you want it to. If you do, you put up too much energy into it and now you have all of this suffering from the restlessness. But the hindrances quite often don't come up just one at a time. It's like: 'beat the kid when he's down'. So, the restlessness comes up and: "I don't like that. I don't want it to be like that." So, you have aversion and restlessness to work with. How lucky can you get? When you see that restlessness arises, the wish you make for yourself is feeling peaceful and calm; feel that. Now, restlessness can be really tough. You feel like jumping out of your skin. You feel like you have to move: "Can't stand it." And there can be all kinds of different pains that arise in your body: "Well, if I just shift a little bit that'll make it better. Oh, what's one of the rules? Don't move." Watch how mind moves. Okay?

Now, one of the things that seems to happen on retreats - and I tell people about it over and over again, but they still do it, and I tell them not to - is they think sitting is more important that walking. So, they'll be sitting in meditation and then they'll go: "Well, this sitting is really good. I'll just do this. Now, I'll just sit for longer." And what happens is, your body energy starts to go down, and when your body energy starts to go down, you'll hit some places that you'll think: "Oh, I really have a good meditation now. It's really something. I just had a period of five or six minutes where it just like somebody took an eraser and erased everything that could happen in five or six minutes. This is great meditation!" And you come running to me and you tell me about this, and I look at it and I go: "You're just getting caught by your sloth and torpor. You have to walk more!" It's not any spiritual attainment, I promise. The walking is very necessary. If you feel like you have to change your posture - after thirty minutes - then get up and walk. It's every bit as important as sitting.

Now, everybody is going to have a job. I think you already talked about that, but that doesn't mean it's time to just let your mind ho-hum around, and do the job, and get it over with so I can go meditate. That's the time for you to learn how to do a job while you're meditating, while you're watching what your mind is doing. So, you can let go of that distraction, come back to what you're doing, smile, have fun doing it. There's nothing to accomplish, there's just doing. Okay?

Now, every day, I want everybody here at 5:25AM.

We used to say 5:30, and then it was 5:35, and then it gets to be 5:40 because one person doesn't come, and we're not going to start the meditation until everybody gets here. So, I want you here a little bit before 5:30, so we can start at 5:30. We'll sit in meditation and you can do your walking if you want to walk after a half an hour, go outside and stay with your meditation and walk, come back in, you can sit until seven o'clock, and then that's breakfast time.

Okay. After breakfast, you'll have time to do your personal things; brush your teeth, whatever. And then there's a work period for one hour. After that then it's walking and sitting here, in the meditation hall, until eleven o'clock. At eleven o'clock, the bell will be rung and we'll have lunch. After lunch, you'll have a period of time until one o'clock that you can lay down and take rest if you want. You can sleep, whatever you feel like; it's up to you. If you feel like going for a walk, that can be restful too; it's up to you. Be here at one o'clock. And then there's walking and sitting until 5:30PM, and at 5:30 you can have some tea.

How many people here have physical problems and need to take some kind of food if they have medicine? Okay. I'll talk to you... Okay. At six o'clock, please be here. After the Dhamma talk, it's not time to chitchat, it's time to do more meditation. Now, after the Dhamma talk, it's good to go out and do some walking because you're sitting here for an hour, hour and a half, sometimes two. I get long winded, so sometimes it's a little bit longer than that. But get up, do your walking meditation, come back in. Don't go to your room and say: "Well, that's enough meditation for the day. I'm going to lay down and go to sleep." Stay in here until ten o'clock, please. And then at ten o'clock, go to your room, lay down, take rest 'til five o'clock in the morning. That's seven hours.

Do you see how it works? Anybody that's done any of the retreats like I've done, like Vipassanā retreats when I went to Mahasi Centre in Rangoon; I had to go to bed at eleven o'clock, get up at three o'clock, and it was meditation for the rest of the day. These retreats are long and can be very hard to do. I'm giving you seven hours rest, plus an hour after lunch! You see how this is a walk in the park! Right? So, you're not going to be run down, you're not going to be overtired. If you do get overtired, come and tell me and we'll work something out. I don't want you to be sleepy all the time.

Now, right before you lay down, starting to relax, right before you go to sleep, make two determinations. One, that you're going to wake up at a particular time: "I'm going to wake up at 4:59 in the morning," and try to hit that. The next determination is that you make a determination that you wake up with a smile. Okay? You wake up with a smile on your face; keep it going. Do that every night. Now, these kind of determinations - although it's just like you're just starting out, they don't seem so important - they get important later on. I had a student in Missouri that I started teaching about determinations and how to gain mastery in going in and out of jhāna. And working with determinations, now, helps set you up so that I can teach you mastery in the future. So, it's real important that you start doing that. Okay?

Whatever kind of distraction you have, learn to use the 6R's. (That is Recognize, Release, Relax, Re-Smile, Return, and Repeat.) Learn to see where your attachment to that is. What are hindrances when they arise? They're something that happen because of past actions. They arise in the present moment. What you do with what arises in the present moment dictates what's going to happen in the future. If you resist the present moment, if you fight with it, if you try to control it, if you try to force it to be the way you want it to be, you can look forward to more and more suffering. Or you can 6R it, and eventually that hindrance will start to fade away. And when it fades away, first thing that happens is you will feel great relief, and right after that you will feel joy arising. And the joy is going to make you smile whether you want to or not. I mean this is good stuff. Okay? You're going to feel like smiling. The joy will be there for a little while, and then you'll feel very tranquil, and you'll feel very comfortable in your mind and in your body.

Now, what I just described to you is the first jhāna. Jhāna is a Pāli word that means "a level of understanding." When you get into the first jhāna, you're beginning to understand how mind is working, and all of these different levels of jhāna are different levels of your understanding. And that's one of the things that makes the meditation real fun because you feel like you're progressing, you feel like: "I'm starting to get this. I'm starting to understand it."

So, the more you can remember to use the 6R's, the more you can allow whatever arises to be there by itself, without getting involved in your thinking about, the easier the meditation becomes. That's a promise. The more you resist or fall back into your old habits of meditation: "Well, I'll try. I used to do this for twenty years. I think I'll try that again." Now, that stops your meditation. That stops your progress, and then we have to start digging around to figure out what you're doing,

Orientation

so that we can get you back on the path that has progress in it. It's real important to just follow these directions without adding anything or subtracting anything. Just follow the 6R's. Smile. Okay?

"But I don't feel like smiling." I don't care... Why? Because the corners of your mouth are incredibly important. When the corners of your mouth go up, so does your mental state. What's the point of doing the meditation? To have an uplifted mind, so you can be happy more of the time, and you can start recognizing when you cause yourself suffering, and you can let that go so you can be happier. So, if I see you're not smiling... (I will remind you to smile!) Have fun with this meditation. Don't get serious. Anytime you get serious, there is an attachment. There is the belief that: "I am this. I am that," and then there gets to be the want to control.

See, we're made up of five different things. You have a physical body. There is feeling: feeling is pleasant, unpleasant, or neutral, doesn't have anything to do with emotion. It's just a pleasant feeling, a painful feeling, neither-painful-nor-pleasant feeling.

You have perception: perception is a part of the mind that names things. This is a cup. Perception is a part of the mind that recognized that.

You have thoughts, and you have consciousness.

What happens is, a painful feeling arises, and then you try to control the feeling with your thoughts. And the more you try to control your feeling with your thoughts, the bigger and more intense the feeling becomes, and the more thoughts you try to put into it to control it, and that makes you suffer.

So, the first thing you have to do - it doesn't matter whether it's a pain in the body or in the mind - is recognize: "This is how this process works." First thing you do, let go of the thoughts (Let them be without getting involved with them.) and relax. Let go of that tight mental fist around the feeling, and allow that painful feeling to be there by itself. It's only a feeling. It's not even yours, you didn't ask it to come up. Let the feeling be there, relax, smile, come back to your object of meditation. Now, depending on your attachment to it, you might have to work with that for a little while. But like I told you, the hindrances come up and they are your teacher. They are showing you exactly where your attachment is. So, what do you do? Let it be, relax, smile, and come back. Does it again? Okay, let it be, relax, smile, come back.

Now, another thing that I'm finding out that people are doing, and this is that they're trying to use the 6R's too much. So, a thought comes up and they don't... it doesn't pull their attention away, but they put their attention on the thought and then try to 6R it, and they can't get quite done before another thought comes up. So, they're trying to: 6R... 6R... 6R... 6R... 6R (as a means to control it). Only 6R if your mind gets pulled away (from your object of meditation), otherwise ignore it. Okay? So, there's a thought there: "It's not pulling my attention to it. Let it be." Stay with your object of meditation. Don't try too hard. Almost everybody that comes - especially if they've done a retreat with anybody else - they come and they start practicing, and they try too hard: "Well, it can't be that easy." It is. Believe me, this is easy. All you got to do is smile. All you got to do is 6R and come back to your object of meditation, without putting too much effort into it. "Well, my mind keeps getting distracted." Okay, so? That means you have a working meditation. Good! That's helping your mind, your mindfulness to get stronger so you can see how the process works more easily.

Okay. So, does anybody have any questions? Okay.

ST: The first one is, if we're not experiencing sloth and torpor, do you still want us to walk and then walk backwards?

BV: Only when you have the sloth and torpor. That helps to pick up your energy.

ST: The second question is, the first ten minutes is loving-kindness to myself?

BV: Yes.

ST: And then it's loving-kindness to a spiritual friend, and stay with them?

BV: To a spiritual friend, same spiritual friend... stay with the same spiritual friend the rest of the time. Then when you come and...

ST: Does the time being a whole week? The rest of the time...

BV: I'll tell you when to quit. But, every time you come to sit, the first ten minutes to yourself, the rest of the time with your spiritual friend. That's when you're doing your walking, when you're doing your daily activities...

ST: So, we're staying with the spiritual friend.

BV: Staying with the spiritual friend...

ST: The whole time?

BV: The whole time, until you come and sit, and then the first ten minutes for yourself.

ST: And we're making a wish for our spiritual friend just as we were doing for ourselves.

BV: Yes, and feel the wish. That's really, really important.

ST: I have just a comment. I'm sitting here thinking... I sat here a year ago, and I heard these instructions and I thought: "This is just too simple. It can't be this simple." And so, it is! It is that simple, it is that easy. And I'm a kind of a go-for-the-gold kind of guy and...

BV: That gets in your way.

ST: That is, it doesn't work...

BV: It doesn't work.

There is a running joke between a student and I about kicking a tree. But one day he wrote to me about a hindrance that he had on the email. And what I try to do is come up with something that's so absurd that it's going to make him laugh.

So, he was telling me about how much this hindrance hurt, and he was really getting tired of it, and he wanted it to stop. And I said: "Well, really get into the pain. I want you to experience the pain completely. As a matter of fact, I want you to take your shoes off and go out to the biggest tree you can find, and kick it as hard as you can. That way you'll really have some pain!" And as soon as I said that, that made him start laughing and the hindrance dissolved. He saw how absurd it was!

Now, the laughing, it sounds really bizarre. I mean, how many meditation teachers have you ever run across that told you to laugh, and told you to have fun, and told you to smile? Well, what does the laughing do? The laughing makes you go from: "I'm mad and I don't like this" to "It's only anger. That's easy to let go of. I don't need that." It helps change your perspective. It's real important because the perspective is everything.

What this meditation will teach you is how everything that arises is just part of a process, and it's not your process, it's just a process. So, why take it personally? Every time you take it personally, it hurts because: "I'm there and I want to control it. I want it to be different than it is." Well, get rid of the "I" and there goes the pain. It's really an amazing thing.

Craving is not particularly strong, but it is particularly persistent. And it comes up in all kinds of things. And you'll be able to start recognizing the tension and tightness in your mind, and in your body. And when you start letting go of that, you're experiencing a mundane - it means "worldly" - kind of Nibbāna. What is Nibbāna? "Ni" - is a negative, "bāna" is fire. So, when you experience "no fire" - no craving - you're experiencing the cessation of craving. And that's where your mind becomes pure, that's where your mind becomes clear, that's where you let go of all of your attachments.

And there's a sutta called the Fire Sutta, and the Buddha talked about: "Everything is burning." What is it burning

Orientation

with? Craving. So, when you let go of the craving, is there any more burning? Now your mind's pure. See how simple it is? But remember that it is a deeply ingrained thing that's going to keep coming up over and over and over again. And as it does, it's helping you to improve your mindfulness, so you can recognize it, and you can let it go more easily that way.

When I was in Germany this time, I was reading a sutta and it started talking about lust, hatred, and delusion, and it dawned on me: lust, hatred, and delusion - "I like it," "I don't like it," "I." That's craving! That's another way of saying: "This is craving." So, what to do? 6R, that's simple. Okay? Anybody else? Yes?

ST: I just want to say that 6R tool is just great! Because it can be applied at the grossest levels of mind, and frustration, and anger, and identity, and everything - throughout the most, most subtle experiences of mind that take place. And so it becomes just a wonderful way of working with the things that are taking place. It can't be overstated.

BV: See, I repeat myself how many times? Now, the thing with the 6R's is, it will take you to Nibbāna. Do it so often that it will become automatic, and that means when something just starts to come up, your mind recognizes it, and you can start 6R'ing right then and let it go. And it's going to be somewhat difficult at first. You're not used to it, but that's okay. It's a learning process. You're teaching mind, you're teaching yourself, you're teaching yourself where your attachments are, and you're teaching yourself how to let go of those attachments, so that you can have a pure mind and a happy mind all the time. Easy, right? No! Simple, yes, not easy... because of our attachments.

We start thinking that some of our concepts are really the most important things in the world and this is the way it's supposed to be, and concepts are part of clinging. Now, every thought that you have that arises is a concept. What's a concept? This is a chair, right? Where is it? Where is the chair? Is it the legs? Is it the seat? Is it the back? Is it the arms?

Where's the chair? The chair is a concept made up of a lot of little things put together to make this the concept.

ST: It obstructs the reality.

BV: Oh yes. It obstructs the reality. There's no getting around that at all because that's part of clinging.

ST: It's always a lie.

BV: Well, the craving is the first part of that. That leads to the concepts, and always those concepts involve "me:" "This is who 'I' am." The start of "me" is the craving: "I like this. I don't like that." Then it's tension, and then all of the reasons why you like it or don't like it start popping up in your mind. Those are all the concepts, the beliefs, the opinions, the ideas. So, when you use the 6R's, now you're getting exactly in the present moment without any colored lenses. No concepts, no opinions, only this right now. And this is perfect. Okay? This will become clearer as the week goes by, I promise.

Another thing is when I'm giving a Dhamma talk, if I say something that you don't understand, don't hesitate to ask a question. There's no such a thing as a stupid question. There is no such a thing. If you don't understand what I'm saying, I want to say it in a way that will be clear, so that your meditation can be good. That's more important than sitting and not questioning.

ST: I have a question. Your spiritual friend has to be a Human?

BV: Yes, absolutely. Why? - This is not a bad question.

ST: Can that be all beings.

BV: No.

SK: Not yet.

BV: This is a gradual training, and there's going to be times that you're going to have: "Stay with the same spiritual friend, I'm bored. I want something else to happen." Well, good. Continue on, go through that.

SK: It's part of the process.

BV: But it has to be a human being that's alive, and the reason is: that's how the meditation develops. It doesn't work when you're doing it with an animal. This is a training, and as you go deeper in the training, I will show you other things. And eventually you will get to radiate loving-kindness to all beings, and beyond. But this is called "Breaking Down The Barriers," and this is what we do first.

As long as you follow the directions; that's the key. Don't add anything, don't subtract anything, right now. That doesn't mean always, but it just means for right now because this is your training period. Okay?

> May suffering ones be suffering free
> And the fear struck fearless be.
> May the grieving shed all grief
> And may all beings find relief.
> May all beings share this merit
> That we have thus acquired
> For the acquisition of
> All kind of happiness.
> May beings inhabiting space and earth
> Devas and Nagas of mighty power
> Share in this merit of ours.
> May they long protect
> the Buddha's Dispensation.
> Sādhu... Sādhu... Sādhu...

MN-20: The Removal of Distracting Thoughts (Vitakkasaṇṭhāna Sutta)

Presented by Ven Bhante Vimalaraṁsi on 19th February 2006 at Dhamma Dena Vipassanā Center, Joshua Tree, California

BV: Ok, the discourse I'm going to do tonight is sutta number 20 in the Middle Length Sayings. It's called "The Removal of Distracting Thoughts." Does anyone have any distracting thoughts they want removed?

1. THUS HAVE I HEARD. On one occasion the Blessed One was living at Sāvatthi in Jeta's Grove, Anāthanpiṇḍika's Park. There he addressed the monks thus: "Monks." - "Venerable sir," they replied. The Blessed One said this:

2. "Monks, when a monk is pursuing the higher mind,

Which in Pāli is called Abhidhamma (higher teachings), and here he is referring to getting into the jhānas.

from time to time he should give attention to five signs. What are the five?

3. "Here, Monks, when a monk is giving attention to some sign, and owing to that sign there arise in him evil unwholesome thoughts connected with desire, with hate, and with delusion, then he should give attention to some other sign connected with what is wholesome.

Now, what is this talking about? This is talking basically about the part of the Eightfold Path that is generally called Right Effort. Right Effort is recognizing when your mind has become distracted, letting go of the distraction, and relaxing, coming back to your object of meditation, and staying with your object of meditation.

Now, I talked to everybody today and one of the things that came up quite often was that their mind was very active. This is not bad. Just because you have an active mind doesn't mean that you have bad meditation. Meditation is about being able to recognize the movements of mind's attention from one thing to another; recognizing that attention movement. When a thought arises and it pulls your attention away from your object of meditation - that is the feeling of loving-kindness and making a wish for your happiness or your friend's happiness - when you recognize that your mind is not on your object of meditation, then you let go of the thought, or feeling, whatever it is that pulls your attention away from your object of meditation, you let that be. You don't try to throw down the thought, stop the thought, stomp on the thought, beat the thought up, because it's there; you just recognize that the thought is there. Let the thought be there by itself. Don't keep your attention on it, and then gently relax the tension caused by that mind's movement. Now smile, and gently return to your object of meditation, and stay with your object of meditation as long as you can.

Sometimes, your object of meditation is only going to be there for part of one thought, and then it goes back. Then you do the whole process again. Allow that distraction to be there, relax, smile, come back to your object of meditation. It doesn't matter how many times in a sitting your mind wanders away. Just because you have an active mind does not mean that it's bad meditation. Bad meditation or no meditation is recognizing that you're thinking something, and you notice it, but you continue thinking. Now, you're not meditating at all, you're getting involved with the story, you're getting involved with the liking and disliking of something. The more you get involved, the less likely you are to let it go, and relax, and come back. So, when a distracting thought or feeling arises, and it pulls your attention to it, allow it to be there, but don't give it any more attention. Even if you're in mid-sentence, just let it be.

Every time mind becomes distracted away from your object of meditation, there is tension and tightness that arises in both mind and body. That tension and tightness is what the

Buddha called craving. Craving is the "I like it, I don't like it" mind. Right after craving, clinging arises. What is clinging? Clinging is all of your opinions, all of your concepts about why you like or dislike the feeling, and then your old habitual tendency arises and you always treat this feeling in the same way. Our old habitual tendency is always, when a feeling arises, is to try to think the feeling. The more you think the feeling, the bigger the feeling becomes, the more intense it becomes, the more attached you become to that feeling. So, when you notice that a feeling arises or a distracting thought pulls your attention away from your object of meditation, as soon as you notice it, let it be, relax, smile, come back to your object of meditation.

It's always kind of comical for me because a lot of people, I'll say: "Ok, tell me about your meditation." - "Ah, I had a great meditation, my mind just stayed on the object of meditation and didn't move at all, and it was just a great meditation." And I kind of ho-hum that. "Yeah ok, you had some candy." But if you come and tell me: "Ah, I had the most terrible meditation, my mind was all over the place!" My next question to you is: "Well, did you recognize that? Did you let it be? Did you relax? Did you come back to your object of meditation?" - "Oh yeah, I did all of that but it still kept on running around." - "Oh, you had a great meditation then, didn't you?" It's exactly the opposite of what everybody thinks is a good meditation. Why? Because when you let go of the distraction, relax, smile, and come back to your object of meditation, you are building up your mindfulness muscles. You're building up your ability to observe what is happening in the present moment.

So you had an active meditation, that means you had to roll your sleeves up and you had to do some real work. But it was good meditation, just like lifting weights. You do that, you repeat it over and over again, eventually you start getting pretty strong. When you have an active meditation it means that you are learning how to strengthen your mindfulness muscles, and this is great meditation, it's not just good meditation. Like I said, bad meditation is seeing that you're thinking about something, and then just get so involved with it that you don't want to let it go. Now, you're not meditating at all.

Now, an interesting thing happens when craving arises. It always manifests in the same way as tension and tightness in your mind and in your body. And I told you that craving is the "I like it, I don't like it" mind. What did we start off with here? "I." This is the very start of the atta belief that "this feeling is me, this is mine, this is who I am." And then when craving arises, all of the thoughts about the feeling reinforce that belief that "this feeling is me, this is mine, this is who I am." And it causes mind to contract. And with that contraction comes more of the same, your habitual tendency. In Pāli we call it "bhava." It's always translated by most people as "being" or "experience," but actually… I had a real good long talk with my Abhidhamma teacher, Sayadaw U Silananda, before he died, that it was actually closer to a correct translation that we use the words "habitual tendency." Now, what is a habitual tendency? When this feeling arises, I always act that way. When a painful feeling arises, I always have the same reaction. Somebody says something to you and all of a sudden your mind grabs onto it and there's anger there. How did that occur?

One of the things that I have to ask you to do - and this is a monk thing - and the Buddha said that we cannot give a Dhamma talk if people are sitting in particular ways: crossing your legs, crossing your arms. So, I have to ask you not to do that. And then I found out some years ago by talking with somebody that was a body language expert, and he did some experiments with about a hundred people. And he gave them information, but first he said: "First, I want you to cross your legs and cross your arms;" and then he gave them a test on the information he gave them. They got about sixty per cent correct. And then he said: "Ok, uncross your arms, but keep your legs crossed;" and they got about seventy per cent correct. And then he said: "Ok, now open up, don't cross your legs, don't cross your arms;" and he gave them more information, they got close to 90 per cent of what he was saying. So, this is why the Buddha said that monks can't give talks when there are certain kinds of body postures.

When we have craving arise, it always manifests as tension and tightness. Now, I'm talking about very subtle, I'm not talking about gross tensions, although it can turn into gross tensions. There is - it's like a sack around your brain called the meninges - and every time your mind has a thought in it, it contracts a little bit. It's not real big, but it is noticeable once you learn about it. So, when I say to let go of the tension and tightness in your body, I'm meaning the gross tensions and tightnesses of holding your hands tight, or your shoulders tight, or your back, or wherever it happens to be, but I'm also talking about the subtle tension and tightness that's in your head. Now, everybody here right now has tension and tightness in their head. Notice that there's this subtle tension, and let it go. When you let it go, you'll feel a kind of expansion happen in your head, a release of tension, and right after that your mind becomes calm. You'll notice for a brief moment that there's no thoughts. There's only this pure awareness, and you bring that pure awareness back to your object of meditation.

Now, I know that there are some of you that have been practicing different kinds of meditation, and I'll show you exactly why the Buddha's meditation, the way he taught it, works so well and is immediately recognizable and effective. When you practice normal meditation and your mind is on your object of meditation, it gets distracted. Now, there are three or four different methods of dealing with this. One of them says you note it until it goes away; another one says you let it go and you come back immediately. But what you're doing, when you practice, in this way is, you're bringing that craving - that you haven't let go of yet - back to your object of meditation. And eventually your concentration starts to develop so it becomes very deep, and it will start suppressing hindrances when they arise. Now, there's a little problem with this because your hindrances are where your attachments are. So you practice absorption concentration, you can get real peaceful and calm while your mind is absorbed, but when you lose that concentration then you have hindrances coming at you really heavily. And you're not really very aware of it.

Now, the Buddha's practice is this: your mind is on your object of meditation - that's the same; your mind gets distracted - that's the same; you let go of your distraction - that's the same; but where the Buddha's teaching is different, is the Buddha said: "Tranquilize your bodily and mental formation" - mind and body - before coming back to your object of meditation. Now, it says this often. It says it in the Satipaṭṭhāna Sutta (MN-10), it says it in the Mindfulness of Body Sutta (MN-119), it says it in Mindfulness of Breathing Sutta (MN-118), it says it in sutta number 62 where the Buddha's giving instructions on how do to the breathing meditation to Rāhula, his son. I'm going to read that to you just so I can let you know that this isn't my idea.

Okay, this is the Mindfulness of Body Sutta number 119. It says "Mindfulness of Breathing."

MN-119:4. "Here a monk, gone to the forest or to the root of a tree or to an empty hut, sits down; having folded his legs crosswise, set his body erect, and established mindfulness in front of him, ever mindful he breathes in, mindful he breathes out. Breathing in long, he understands: 'I breathe in long;' or breathing out long, he understands: 'I breathe out long.' Breathing in short, he understands: 'I breathe in short;' or breathing out short, he understands: 'I breathe out short.'

Now, did you hear me say "nose," "nostril," "upper lip" or "abdomen?" No. It says you understand when you take a short breath, you understand when you take a long breath. Now, the real instruction occurs:

He trains thus:

These are key words - "he trains thus."

'I shall breathe in experiencing the whole body;'

Not "body of breath." The whole "body," physical "body."

he trains thus: 'I shall breathe out experiencing the whole body.' He trains thus: 'I shall breathe in tranquilizing the bodily formation;' he trains thus: 'I shall breathe out tranquilizing the bodily formation.'

That's the entire instructions in how to practice mindfulness of breathing. And you have no idea how many times I've gotten in discussion with monks in Asia, with monks here, with laymen teacher here, and I'll say: "It says that on the in-breath you tranquilize your body formation, on the out-breath you tranquilize your body formation. You tranquilize your body formation on the in-and-out-breath. Do you do that?" - "Well no, I practice this way." Well, but the instructions that the Buddha gave, very specifically said you tranquilize on the in-breath and you tranquilize on the out-breath. In other words, when you breathe in, you're not focusing on the breath; you see the breath and you relax; on the in-breath, you see the breath and you relax; on the out-breath, and you relax; on the in-breath, you relax; on the out-breath... that's quite different from the way, in this country in particular, meditation is being taught. Meditation is being taught to focus very deeply on the tiny sensation of the breath, but there's no relaxing that's occurring.

And I've run across a lot of people that have said: "Well, I become real peaceful and calm and serene." When you're practicing without the relaxation, your mind becomes absorbed, there's no hindrances that can arise, you can have all sorts of things that are very nice states that your mind focuses on, but you're not practicing insight while you're practicing your breath meditation. You're practicing a form of absorption if you don't have that relaxing. Now, coming back to the mindfulness of mettā - because that's what I teach, I teach insight in mettā - there is that relaxing. I'm continually talking about: you see a distraction, you relax; any tension or tightness in your body, in your mind, let it be and relax. So, this is basically the same kind of instruction that the Buddha was giving for the mindfulness of breathing.

When the Buddha was a Bodhisatta, he practiced the absorption kinds of concentration where he got to very deep states of absorption, but then he went to the teacher and he said: "Is this all there is?" And the teacher said: "Yeah, this is it, this is as far as you can go." You can get to, the first teacher said, the Realm of Nothingness; the second teacher said the Realm of Neither Perception nor Non-perception. Can't get any higher, that's it. And the Bodhisatta said, "I'm not satisfied with that. There's still something there that I'm seeing." He said "There has to be another way." Now, the meditation, the absorption meditation, has been taught from time immemorial. Everybody practices that in one form or another. It doesn't matter what religion you're talking about. When they're talking about some form of concentration, they're talking about absorption types of concentration.

I was in Burma for almost three years. I had the opportunity to go and study with some really, really good scholars. Now, one of the scholars was at the Sixth Buddhist Council, and he was the chief answerer for the Sixth Buddhist Council. He's called the Mingun Sayadaw. He had memorized over twelve thousand pages from the suttas and commentaries. He took a test. Now, you know how everybody here, they complain because "There's a four-hour test I have to take when you're going to college. Ah, it was a killer!" He took a test ten hours a day for thirty days in a row. He got better than ninety percent correct on everything that he did. I mean this man had an amazing mind. He knew the suttas unbelievably well. So, I went to him and I said "Bhante, where in the suttas does it mention 'access concentration' or 'moment-to-moment concentration'?" And he said, "It's not in the suttas. That's in the commentary." I asked him a lot of... in a lot of different ways basically the same thing about absorption concentration: "Is that really what the Buddha taught?" And he said: "No, it was different because of the tranquilizing." - "Well, why aren't we teaching that now?" - "Because the commentaries don't agree with that and we go with the commentaries."

When I let go of the commentaries, and I still use the commentaries occasionally because there's some real good points in the commentaries, but I always check it against what it says in the suttas now. When I started going to the suttas, I started seeing a definite different type of meditation that the Buddha was teaching.

Now, in this country in particular there's an awful lot of people that are very much interested in quote "straight Vipassanā." When you look up the word "vipassanā" in the suttas and you get all of the different references, the suttas that it goes to, and then you look up the word "samatha" and you go to those references; you start seeing that "vipassanā" and "samatha" are always mentioned together. The word "vipassanā," in the suttas, is mentioned just over a hundred times, I don't remember the exact number. The word "jhāna" is mentioned thousands of times in conjunction with "vipassanā" and "samatha." So, what did the Buddha teach? Did he teach straight Vipassanā or did he teach samatha-vipassanā? There's a Sutta 149 in the Middle Length Sayings that kind of clears everything up. Now, let me see if I can find this part, it's not there... okay, this is section number 10 if you want to go to it and read it yourself:

MN-149:10. "These two things - serenity (samatha) and insight (vipassanā) - occur in him yoked evenly together.

It says, these two things - serenity and insight - occur in him yoked, held together, evenly together. So there's a little interesting sidebar for you to think about.

What the Buddha taught was how to have a still, alert mind that saw how things occur - how they occur. We don't care about why - why is for the psychologist and the therapist. How does anger arise, what happens first, what happens after that, what happens after that? You can be sitting in your meditation very peacefully, very calmly, and all of a sudden somebody slams the door, they make a sound, doesn't matter what the cause is. And your mind goes "God, I hate that. I wished it'd stop." Now, how did that arise? Okay, first there was a sound, and then there was a feeling, and it was a painful feeling. And then there was craving, "I don't like," and tension, and then there's clinging, and then there's your habitual tendency of: "When this kind of feeling arises, I always act with dissatisfaction." So, you're reacting over and over again to a sound. Whose reaction is it? "It's mine, I don't like it, I don't want it to be there, I don't like being disturbed." - "I," "I," "I," "I," "I." When in fact, sound arose - that's not good, bad, or indifferent - but it was kind of loud and it was a painful sound. When your mindfulness is sharp, you will see that painful feeling arise - and immediately relax. Then the craving doesn't arise, and the clinging doesn't arise, and your habitual tendency doesn't arise. Your mind is alert, bright, and you bring that mind back to your object of meditation. It takes some degree of practice because these things happen very quickly, and it's hard to recognize them. Now, what actually happened? When the sound arose, there was a painful feeling and then that "I don't like it" tension, and your concepts, and opinions of the way things should be is fighting with reality, and that causes pain, that causes suffering, that causes all kinds of disturbance.

Now, the way Dependent Origination works is very fast. Every thought moment, it has Dependent Origination in it - {snaps finger} - that was a million times. It happens over and over again very quickly. The more you identify with the dissatisfaction, the more the dissatisfaction keeps arising; the more you identify with it, the more pain you experience. How to let go of the pain.

I used to get a kick out of one of my friends that was a Zen teacher, and he would teach people about Buddhism and he would say "Buddhism is about pain." And then he'd just sit there and he wouldn't say anything more. He didn't say anything about the cause of the pain, or the possibility of the cessation of the pain, or the way to do it. He just said, "Buddhism is about pain!" And I know some people that are teaching vipassanā, that they want you to have pain arise. So they tell you as soon as a painful sensation arises, you put your attention right in the middle of that pain and watch, quote, "its true nature." So you stare at that pain in your knee, or wherever it happens to be, and you watch all these different characteristics arise and pass away, but you're missing something when you do that. You're not seeing mind's reaction to the pain, which is tightened around it, "don't want it there." Pain by nature is a repulsive thing. So, is the Four Noble Truths being taught, when they say, "Put your attention right in the middle of the pain?"

Now, what I'm telling you is, when this feeling arises - pain is going to arise - welcome to having a human body. What do you do with it? First you notice all the thoughts about the pain, and you let those thoughts go and relax. Now, you notice a tight mental fist around that pain. Now, the truth is when these kind of sensations arise, they are there. Anytime you try to fight with the truth, anytime you try to control the truth, anytime you try to make the truth be something other than it is, that is the cause of suffering. So, what do I tell you to do? Allow the pain to be there. "It hurts." Yeah okay, it's a painful feeling. But it's okay for that painful feeling to be there; it has to be okay because that's the truth.

Allow the painful feeling to be there and relax into that. Now, bring your smile back to your object of meditation. The nature of these kinds of sensations is they don't go away right away. So your attention is going to go back to it. So you treat it in the same way again. Let go of the thoughts about it, relax, allow the space for that sensation to be there, relax. Come back to your object of meditation. What are you doing when you do that? You're practicing the entire Eightfold Path. You're changing from: "This is my pain and I don't like it" to "It's this sensation and it's okay for it to be there because that's the truth, it's there." You've changed your perspective. You've changed your view from "This is me, this is who I am" to "It's only that." Every time you change your perspective, there is a lessening of tension and tightness. There is the learning how to lovingly accept whatever arises in the present moment. Anytime you try to fight with what's happening in the present moment, anytime you don't like what's happening in the present moment, you can look forward to dukkha. You can look forward to pain, you can look forward to suffering, you can look forward to stress. I don't care what name you put on it; it hurts.

What is the cause of suffering? The Second Noble Truth: the cause of suffering is craving. How does craving arise? Craving arises as tension and tightness in your mind and in your body. Every time you let go of the tension and tightness in your mind, in your body - that's the Third Noble Truth - that's the cessation of the suffering. And the way you do it is by practicing the Eightfold Path, which we'll get into at another talk down the way. So, every time there's a distraction, every time your mind gets pulled away from your object of meditation, there is this craving, there is this tension and tightness. And every time you see it, you allow it to be and relax, you are practicing the Third Noble Truth.

Now, one of my monk friends - it was another scholar in Australia - we got in a big discussion about the word "Nibbāna." What is Nibbāna? And he kept on saying there's two kinds of Nibbāna. I'd never heard of that before. How can that be? So, there's a mundane kind of Nibbāna: "Ni:" no - "bāna:" fire. Putting out the fire. The fire of what? The fire of craving. You must experience the cessation of craving - the tension and tightness - many thousands, many tens of thousands, many hundreds of thousands of times before you will be able to experience the supra-mundane kind of Nibbāna. Letting go of that tension and tightness every time it arises gets you one step further, one step closer, to the supra-mundane Nibbāna. You will hear me say over and over again: "When a sensation arises, allow it to be, relax, come back to your object of meditation.

MN-20:3. **"When he gives attention to some other sign connected with what is wholesome, then any evil unwholesome thoughts connected with desire, with hate, and with delusion are abandoned in him and subside. With the abandoning of them his mind becomes steadied internally, quieted, brought to stillness, and collected. Just as a skilled carpenter or his apprentice might knock out, remove, and extract a coarse peg by means of a fine one, so too... when a monk gives attention to some other sign connected with what is wholesome... his mind becomes steadied internally, quieted, brought to stillness, and collected.**

I was telling some of you today about the five Rs: Release, Relax, Re-smile, Return, Repeat... but, I came up with another one. So, there is six of them. First is Recognize; recognize that your mind is pulled away from your object of meditation. Then Release the distraction, and Relax, Re-smile, Return, and continue doing it, continue on smiling, continue on with your object of meditation, Repeat. Anyway, when your mind is on your object of meditation, it's very peaceful and calm, and it's wholesome, it's staying with a wholesome object. When your mind gets distracted, that's when the craving, the clinging, and the pain begin. The more you get involved with that distraction, the more there is the "This is me, this is who I am, and I want to control it, and I want it to be the way I want it to be." And it never is, so there's your suffering.

But what I want you to get in the habit of doing is seeing how this distraction arises. Again, we don't care about why it arises - well, the door slammed, that's why - who cares? It's just a sound. It's just sound waves hitting the ear. Your ear is in good working order, the sound wave hits the ear, ear consciousness arises. The meeting of these three things is called ear-contact. With ear-contact as condition, ear-feeling arises. Feeling is pleasant or painful, or we could go all the way up to 108 different kinds of feelings, but I don't want to do that. It basically comes to either pleasant or painful. With feeling as condition, craving arises. Craving always manifests as tension and tightness, and it's the "I like it, I don't like it" mind. With craving as condition, clinging arises; all of your opinions and story about. With clinging as condition, habitual tendency arises. "I always think this way when this kind of feeling arises." Every time somebody slams the door, there is dissatisfaction: "I always act that way when that happens." That's the cause of a lot of suffering because "I don't like the door to slam. I don't like that sound. I want the sound to stop so it doesn't, quote, 'disturb me.' But sound is just sound, it's not good, it's not bad, it's just sound. And it's okay for the sound to be there, it has to be okay. Why? Because it's there - it isn't dependent on whether you like it or dislike it, it is there - you don't have any control over it. Your reaction is the cause of suffering: "I don't like it. I hate that when it happens. It disturbs my meditation. It makes me upset and frustrated," and your mind goes off into a thousand different things. And then with that distraction then comes more distraction, and it pulls your mind away further and further away from your object of meditation. Sometimes you can get caught for a long period of time. And then somebody else slams the door or the wind catches it or another sound happens, and your mind takes off with that one. What you think and ponder upon, that is the inclination of your mind. Whenever this sort of thing happens: "I don't like it. I want it to be different than it is," the more you get into disliking something, the more your mind will tend towards that dislike.

Now, in the morning, one of the things that we say is that hatred can never be overcome by hatred in this world; hatred can only be overcome by love. I like to change that around a little bit because hatred is such a hard word. How about aversion can never be overcome by aversion? Aversion can only be overcome by loving acceptance. How's that sound? "Well, you always act in this way!" How many times has that been said in relationships? "You're always like this!" Well no, you're not, but because you think that over and over again, your mind tends towards that and that leads to more and more suffering.

So how to overcome this habitual tendency? Sharpen your awareness to see when something happens and the feeling that arises because of that contact, and relax right then. If you relax that craving right then, then you don't have clinging, you don't have your habitual tendency. Your mind is very alert; your mind is very receptive for whatever else arises; you have gained a state of true equanimity. That's what this practice is for, that's what this practice is all about: sharpening your awareness so you can see how these things happen. That's the question that the Buddha asks: How? Why? Oh, there's millions of excuses of why things happen. "Well, I don't like these sounds because one time when I was in the crib, somebody made a real loud sound and scared the heck out of me and I've never liked loud sounds since." Why? Who cares! Why isn't the question. How did this arise? Now, the whole idea of getting rid of your hindrances is seeing how they arise.

Now, restlessness is a great hindrance, and you better be friends with it because it's going to stick around for a while, until you become an arahat anyway. What is restlessness? Restlessness, first off, is a painful feeling. There's the "I like it, I don't like it," and then there's all the stories about what's happening in the restlessness. Restlessness is every distracting thought. Every thought that pulls you away from your object of meditation is part of restlessness. So, you're sitting in meditation and all of a sudden you think about what happened last year, what happened last week, what happened yesterday - doesn't matter - what's going to happen tomorrow, doesn't matter what the distraction is. As soon as you recognize that your mind is not on your object of meditation, then let go of that distraction, relax, smile, come back to your object of meditation. The nature of these kinds of distractions is they're not going to go away right away. So, your mind gets pulled back and starts thinking again. How did that happen?

Take more interest in how the movement of mind's attention got from being very peaceful and calm on your object of meditation, to being distracted. How did that happen?

As you take more and more interest in how your mind gets distracted, you start becoming more familiar with the process because it is a true process. A lot of people will take words like "restlessness" or "automobile" or "pain;" all of these words are concepts. Now, we'll take automobile as a great concept. Go outside and show me where your automobile is. Is it the wheel, is it the bumper, is it the headlight, is it the steering wheel, is it the motor? You can go on and on and on. This is a thing that has many little parts that are put together to make up this idea that this is one thing. The same thing happens with pain. What is pain? Is it heat, is it anxiety, is it dislike, is it vibration? And it can be made up of all of those things. But when it's pain, it turns into "my pain." When you start taking it apart and saying "Well, this is heat, and here's some vibration, and here's some dislike of it, and this feeling arises, and all of these different parts." You start seeing that it's not yours, its just part of a process that arises. It happens in the same way every time. Tell me how it happened.

With restlessness, what happens first, what happens after that, what happens after that? When you become familiar with how your mind becomes distracted, you start letting go a little bit more quickly because you're recognizing this process. It's not "me," it's not "my restlessness," it's not "my thoughts," it's just a bunch of little things that are put together to make up this concept. Now, you're taking the concept apart and you're starting to see these little things arise. As you become more familiar with how they arise, you can let go of them more quickly, more easily, and that process is called Dependent Origination. There's not very many people in this country that will teach Dependent Origination in a meditation retreat because people, to be quite honest, don't really understand how it works. And you'll be getting more of that later, I promise. But Dependent Origination - sometimes there's five links that you look at, sometimes there's seven, sometimes there's nine, sometimes there's eleven. It just depends on the situation and how clear your mind is at that time, how good your awareness of this process is at that time.

Now, one of the big thing that's happening in this country is everybody is talking about the importance of impermanence, suffering, and the not-self nature of everything. In the Mahavagga - that's one of the books of the discipline - and anytime that's brought up, everybody thinks: "Oh, the book of discipline, rules for the monks!" It's a lot more than that! It has a lot of suttas in it. It has a lot of direction in how to do the meditation. In the Mahavagga it says: **"You can see anicca, dukkha, anatta, without ever seeing Dependent Origination, and you can never see Dependent Origination without seeing anicca, dukkha, and anatta."** That's a pretty powerful statement right there. That's pretty important, actually. You can always see impermanence, suffering, and the impersonal nature of everything when you see the process of Dependent Origination and how it works. You will become more and more familiar as your mind begins to calm down. And, don't be impatient. You play with this, you make this a game, and your awareness will take off, and you'll be able to recognize these things. Not all of them at once, you'll see one thing at a time, but that's ok. The thing that you want to be aware of - that the weakest link in Dependent Origination is craving. You can recognize it because there is tightness in your mind and in your body. And as soon as you see that you can start relaxing and letting it go. Then the suffering doesn't arise so much anymore. And you start gaining more of a sense of balance in your practice, in your everyday life.

Now, one of the things that I found, especially coming back to this country is: everybody assumes that the hindrances only arise really while you're sitting on the cushion; that's the only time you need to take a look at them. Wrong. Hindrances are arising all the time. When you're sitting on the cushion is the time that you can really spend watching how it arises. And you become more familiar with that, so when you get caught by a hindrance out there, you won't get caught for as long. You'll be able to recognize it, see it for what it truly is. See, this is an all-the-time practice. That's one of the reasons why I try to impress the idea that, while you're doing your daily activities - I don't care what you're doing - I want you be watching the movements of mind's attention. Stay with your object of meditation. If you can't stay with your object of meditation, at least smile; at least. Why? Because when your mind is uplifted, your attention is very quick, alert. And your mind is very agile; it sees things much more quickly when you have an uplifted mind.

I'm told that I'm crazy quite often because I try to get people to smile and have fun. But most people think; "Well, meditation is supposed to be serious." - "Life is supposed to be serious." I'd like to catch the guy that wrote that statement and smack him one. Who said life is supposed to be serious? I mean really! We all have this idea that that's the way quote "grownups" are supposed to act. But I'd rather be a kid; I am a kid. Who am I kidding? When you have a mind that has joy in it, you have a mind that is not attached at that time. But one of the mistakes that happens in Asia is: the monks that do the teaching of meditation, they're pretty severe. Because all the people in Asia, they're around monks all they time, they're happy-go-lucky folks, they're not real serious, they like to play and laugh and talk and have a good time, and then when it's time for them to do meditation, the monk has to be really severe. And they have joy coming up all the time, so they go to the teacher and they say: "Well, I have some joy coming up and it's really neat." The first thing the teacher says is: "Don't be attached!" Well, what happens when

Westerners - who are very serious minded and goal oriented and hard working - go to Asia and get a teacher like that? They tell us we got to try harder. "You got to note fifty thousand times in an hour! You have to really put out the effort!" Well, we knock ourselves out doing that, and as a result the progress in the practice is not very good because we're trying too hard, we're putting out too much energy, too much effort.

And it's only taken me a few years of being back in this country to really figure this out. I tell people just the opposite. You're already goal oriented, you're already trying too hard, lighten up, have some fun, relax! Why? Because that puts your mind in balance. In Asia they had to do it the other way. They were already too light, they had to get serious, they had to get pushed into getting in balance. But here we don't need that. I've seen an awful lot of retreats - except the ones that I give - where nobody smiles. And you see these deep wrinkles in their forehead where they're really trying hard. Well, if I see you doing that, I'm going to come and thump you on the head. Don't do that, relax, have fun! We need that kind of balance. And from my experience, it's the opposite... I haven't run across any Asian teachers that don't stress putting in a lot of effort, and a lot of energy. So, I'm starting up a meditation where you don't have to do that so much. I'm starting up a place where we can have fun and get in balance, and still have a really good practice.

I practiced straight Vipassanā for twenty years. I put a lot of effort into it. I went to a lot of different teachers. When I started practicing according to the way it teaches in the suttas, I started recognizing that I didn't have to put out that much effort. I didn't have to put out that much energy because I was already serious and trying hard as it was. I didn't need to add any more to it. It actually slowed down my progress in the meditation. And it was funny when I was in Malaysia because there was a lot of people that were practicing straight Vipassanā, and they would come out of a one-month retreat, and they were miserable. And they were saying things to other people that were horrible things, they were hurting people's feelings. And they'd come running to me and they'd say: "I need to take one of your retreats!" I only gave a one week retreat. "Ok, you come and do a mettā retreat. I'll teach you how to re-smile again." And then their mind got in balance, and then they were off to the races, do whatever they were going to do. But I didn't let anybody walk around being serious; you hear me laugh fairly often. Why? Because I want you to laugh. I want you to not try so incredibly hard that you turn out to be your own worst enemy. I want you to try, but be happy while you're doing it. Lightly, not in a heavy way. The Buddha's practice was always about balance. So, we need to practice smiling to have that balance.

When a hindrance arises, try to see how it arises, and have fun with it. Treat it like it's a partner, it's a game. "Well, this anger, I don't feel like smiling, I don't feel like playing, I feel like being mad!" Ok, you be mad, you suffer, you make yourself miserable, your choice. You can do that or not, it's up to you. Me, I like to laugh, makes my body feel good, makes my mind light. Let go of all kinds of attachments when I can laugh at how crazy my mind truly is. And I got a whopper, I'll tell you. But this is like going in and teaching people: "Well, I've always been running a circle this way," and now I'm coming along and saying "Well, I want you to go the other way." - "Well it's hard." - "Well, your old habits, hard to let go of. Your old habits of being grumpy, your old habits of being fearful, your old habits of having anxiety, or depression, whatever the catch of the day happens to be, it's hard to let go of." Why? Because we've thought about it a lot and our inclination of mind tends towards that. Now, I'm saying: "I want you to smile, and I want you to think loving and kind thoughts, and feel those thoughts in your heart." Change your old habit into a new habit. The more you do it, the easier it becomes, I promise.

MN 20: Removal of Distracting Thoughts   45

The first day of the retreat, it's the pits. It's always hard because your mind is still running around just like it always did out there. So, it starts to take to the discipline and then it says: "Well, I'm going to get sleepy for a little while, I'm going to run around and get restless for a little while, I'm going to dislike this, and I'm going to like that, and I'm going to hold on to this, and... " And you're doing all the things that you normally do, and I'm showing you a way of changing that habit, at least for a period of time. How much you change, how closely do you follow the directions? Don't add anything, don't subtract anything. Just smile. Feel that radiating feeling of love, the wonderful glowing feeling. Make a wish that you want to feel yourself, and then put that wish in your heart, and give it away! And keep giving it away.

One of the things that is not really brought up in this country in particular, is that there's three parts to meditation. The first two - they're never talked of; only sitting and walking, that's meditation. The Buddha said it's dana, sila, bhāvanā; that's what meditation is. Dana is giving: "Oh, the monk's talking about giving, he wants to get rich." No, I'm not talking about that. There's three ways to give: you give with your speech; you give with your actions; you give with your mind. I'm asking you to give with your mind. Every time I'm saying: "Stay with your spiritual friend, and wish them well," you're practicing your generosity that way. Now, there's three ways of giving too. Prepare your gift with a happy mind; give your gift with a happy mind; reflect on giving that gift with a happy mind. There's a lot of happy around here, isn't there? Do it often, as much as you can remember to do it, and not only while you're sitting on the cushion. Right now, I want you to do it all the time. I don't care if you're eating, I don't care if you're going to the toilet, I don't care what you're doing, keep giving. It feels good, makes you happy.

The next part is practicing your precepts. And this is incredibly important stuff, and this is something that most retreats that I've been to in this country, the teacher will give the precepts one time in Pāli, and never mention it again. And you never really get a feeling for it. We do it every day, we do it every morning. Not as some kind of rite and ritual, but as a reminder to keep your precepts. You break your precepts, you can look forward to a restless mind, fear, anxiety, depression. Now here we're taking eight precepts. When you get off retreat, I will give you five precepts. But don't just take the precepts and say: "Yeah, yeah, yeah, yeah, yeah." I highly recommend that you take the precepts every day to keep them in your mind. You break the precept and you can look forward to a lot of restlessness, anxiety, fear, depression, all of the stuff, all of the negative mental states arising. What do you think the hindrances are all about? They're about breaking precepts. The hindrances arise because you don't keep your precepts as good as you could.

I know people that they've done lots of retreats. They get off retreat, they forget about their precepts, go back to life the way that they normally live it. Come back, do a retreat, the retreat is two weeks long, it takes them a week to calm down, so that they can actually get some benefit from the retreat. Well, they're not being very serious about what the Buddha is talking about, or practicing. This is an all-the-time practice. Keep your precepts as closely as you possibly can. If you break one of the precepts for whatever reason, then stop right then, forgive yourself for making a mistake, make a determination not to break the precepts again, and take the precepts again, right then and there. "Ah, but a glass of wine is good after a meal or with a meal." Now, the precept says: "Don't take any drugs or alcohol." There's a real good reason for that. You take drugs and alcohol, one: it dulls your mind out right then, and you have a tendency to break the other precepts. But, more importantly, it affects your meditation in a negative way. Your mind gets dull for periods of time, and that's directly from taking alcohol. "Oh, it's only one glass, once in a while it doesn't matter." Yes it does, it does matter. Don't do that, not if you really want to purify your mind.

Keep your precepts as closely as you possibly can, all of the time.

Now, I've told this story over and over again, but I'll tell it again. I had a lady that, she was in Malaysia, she came to me and she said: "I want you to teach me how to meditate." She had never done any meditation before. She kept her precepts really closely. She was real kind and helpful to a lot of people. And I said: "Fine. I'm giving a weekend retreat. Come." So she came, and her first few sittings were hard, right after that I walked by her and I saw she had kind of a frown on her face. I said: "Come on, let's talk!" I said: "How's your meditation going?" And she said: "Well, I can only sit for about forty-five minutes!" And I said: "Well, why don't you sit longer?" She said: "I have such pain in my legs I can't believe it!" So, my being an American, I said: "Well, then don't sit on the floor. Try sitting in the chair." Now, this is one day of meditation, right? She had a four-hour sit. She got it! She got the meditation very well and very easily because she had spent her lifetime living by the precepts. And the Buddha said, if you keep your precepts really closely, your mind will naturally tend towards tranquility and calmness. I know people that for years and years of practice and they finally get a little bit of concentration. This is a lady that did it one day and she progressed further than many people. It was amazing. She was so good I wanted to smack her in back of the head. Nobody's that good.

This is all intertwined and interconnected. You don't just take one part of what the Buddha is teaching and say: "Well, I'm going to perfect that, the heck with the rest of it." Doesn't work. You're going to spend years and years of getting frustrated and then - like what's happening in this country - well, we'll try yoga Vipassanā, and we'll try psychotherapy Vipassanā, and we'll try Hindu Vipassanā, and Christian Vipassanā! Well, what's the matter? Why is that happening? Why is it there are so many people that have been practicing twenty years or more that don't have any real progress in their practice, so they start going to other things and incorporating it? Why is that happening? Because they're not following the Buddha's teaching completely. And they're starting to throw in some New Age ideas about this and that.

Now, I've gone off of the sutta a little bit, but it agrees with what I'm talking about and I am talking about what this Sutta is talking about.

How do you get rid of a hindrance? How do you get rid of a distraction? Now, one of the things that has happened in the suttas is, over the years there have been some things that have been added. This particular sutta was added some time later than the time of the Buddha, because he wouldn't have given these kinds of instructions. The kind of instruction I'm talking about is the favorite quote, in Burma, from their teachers to the students: When you have a distraction that's so bad…

7. "If, while he is giving attention to stilling the thought-formation of those thoughts, there still arise in him evil unwholesome thoughts connected with desire, with hate, and with delusion, then, with his teeth clenched and his tongue pressed against the roof of his mouth, he should beat down, constrain, and crush mind with mind.

That's one of the instructions. That has to do with absorption concentration. That doesn't have anything to do with what the Buddha was teaching. This particular sutta was added by some Brahmans about three hundred years after the Buddha had died, and it got into the suttas, and it's basically been overlooked every time there's been a Buddhist Council; that happens occasionally.

What this "teeth clenching" passage seems to have come from is Majjhima Nikāya sutta 36, section 20 (section 20 - isn't that ironic…). Here it has a completely opposite meaning. Let's see what sutta 36 says:

MN-36:20. "I thought: 'Suppose, with teeth clenched and my tongue pressed against the roof of my mouth, I beat

MN 20: Removal of Distracting Thoughts

down, constrained, crushed mind with mind. While I did so, sweat ran from my armpits.

But what follows changes the meaning entirely...

"But although tireless energy was aroused in me and unremitting mindfulness was established, my body was overwrought and uncalm because I was exhausted by the painful striving..."

So we see here that the Buddha is saying that this leads to uncalm and restlessness and it is what not to do. We must relax and 6R gently all of the hindrances, and never force them away or repress them.

There are some other suttas... one of the suttas says that the Buddha said that there would never be a country run by a female. And that's the most ridiculous thing I've ever heard. The Buddha would never say anything like that, but that is in one of the suttas. And it just gets kind of overlooked because it's not any major kind of teaching, so the heck with it.

But the way you overcome any hindrance, any distraction, is by recognizing that your mind has been pulled to that distraction, let the distraction be, relax, smile, and come back to your object of meditation.

Be more alert as to the process of the distraction. Let's say with dullness, sleepiness, okay? How does sleepiness arise? Well, you're kind of on your object of meditation; and then you kind of let your mind ho-hum and think about this and think about that; and then your mind starts to get a little bit more dreamy; and then your back starts slumping; and then all of a sudden you almost fall over because you're asleep; and then you try to put in a lot of effort and straighten up real fast. But you haven't put in the right kind of effort and you still have those ho-hum thoughts, and the whole process happens again. So, how do you overcome the sleepiness?

You don't overcome it at the start, you overcome it at the end. You become more familiar with how this arises. When you start seeing that your back is starting to slump, if, right then, you recognize that and let go of that, straighten your back, come back to your object of meditation, then you'll go only that far. You won't go till you're bobbing! And then you see the process of what happens right before that. As you do this a few times, you'll start to see: "Oh, this is how that works!" As you recognize this more quickly, you start to let go more quickly. As you let go more quickly and relax into that, you stop identifying with that as being yours. And the hindrance eventually gets so weak that it won't even come up any more. If you laugh with yourself about getting caught again then the sleepiness will fade away.

What happens then? A real sense of relief. Right after the relief, you feel joy coming up big time, very light in your body, very light in your mind, happy feeling, really, really happy. There's some excitement with it. When that fades away, then you feel more comfortable than you've ever felt. Your mind feels comfortable, your body feels comfortable. Your mind stays with your object of meditation, doesn't move.

What I just described to you was the first jhāna. How did you get to that first jhāna? By understanding the process of the hindrance, how the hindrance worked, and letting go of that attachment to it. What's the attachment? "I, this is me, this is mine, this is who I am." You've broken it down enough, so that you see that this is part of an impersonal process. It's just stuff coming up, it always comes up in the same way, so you start letting go as you recognize it. You've let go of that attachment (craving). And for that, you get some candy.

Now, the hindrances are incredibly important. Your mindfulness is going to be real good and sharp for a period of time, and then, for one reason or another, it starts to get weaker. And before long, there's another distraction. So you get to work with that. Every time you let go of a distraction, relax, smile, come back to your object of meditation, your mindfulness gets a little bit clearer, stronger, you're able to watch it more clearly and not identify with the hindrance so much any more. You're starting to see every hindrance as part of a process. So, the hindrances are absolutely a necessary part of your practice. It's good that they arise. Why? Because it makes you go to work. So you have to let go of them. It helps you to see how the process works more and more clearly. And this happens going from one jhāna to the next. Every time you let go of a hindrance, you'll be able to experience a deeper kind of jhāna because your understanding in how the process works becomes more clear.

When the Buddha was talking to someone about the way to experience Nibbāna, he described it in dozens of places in the suttas that the way that you experience Nibbāna is by seeing Dependent Origination. That's the way you experience Nibbāna... not by seeing anicca, dukkha, anatta; you see that automatically. But it's seeing and recognizing the process as being an impersonal process, and that's the way it works. Your understanding is the thing that gets you to Nibbāna. It's not a mystical, magical pop... there it is. It's your understanding of the process.

That is what the Blessed One said. The monks were satisfied and delighted with the Blessed One's words.

Let's share some merit, then.

May suffering ones be suffering free
And the fear struck fearless be.
May the grieving shed all grief
And may all beings find relief.
May all beings share this merit
That we have thus acquired
For the acquisition of
All kind of happiness.
May beings inhabiting space and earth
Devas and Nagas of mighty power
Share in this merit of ours.
May they long protect
the Buddha's Dispensation.
Sādhu… Sādhu… Sādhu…

MN-10: The Foundations of Mindfulness (Satipaṭṭhāna Sutta)

These days there are heaps of books on Buddhism. People read this and that from different Buddhist teachings and become thoroughly confused. Where to go from there? The practice of Dhamma is the answer. This can only be done using the principles of this profound and wide ranging Sutta. This is the cornerstone of the Buddha's instruction, for nothing good can be accomplished without mindfulness. Generosity cannot be practiced without it, neither can the moral precepts. And how far will one get with the development of the mind without mindfulness? The principles of this Sutta, when practiced, establish mindfulness or awareness in the mind as immovably as a foundation stone. This means that forgetfulness, distraction, boredom, worry, dullness-all deluded states of mind are gradually replaced by mindfulness, full awareness and wisdom-understanding. All kinds of mental troubles, whether born of greed, hatred and delusion, however strong they are, can be overcome with mindfulness. This is because to be mindful, as taught in this Sutta, is not to add something new to the mind, it is strengthening a mental factor which is already there, making the occurrences of the mindful mind stronger and more frequent than they had been. The wandering mind distracted by the sense here and there and pursuing all sorts of unwholesome thoughts occurs less frequently. This makes for more happiness and less suffering. Try out the Satipatthàna Teachings and find out for yourself! But when you do it is advisable to have someone who can guide your efforts and help with your problems.[1]

Presented on 21st and 22nd February 2006 at Dhamma Dena Vipassanā Center, Joshua Tree, California

BV: Ok, the sutta tonight is the Satipaṭṭhāna Sutta, The Foundations of Mindfulness.

---

[1] *A Treasury of the Buddha's Words: Discourses From the Middle Collection*, translated by Nyanamoli and edited by Phra Khantipalo, with notes by Phra Khantipalo. (Mahamakut Rajavidyalay Press, Bangkok, Thailand. Publication date unknown)

1. THUS HAVE I HEARD. On one occasion the Blessed One was living in the Kuru country where there was a town of the Kurus named Kammāsadhamma. There he addressed the monks thus: "Monks." - "Venerable sir," they replied. The Blessed One said this:

2. "Monks, this is the direct path for the purification of beings, for the surmounting of sorrow and lamentation, for the disappearance of pain and grief, for the attainment of the true way, for the realization of Nibbāna - namely, the four foundations of mindfulness.

3. "What are the four? Here, Monks, a monk abides observing the body as a body, ardent, fully aware, and mindful, having put away covetousness and grief for the world. He abides observing feeling as feeling,

This translation says: "feelings as feelings," but we got to take the "s" off of that because it's way too misunderstood, so we want to say "feeling as feeling."

ardent, fully aware, and mindful, having put away covetousness and grief for the world. He abides observing mind as mind, ardent, fully aware, and mindful, having put away covetousness and grief for the world. He abides observing mind-objects as mind-objects, ardent, fully aware, and mindful, having put away covetousness and grief for the world.

Now, the first part is the contemplation, or observation, of the body, and it starts out with mindfulness of breathing. Now, an interesting thing is that the instructions of mindfulness of breathing are exactly, word for word, letter for letter, the same here as it is in the Anāpānasati Sutta, the Kāyagatāsati - Mindfulness of Body - Sutta, and sutta number sixty two (MN-62, The Mahārāhulovāda Sutta), where the Buddha gives instructions in mindfulness of breathing. So these instructions are pretty much standardized through all of the different kinds of meditation.

MN 10: The Foundations of Mindfulness   55

4. "And how, Monks, does a monk abide observing the body as a body? Here a monk, gone to the forest or to the root of a tree or to an empty hut, sits down; having folded his legs crosswise, set his body erect, and established mindfulness in front of him, ever mindful he breathes in, mindful he breathes out. Breathing in long, he understands: 'I breathe in long;' or breathing out long, he understands: 'I breathe out long.' Breathing in short, he understands: 'I breathe in short;' or breathing out short, he understands: 'I breathe out short.'

The key word to this part of the instructions is "he understands." He knows when he's taking a long breath and when it's short. He knows when the breath is very fine and when it's coarse. He knows when it's subtle, and when it's not. He understands. It doesn't say: "he focuses on." It doesn't say: "he puts his strong attention only on the breath," it says he understands the breath. And again, you want to notice that it doesn't say "nostril tip," "nostril," "upper lip," or "abdomen," or any combination of those. You just understand what the breath is doing in the present moment. Now...

He trains thus:

These are key words because this is the actual instruction in the meditation itself.

'I shall breathe in experiencing the whole body;'

In the first edition of The Middle Length Sayings, Bhikkhu Bodhi, I talked to him about this, he was obliged to put in brackets "(of breath)" behind "experiencing the whole body." That was when Nyanaponika was still alive, and Nyanaponika was Bhikkhu Bodhi's teacher, so he felt obliged to put that in. After Nyanaponika died, he came out with a second edition, and he took "of breath" out because it's misleading. It makes you, if you put "of breath" behind "experiencing the entire body," it implies that you're focusing very deeply just on the breath to the exclusion of everything else, which is a form of absorption concentration. But you'll see in a moment that that is not the case. So when he came out with the second edition, he took that out in every place except The Mindfulness of Breathing sutta. He forgot to take it out in that one, but he took it out everywhere else.

he trains thus: 'I shall breathe out experiencing the whole body.' He trains thus: 'I shall breathe in tranquilizing the bodily formation;' he trains thus: 'I shall breathe out tranquilizing the bodily formation.'

Now, this is the entire instructions in the meditation of how to do mindfulness of breathing. I have had many, many discussions with many, many monks who are practicing meditation and teaching meditation, and I say: "Well, how do you practice mindfulness of breathing?-Well, I put my attention on my nostril or upper lip, and I keep my attention there very strongly." Now, that doesn't match the instructions of "he trains thus." He trains thus: tranquilizing the bodily formation on the in-breath, and tranquilizing the bodily formation on the out-breath. They're just taking the breath without the tranquilizing. This last part of the instruction is the very thing that makes the Buddha's meditation different from everybody else's teaching.

All of the brahmins and Hindus of the time, they were doing breath meditation, but they were focusing just on the breath. They didn't put in that extra step of tranquilizing the bodily formation. Now, what is tranquilizing the bodily formation mean? Most people, especially in this country, when you talk to them about the body, to them the body is from the neck down, and the mind is from the neck up, when in fact the body is from the top of the head all the way down.

Now, when it says tranquillize the bodily formation, what it's talking about is there is subtle tensions and tightnesses in your head, in your mind, in your brain. You relax on the in-breath, you feel an opening and a calming, you relax on the out-breath, you feel an opening and a calming, opening and calming. You're using the breath as the reminder to relax, to tranquillize your bodily formation. Now, this means also that if there's any tension anywhere in your body, if you see that tension, you relax that, also relaxing this. {BV point at his head} The subtle tightness that's in your head is also a tightness in your mind. So you're actually tranquilizing both the bodily formation, and the mental formation by relaxing.

How many times have you heard me say: "When there's a distraction, let go of that, relax, smile, come back to your object of meditation?" The more you can relax the tension and tightness that is very subtle in your head, the faster your meditation deepens. And when I've talked to the monks and the other teachers that are teaching mindfulness of breathing, and I come to this statement of tranquilizing the bodily formation on the in-breath and the out-breath, and I say: "Do you do that?," and there's a very blank look. "No, we don't do the meditation this way. We follow the Buddha's teaching another way." But this extra step is the key to changing your entire meditation so that it becomes immediately effective. The progress in meditation is so much faster when you follow all of the instructions when you're doing mindfulness of breathing that he gave.

Now, I know that a lot of Vipassanā people, they say they practice the Mahasi method, and the Mahasi method says that when there's a distraction, you put your attention on that distraction until it goes away and then immediately come back to the breath. They don't have any relaxing in it. If there's no relaxing then you have things like access concentration and moment-to-moment concentration. When you have this kind of one-pointed concentration, when your concentration gets deep enough, the force of the concentration pushes down the hindrances so they don't arise. And they call that purifying the mind, and in a way they're right. But it's not the way that the Buddha taught.

It's a little bit different than that. The way the Buddha taught to tranquillize your mind was by letting go of the tension and tightness caused by distraction. How do you let it go? You relax. What are you relaxing? You are relaxing the tension and tightness caused by craving. Craving always manifests as tension and tightness in your mind and in your body. So every time you let go of that tension, especially the tension that's in your head, you'll feel an expansion, and your mind takes a little step down and becomes calm. Right after that you'll notice that there's not any thoughts. But there's real, good, strong, pure awareness, and you bring that mind, that has no craving because you've let it go, back to your object of meditation.

Now, this is day three of the meditation and some of you are doing incredibly well-that's not a good word-very, very well, and it makes me very happy that you're following these instructions like you are because you're starting to progress; you're starting to have happiness and joy arise; you're starting to feel more at ease with the meditation; and you're starting to understand what this is all about. And that comes from following that one extra step of relaxing. I've been to many, many retreats practicing the Mahasi method, and I started noticing after the first seven or eight years that it takes about five years to really understand what the meditation isn't, before you start understanding what the meditation is. But, that's not happening with this retreat. You're all starting to understand what the meditation is, right now. You don't have to go through the five year period that most people do. You're really starting to grasp it, and it makes me incredibly happy to see how well you're all doing. It's hard work, but you're getting it.

So this extra step of tranquilizing the bodily formation, letting go of the tension and tightness, means that you're letting go of craving. And what is craving? That is the cause of suffering. And when you let go of that craving, and your mind becomes... you feel that expansion and calmness, that pure mind, that is where the cessation of suffering is. And you're bringing that cessation back to your object of meditation. So it's kind of an amazing phenomena that so many people are so interested in practicing the Buddha's teaching, but they're not following the instructions. This is only four lines in the instructions, four sentences, but they're not following them exactly. When I first started practicing meditation, it happened to be with the Mahasi method, and I was just... I considered myself a dumb American, I didn't know anything. So whatever the teacher said that I was supposed to do, that's what I did. It took me twenty years to finally go and understand what these instructions were talking about because I was always following what the teacher said without investigating more deeply on my own. So I want to encourage you not to believe anything that I'm saying. I want you to investigate on your own and see whether this really works or not, and you're starting to do that.

Just as a skilled lathe-operator or his apprentice, when making a long turn, understands: 'I make a long turn;' or, when making a short turn, understands: 'I make a short turn;' so too, breathing in long, a monk understands: 'I breathe in long;' or breathing out long, he understands: 'I breathe out long.' Breathing in short, he understands: 'I breathe in short;' or breathing out short, he understands: 'I breathe out short.' He trains thus: 'I shall breathe in experiencing the whole body;' he trains thus: 'I shall breathe out experiencing the whole body.' He trains thus: 'I shall breathe in tranquilizing the bodily formation;' he trains thus: 'I shall breathe out tranquilizing the bodily formation.'

As you begin to see when distractions arise in your mind and you let go of the distraction and relax, smile and come back to your object of meditation, you're beginning to see how mind moves, mind's attention moves. And with that you're starting to develop wisdom, little bit by little bit. Now, if you have an active mind, but you see that as soon as you notice, you let go of the distraction, relax, smile, and come back, you're starting to improve your mindfulness. Improving your mindfulness means you're starting to see how mind's attention moves from one thing to another. You know, you're sitting in meditation and your mind is on your object of meditation, breathing or whatever, and all of a sudden you're thinking about what happened yesterday. How did that happen? When I was studying about the seven factors of awakening, I started thinking that there actually... there needs to be another one or two added into that. The first thing has to have, you have to have curiosity. You have to want to know: "What happened? How did that work?" Not getting involved in "why" did that work that way, but "how" did it work? That's the key question that the Buddha was always presenting: How? How does that arise? How does that work?

Since coming back to this country-I spent twelve years in Asia-and coming back to this country, there was a lot of talk about stress, and a lot of talk about depression, and a lot of talk about drugs to overcome the depression, and drugs to overcome the stress. When you start looking at how mind's attention moves, you don't need any drugs for that. All you have to do is start to pay attention to how this arises. So how does stress arise? A feeling arises, most often it's a painful feeling: "I don't like this." Critical mind is real big in this. "I want it to be different than it is." Right after the feeling, the "I like it, I don't like it" mind. Right after that, the story about why you like or don't like that feeling, and your habitual tendency of really getting involved with trying to think your feeling away.

Now, on one of the charts that we handed out, the top one as I remember, is the five aggregates, and it shows how those turn into the four foundations of mindfulness. Now, when your mindfulness becomes weak or distracted, then you look at the bottom line and you see all of these hindrances that are there. When your mindfulness gets weak then a hindrance will arise. The hindrances are not the enemy to fight with, they're friends to welcome in. They are your best friends because they're showing you up close and personal where your attachments are. And what is an attachment? Attachment is the belief that: "I am that. I am this feeling. I am this thought."

But you know, I've talked to an awful lot of people and I say: "Well, you have this depression. Did you ask that feeling to come up?" Did you say: "Well, I haven't been depressed for a few days, it's time to get depressed?" No, nobody's crazy enough to do that. Well, maybe some people are. But it arises because there's an expectation of something being the way "I want it to be." That's your opinions and your concepts and that sort of thing. When reality doesn't meet that expectation, a painful feeling arises, and the "I don't like it" mind grabs onto that and you get more and more involved in all of the concepts and opinions, and ideas about why you want it to be other than the way it is. But the truth is, it arises because of past action. What arises and is in the present moment is the truth. It's ok for that feeling to be there. It has to be ok because it is the truth. What you do with what arises in the present moment dictates what happens in the future. If you fight with the truth, if you resist the truth, if you try to change the truth to match your ideas, you can look forward to suffering.

Now, the more you think about a feeling, the bigger and more intense that feeling becomes, until just a regular feeling turns into this huge emergency. "And I can't sleep, and I can't eat, and I'm so depressed all the time!" Why? Because you continually are resisting a feeling and trying to think your feeling away, and it doesn't work. Why doesn't it work? Because you can't control whether feeling arises or not. It arises because conditions are right for it to arise. What you're learning how to do right now is to recognize that tension and tightness that arises right after the feeling arises. That tension and tightness is craving.

That's the start of that false idea that "This is me. This is mine. I don't like it. I want it to be different than it is." Then you have the clinging. And the clinging is the story, all of the ideas, all of the concepts, all of the opinions about why this feeling should be other than it is. So you keep trying to think the feeling, so the feeling gets bigger and more intense. Like it has a lot of energy, and all of a sudden you're trying to push it back down, and it pushes back and gets stronger. So you have to finally wind up saying: "Well I can't stand this, I'm going to take some drugs. That'll control it." And these drugs wind up dulling your mind and causing your body all kinds of different problems, and it doesn't solve the problem. What's going to solve the problem? Practicing meditation the way the Buddha taught.

And I told you the first night, the Buddha didn't just teach sitting like a rock-that's meditation. He said you have to practice your generosity. Anybody that's really into their depression, be a friend to them-take them to a hospital where somebody is dying of cancer and say: "You think you got problems? What are you depressed about? Here's somebody that's got some real problems." Then you suggest what their job is, is to go visit this person in the hospital and make them smile and feel at home and at ease. Practice your generosity, practice it as much as you possibly can. Practice giving in your speech; saying things that make other people feel good; in your actions, helping in whatever way is necessary; and with your thoughts. Now, you're practicing Loving-Kindness Meditation; you're doing that. You're practicing all of these things and keeping your precepts. Now, your meditation is starting to blossom. I mean, I just look at your faces and it makes me smile because one of the advantages of practicing Loving-Kindness Meditation is your face becomes very beautiful. Your face starts to get radiant and glowing, and that's what I'm seeing. It's great! You're practicing giving that loving-kindness to your friend. Giving it away. Now, when you get home, call up your spiritual friend and ask them if they've noticed any difference in the last week or so. It's amazing.

MN 10: The Foundations of Mindfulness

The whole point of The Satipaṭṭhāna Sutta is to try to teach us how to let go of craving. How to improve our observation power, and watch how mind's attention goes from one thing to another. That's what mindfulness is, seeing attention go from one thing to another. Relaxing, letting it be, smiling, coming back. Staying with that as much as you possibly can. But you can't criticize yourself because you're not as good as you think you should be. Criticizing is no fair. You're as good as you are, and that's great. You have to let go of the expectations. You have to develop what Suzuki Roshi used to phrase as "the beginner's mind." Do you know what's going to happen five minutes from now? I don't either. The roof could fall down. An airplane can come right here and drop right in on us. Who knows? Why do we have to try to expect something to be in a particular way? The more we have expectations, the more suffering we cause ourselves when those expectations don't arise.

5. "In this way he abides observing the body as a body internally, he abides observing the body as a body externally, he abides observing the body as a body both internally and externally.

Now, what's it talking about here? How are you observing? First off, I really don't like the word original word "contemplating" because it implies thinking, and this is observation. So I changed that here. How are you seeing the body as a body internally? How do you do it? You see when there's tension and tightness and you relax. On the in-breath you relax, on the out-breath relax.

{repeats} he abides observing the body as a body externally,

You're using the breath as the reminder to relax. That's the external part of the body. And you're doing both internally and externally.

He abides observing in the body its nature of arising, he abides observing in the body its nature of vanishing,

You're seeing that all the time. You're seeing the nature of both arising and passing away, but it's not just of the physical body, it's of the tension and tightness and the mental body that you are seeing relax.

he abides observing in the body its nature of both arising and vanishing. And he abides independent, not craving or clinging to anything in the world.

How are you independent, not craving or clinging to anything in the world? Remember, craving is the start of the ego-identification or "I am that," and clinging is the thinking about that. You're independent because you're letting go of that "I like it" or "I don't like it" mind, craving. Just letting it go. You become independent, you become very clear without the cloudiness of the false belief that "This is me. This is who I am."

That is how a monk abides observing the body as a body.

6. "Again, Monks, when walking, a monk understands: 'I am walking;' when standing, he understands: 'I am standing;' when sitting, he understands: 'I am sitting;' when lying down, he understands: 'I am lying down;' or he understands accordingly however his body is disposed.

7. In this way he abides observing the body as a body internally, externally, and both internally and externally... And he abides independent, not craving or clinging to anything in the world. That too is how a monk abides observing the body as a body.

Then we get into the four postures, and I've always thought that this was kind of comical, especially when I was practicing with the Mahasi method because they said: "Well, know what posture you're in, and note it ten or fifteen times: sitting, sitting, sitting, sitting, sitting, sitting; standing, standing, standing; walking, walking, walking; lying down, lying down, lying down. It always seemed kind of a strange exercise. I know when I'm standing, I know when I'm sitting. It's saying that whatever posture you're in, practice your meditation, practice staying with your object of meditation. Practice, if you're doing mindfulness of breathing: on the in-breath relax, on the out-breath relax, whether you're sitting, standing, walking, or lying down. If you're practicing loving-kindness then stay with that radiating feeling, and making a wish and wishing your friend happiness, whether you're standing, sitting, lying down, or walking.

Now, here's another part that is very interesting, and this is called "full awareness."

8. "Again, Monks, a monk is one who acts in full awareness when going forward and returning; who acts in full awareness when looking ahead and looking away; who acts in full awareness when flexing and extending his limbs; who acts in full awareness when wearing his robes and carrying his outer robe and bowl; who acts in full awareness when eating, drinking, consuming food, and tasting; who acts in full awareness when defecating and urinating; who acts in full awareness when walking, standing, sitting, falling asleep, waking up, talking, and keeping silent.

Now, the question is, full awareness of what? It's a real easy answer. Full awareness of your object of meditation. What this is trying to tell you is, it doesn't matter what you're doing, stay with your object of meditation. Doesn't matter whether you're eating or going to the bathroom. You stay with your object of meditation, when you're sitting, when you're standing, when you're walking, when you're falling asleep, when you're waking up. Stay with your object of meditation. Smile. Wish your friend happiness. Easy, right?

9. "In this way he abides observing the body as a body internally, externally, and both internally and externally... And he abides independent, not craving or clinging to anything in the world. That too is how a monk abides observing the body as a body.

It doesn't matter what your body is doing at the time, stay with your meditation as much as you possibly can. Be fully aware when your mind is uplifted and when it's not. Be fully aware when your mind is tight, and when it's not. Be fully aware when there's a hindrance, and when there's not. Know what to do with all these things; stay with your object of meditation. If your mind is pulled away to something, let it be, relax, smile and come back to your object of meditation, continually. Do that fifty thousand times an hour. Or smile and have fun with it. Keep your mind light, keep your mind uplifted. That's why the corners of your mouth are so important because the corners of your mouth go up, so does your mental state. With your mental state uplifted, it's very easy to see when you start too heavy out and get heavy emotional states in it. It's very easy to see when you get caught, and it's also very easy, with practice, to let it be, relax and smile, unless your attachment is really, really strong. Then you have to roll up your sleeves and go to work with it.

But let's say that, you get up in the middle of the night; you got to go to the bathroom; you think: "No, I'm not going to turn the light on, I'll just go in there." And you stub your toe. What happens in your mind? First thing, there's a painful feeling. Next: "I don't like that painful feeling." Next: "I hate it when I stub my toe, that really hurts, and grrr, grrr, grrr, grrr, grrr." And limping around and cursing, and all of those sorts of things. Is your mind alert, uplifted, or not? So what do you do? You know, anytime you have a physical pain arise in your body, your mind and your body is telling you right then: "It hurts and I need some love." And what do we always give it? "I hate this feeling when it arises, I wish the pain would stop; oh that hurts so bad, I hate that." You're giving it aversion.

Now, this is something that I've practiced a lot because when I was in Asia I was barefoot a lot. And they have this bad habit in Asia of having these little steps that are about an inch high, that lead into the bathroom, and I've broken a lot of toes because of that. And I actually got quite good at being able to recognize the dissatisfaction of the pain when it arose, and I really was able to see how all of these things arose because it happened often enough. And when I would notice that my mind got onto the dissatisfaction of that pain, I would let that go and relax, and start sending loving-kindness and relaxing my mind and love my toe. And then I would keep doing that for a little while, while I hobbled into the bathroom and did whatever I did, and then I hobbled back out and I laid down. Next morning I'd wake up then start moving around and I looked down at my foot and it's all bloody. And I'm starting to think: "Well, what in the world, how did that happen?" And then my memory kicks in, and it says: "Oh, I kicked that real hard last night, I stubbed my toe." But there's not so much pain in that. As you begin to put loving-kindness into a pain, and let go of the dissatisfaction, the endorphins in your body start flowing all through your body. The endorphins are about ten times more powerful than morphine. It takes away that pain and you don't even feel it anymore. And this has happened, not a few times, this has happened a lot, my toes are real crooked because of it.

So when your awareness is up, and your mind is uplifted, those kinds of things will automatically start to happen more often. Your mindfulness starts to improve more as you have a happy mind. Remember the other day, I was telling you, in sutta number nineteen (MN-19, The Dvedhāvitakka Sutta) the Buddha said: "What a person thinks and ponders on, that is the inclination of their mind." You think and ponder on dissatisfaction and having critical thoughts, your mind is naturally going to tend towards that. You start thinking more and more loving and kind thoughts and giving those thoughts to other people, then your mind is going to tend towards that all the time. Takes practice, but what else have we got to do? So, the more you practice smiling and having a light mind, the more your mind will tend to smile and be light. This is what this instruction of full awareness is all about. No matter what you're doing, stay with having that light mind and wishing yourself and other people well, and as you do that you will tend to have that happen more and more often, and that leads to happiness. But it also leads to a kind of awareness that's very much more alert when your mind gets pulled down. So if you stub your toe, you don't go to bed cursing, and waking up in the morning cursing because the pain didn't go away.

When I was practicing the Mahasi method when I was in Burma, they were encouraging us very much to eat very, very, very slowly, and watch each little movement as you had it occur. And sometimes it would take us an hour to finish; this is of constant movement, to finish a meal. I never was able to translate those kind of slow, meticulous actions into everyday living. I never did quite figure out: "Why are we doing that?" When I was doing a walking meditation, I was seeing five hundred, a thousand or more, little tiny movements as I was picking the heel up; and then I saw that, that many again as I was picking the toe up; and then I saw that many again as I was moving my foot forward; and I saw that many again as I was dropping it. It took me forty-five minutes to walk the length of the meditation hall, one time. But how does that translate into everyday life? "Well, you need to see the intention before every movement." It made me wonder-was that practicing full awareness? When I started getting back into the suttas, I started reflecting on those times when I was moving very slowly all the time, and I started thinking about the things that they were talking about, of watching all of these tiny movements of the body. But one thing they never told me to watch was what my mind was doing.

They wanted me to focus my attention on actions of the body and completely left mind alone. I don't think that's what the Buddha had intended when he was teaching the Satipaṭṭhāna Sutta. I think the Buddha had intended that he wants you to watch what mind is up to all the time no matter what your actions are. He wants you to see when craving arises; he wants you to see when clinging arises. How do these movements of mind's attention occur? That's how you start to

MN 10: The Foundations of Mindfulness 69

begin to see what Dependent Origination is all about. Not by keeping your attention in an external way on a movement, but by keeping your attention on mind's movement, when it goes from one thing to another. Now, that doesn't mean that you don't pay attention to what you're doing while you're doing it, you can really hurt yourself if you don't, but you watch what mind is doing as much as you possibly can.

Now, with all of these jhānas that I was talking about last night, can you experience joy and happiness while you're walking from here to there, or while you're washing your body, or while you're washing your clothes, or while you're eating a meal? Can you see joy and happiness and stillness of mind while you're doing that? If your mindfulness is good, yes. Can you experience equanimity when you're walking to your car? That doesn't mean letting your mind ho hum and think about this and think about that. It means seeing that there's this distraction, letting go of that, coming back into the present moment while you're walking. Can you do that? That's what this is all about. It's about teaching ourselves how to have this incredibly balanced mind that's very alert and that tends towards happiness. And this is not the kind of happiness that's giddy and you feel like laughing; it's a sense of relief because there's no suffering.

The jhānas can be experienced with whatever you're doing, but it takes strong mindfulness, it takes strong attention, and observation of how mind's movement arises. And when it gets distracted, that distraction is a hindrance. Letting go of the hindrance, letting go of the craving, smiling and coming back, keeping your mind uplifted and light-that's the meditation! Too many people have the idea that meditation is only about sitting like he's doing, not moving. {BV nods at the Buddha statue.} Well, I know chickens that can do that, and they can sit for hours on end, but is that a useful thing? The whole point of the meditation is to be able to take it out into your life and use it daily, be able to see how you cause your own pain by these attachments. Like when you stub your toe and curse it, and then you try to push the pain away so you can do something else, and the pain keeps coming back, and you keep disliking it-does that lead to the cessation of suffering? No. Why? Because there's still attachment there, there's still the "I believe this sensation is mine and I don't like it. I want it to be different than it is." This is fighting with the truth, fighting with what is happening in the present moment. The Buddha was very much in favor of learning how to lovingly accept whatever arises and see that with balance. That's what the Satipaṭṭhāna Sutta is trying to teach.

Now, one of the things that the Buddha said in one of the discourses, and I don't remember which one it was right off, but he said basically there's three kinds of personality. The personality like Sāriputta; his mind tended very much towards intellect; his mind was very bright, but he was not very sensitive to feeling. Then there was the mind like Moggallāna; he was an intelligent man, but his mind tended more towards feeling, and he was very sensitive to different kinds of feeling. And then there was the kind of person that was like the Buddha, that was a mixture of these two; he was very sensitive to feeling and also very intelligent. For people that are very sensitive to feeling, they have a tendency to get caught in lust and physical desires a lot. They have a tendency to indulge in that. So the Buddha came up with a meditation for that kind of personality type, and this is called the foulness meditation. This is the meditation of the body parts. And when I first became a monk, it was highly recommended that all of the monks practice this meditation for a period of time, so that they wouldn't have lust coming up in their minds so much.

10. "Again, Monks, a monk reviews this same body up from the soles of the feet and down from the top of the hair, bounded by skin, as full of many kinds of impurity thus: 'In this body there are head-hairs, body-hairs, nails, teeth, skin, flesh, sinews, bones, bone-marrow, kidneys, heart,

liver, diaphragm, spleen, lungs, intestines, mesentery, contents of the stomach,

And this is where it gets real good. This always made my mind completely balanced when I got to this part.

feces, bile, phlegm, pus, blood, sweat, fat, tears, grease, spittle, snot, oil of the joints, and urine.' Just as though there were a bag with an opening at both ends full of many sorts of grain, such as hill rice, red rice, beans, peas, millet, and white rice, and a man with good eyes were to open it and review it thus: 'This is hill rice, this is red rice, these are beans, these are peas, this is millet, this is white rice;' so too, a monk reviews the same body... as full of many kinds of impurity thus: 'In this body there are head-hairs... and urine.'

Everybody's body has it. Every time I got to the phlegm and bile and pus and blood and all of these kinds of things, my mind would lose any desire for any kind of physical gratification.

11. "In this way he abides observing the body as a body internally, externally, and both internally and externally... And he abides independent, not craving or clinging to anything in the world. That too is how a monk abides observing the body as a body.

Now, I had one retreat that there was an awful lot of people that were the kind of, they were lust temperament types of persons. So I said "Ok, I want you, for three days, I want you to look at every other person's body in the room, and I want you to see them turned inside out. And tell me what's beautiful about that. Hey, you have some great intestines. What a liver! Oh that pus is really an interesting color." See how it balances your mind though. Now, this meditation is not for everybody. A person that has a kind of an angry temperament, they can get into the foulness of the body so heavily that they have a tendency to commit suicide and things like that. So it's not for everyone.

But I practiced this particular meditation for six months. And what I wound up doing in my mind was visualizing a bowl, and you know how everybody's attached to hair? "Oh I have to go get my hair fixed, and it's. I need to cut my hair, color my hair, and it's so beautiful." Well, take a bowl of hair and sit it in front of you: it smells bad. How do you feel when you have a few hairs in your soup? You see it really isn't such a beautiful thing. And the longer that it would sit in the bowl, the worse it starts to smell. Now, I was visualizing these things, but I also am a realist enough to know that: "Yeah, this is real." And when you put every organ that this is talking about into a bowl, and observe: "What is beautiful about that?" It's just this thing, you start losing your attachments.

Right after I did that I'd had the opportunity to go visit, in Bangkok, the big hospital there that was across the river. I can't remember the name of it, huge hospital. But they let monks go in to see the autopsies, which is incredibly interesting. And I went in and there's a man, early in the morning, walking down the street, minding his own business, the car jumped over the curb, hit him and killed him immediately. And here he is, sitting on the table, and his broken bones, and then they cut him open and took out the heart, and they weighed the heart, and the liver and all of these different organs. And then they cut around like this, and they took the skin, and they put it over his face, and they took a hand saw, cut the skull, pulled the brain out, measured the brain, thought he might have had some kind of brain problem, so they started slicing it. Now, just that morning he was a live human being, and now what is that? Where is the being in that? "Am I here? Am I the brain? Am I the heart? Where am I? I am not there. There is no 'I' in this." And that's a big realization. And it does keep your mind very much in balanced. And it was quite interesting.

There was, I think there was four or five people that had died, and one lady, she had... she died of a stroke. So when they

MN 10: The Foundations of Mindfulness 73

took her brain out you could see there was a big bloody spot. So they cut through it and then they found that she had a tumor. But the whole time I was sitting there, after I had gone through this mentally, now I'm seeing it actually as it is, and I'm thinking: "Well, what's so special about this? This is not much, not much of anything. It's certainly not me, not mine." There's a kind of balance that is very real when you do this kind of meditation, but you have to do it with a teacher. Ok, you can have a tendency to get very morbid. So I know how to teach this because I've practiced it enough, but I don't teach it to too many people, only for people that are really having problems with lust. And it might take two or three retreats before I'll even suggest it; I want to see what people will do.

Now, Loving-Kindness Meditation is not for every type of personality. If your mind tends more towards intellect, and is not very sensitive to feeling, it's better to do the mindfulness of breathing meditation. Mindfulness of breathing meditation is for every type of personality type. But I started teaching Loving-Kindness Meditation in Malaysia because in Malaysia the Chinese speak English. That's one of the reasons I like going there because I could actually talk to them and teach them, but they're a third of the population of Malaysia. A third of the population is Indian, a third of the population is Malay. Malay run the government, and they're continually pushing down the Chinese. Chinese are very ambitious, hard working people, and the Malay are not so much, so they're always putting roadblocks in the way and stopping the Chinese from gaining too much. They don't want them to gain too much influence in the country. And the Chinese were walking around being angry.

So when I started teaching meditation there, I didn't think that there's a lot of people that were practicing mindfulness of breathing, but I didn't think that was an appropriate meditation for these people at that time. So I said: "I'm going to teach you Loving-Kindness Meditation." And as you know, I teach loving-kindness in a little bit different way than most people teach it. And they really took to it. And there were major personality changes that started to happen for these folks. After doing a one-week retreat they would go back to work, and then people at work would start noticing that they didn't get angry so easily, and they were more smiling, and they were happier, more uplifted. So that was one of the ways I had the opportunity to help the Malay Chinese so that they didn't become upset or walk around being angry all the time. They learned how to have balance in their life, and that's what the meditation is for, teaching true balance. Just like this meditation.

There is another meditation that the foundations of mindfulness talks about, and it's actually nine different kinds of meditation, and this is called the cemetery meditation. And that's a real hard meditation to do now because it takes a charnel ground. A charnel ground is where they take dead bodies and they let them sit until, well in India at the time of the Buddha, they let them sit there until the family would come and bury them if they didn't have enough money to be cremated and that sort of thing. So you would go to these charnel grounds and there would be all kinds of different bodies in different degrees of decay. And the Buddha recommended that if you have a lust kind of personality or you're very much attached to things, to go and stare at a body that's decaying. It's real sobering. I did get a chance to do that one time with a human body. I've done it with animals. But it's really quite something.

You get to see again how repulsive the body is, but you also get to see that it's… "I'm not there. It's not me. It's not mine. It's just a body." When you start losing your attachment to your body, you start losing attachment to mental states too. And with that comes more and more balance with your practice. Now, an interesting thing is, in this particular sutta, it talks about the elements. And it talks about the earth element, the water element, the fire element, the air element;

MN 10: The Foundations of Mindfulness

it just talks about the four elements. And when you go to sutta number sixty-two (MN-62, The Mahārāhulovāda Sutta), it talks about the elements also. And it's kind of surprising the difference of the elements, because it's just talking about earth, air, water and fire, but here in this particular sutta, it describes what each one of these great elements are. And it says...

MN-62:8. "Whatever internally, belonging to oneself, is solid, solidified, and clung-to, that is, head-hairs, body-hairs, nails, teeth, skin, flesh, sinews, bones, bone-marrow, kidneys, heart, liver, diaphragm, spleen, lungs, large intestines, small intestines, contents of the stomach, feces, or whatever else internally, belonging to oneself, is solid, solidified, and clung-to: this is called the internal earth element.

And then when you're talking about the water element...

MN-62:9. "Whatever internally, belonging to oneself, is water, watery, and clung-to, that is, bile, phlegm, pus, blood, sweat, fat, tears, grease, spittle, snot, oil-of-the-joints, urine, or whatever else internally, belonging to oneself, is water, watery, and clung-to: this is called the internal water element.

12. "Again, Monks, a monk reviews this same body, however it is placed, however disposed, by way of the elements thus: 'In this body there are the earth element, the water element, the fire element, and the air element.' Just as though a skilled butcher or his apprentice had killed a cow and was seated at the crossroads with it cut up into pieces; so too, a monk reviews this same body... by way of elements thus: 'In this body there are the earth element, the water element, the fire element, and the air element.'

Now, the elements, you can say the earth element is hardness and solidity; the fire element is hot and cold; the air element is vibration; and the water element is called cohesion. Now, it's a real interesting phenomena, and I want you all to try this sometime during the retreat. Stick your hand in a bucket of water and tell me what water feels like. What does water feel like? You'll feel hot and cold, that's the heat element. I want to know what the water element feels like. That'll be a fun one for you because you can't feel it. Oh, and I'm hearing some people are saying: "Oh yes I can, I know what water feels like." Oh, you're feeling hot and cold, but you don't feel water. It's one of the darndest things. And this is something that you touch every day, but you never think about.

13. "In this way he abides observing the body as a body internally, externally, and both internally and externally... And he abides independent, not craving or clinging to anything in the world. That too is how a monk abides observing the body as a body.

14. "Again, Monks, as though he were to see a corpse thrown aside in a charnel ground, one, two, or three days dead, bloated, livid, and oozing matter, a monk compares the same body with it thus: 'This body too is of the same nature, it will be like that, it is not exempt from that fate.'

15. "In this way he abides observing the body as a body internally, externally, and both internally and externally... And he abides independent, not craving or clinging to anything in the world. That too is how a monk abides observing the body as a body.

16. "Again, Monks, as though he were to see a corpse thrown aside in a charnel ground, being devoured by crows, hawks, vultures, dogs, jackals, or various kinds of worms, a monk compares this same body with it thus: 'This body too is of the same nature, it will be like that, it is not exempt from that fate.'

17. "... That too is how a monk abides observing the body as a body.

So the charnel ground observation, because you can't really do that with a human body, I think we'll let that go as far as explaining it. In Thailand there were some people that were very highly religious, and they knew that they were going to die, they would go to a monk and say to the monk: "What I would like you to do is take my body and preserve it, so other people can come around and see what a dead body is like." And then there would be monks that would come around and they would sit there and quite often fear arises, at first, when you realize that this dead body will be theirs before long, I mean that's what this is going to be in a little while, and we always hold on to it, we always cling to it. But once you let go of your attachment (craving) and just start looking at a body as what it is, it's just a body, it's just some elements that are all mixed up together, your mind can have a very freeing, opening, experience. And you can develop your jhānas with that. But the meditator needs to continually relax into what you're looking at. Letting go of the clinging, letting go of all of the different mental states looking at a dead body can bring up, and all of the feelings that can arise; letting them be, letting them go, and seeing it for what it really is.

18-24. "Again, Monks, as though he were to see a corpse thrown aside in a charnel ground, a skeleton with flesh and blood, held together with sinews... a fleshless skeleton smeared with blood, held together with sinews... a skeleton without flesh and blood, held together with sinews... disconnected bones scattered in all directions-here a hand-bone, there a foot-bone, here a shin-bone, there a thigh-bone, here a hip bone, there a back-bone, here a rib-bone, there a breast-bone, here an arm-bone, there a shoulder-bone, here a neck-bone, there a jaw-bone, here a tooth, there the skull-a monk compares this body with it thus: 'This body too is of the same nature, it will be like that, it is not exempt from that fate.'

25. "... That too is how a monk abides observing the body as a body.

26-30. "Again, Monks, as though he were to see a corpse thrown aside in a charnel ground, bones bleached white, the color of shells... bones heaped up... bones more than a year old, rotted and crumbled to dust, a monk compares this same body with it thus: 'This body too is of the same nature, it will be like that, it is not exempt from that fate.'

31. "In this way he abides observing the body as a body internally, or he abides observing the body as a body externally, or he abides observing the body as a body both internally and externally. Or else he abides observing in the body its nature of arising, or he abides observing in the body its nature of vanishing. And he abides independent, not craving or clinging to anything in the world. That too is how a monk abides observing the body as a body."

Now, we get into observation of feeling.

32. "And how, Monks, does a monk abide observing feeling as feeling? Here, when feeling a pleasant feeling, a monk understands: I feel a pleasant feeling;' when feeling a painful feeling, he understands: I feel a painful feeling;' when feeling a neither-painful-nor-pleasant feeling, he understands: 'I feel a neither-painful-nor-pleasant feeling.' When feeling a worldly pleasant feeling, he understands: 'I feel a worldly pleasant feeling;'

What is a worldly pleasant feeling?

ST: Hot chocolate?

BV: Hot chocolate! {Laughs} Chocolate of any kind, eh?

ST: Joy?

BV: Yes, that's true. Joy is a very pleasant worldly feeling, but what makes it worldly?

ST: "I want more."

BV: I want more. Yes. It's the identification with that feeling: "I am that." Ok, and...

when feeling an unworldly pleasant feeling, he understands: 'I feel an unworldly pleasant feeling;'

BV: What is an unworldly pleasant feeling?

ST: Joy from experiencing a jhāna?

BV: Still joy, but there's not the identification with it.

That's what makes it unworldly. See, this is a very subtle way of talking about the difference between a person who has mental development and a person who doesn't have any mental development. A person who doesn't have any mental development, when joy arises, they really indulge in it and try to hold onto it and make it last for as long as they can. And they take it as theirs. A person who has mental development sees it for what it is. It is a pleasant feeling, let it be, relax, come back to your object of meditation.

when feeling a worldly painful feeling, he understands: 'I feel a worldly painful feeling;'

Basically, it's the same thing as a pleasant feeling. Yeah, the chocolate is all gone. Oh, dukkha, dukkha! Ha Ha!

One of the things that happens in the suttas, that people don't really realize, because they talk a lot about pleasant feeling and attachment to pleasant feeling. The suttas don't really talk much about painful feeling because it's supposed to be understood. But painful feeling and pleasant feeling are the same coin just different sides. The craving is like that: "I like it. I don't like it." It's still craving. But one of them is a pleasurable thing and one of them is a painful thing.

when feeling an unworldly painful feeling, he understands: 'I feel an unworldly painful feeling;'

What is that? When a painful feeling arises, you see it as painful, allow it to be there, relax into that, and come back to your object of meditation.

ST: It's impersonal.

BV: It's impersonal, that's it. That's it exactly. Both the pleasant worldly feeling or unpleasant worldly feeling, they are still feeling, but when it's unpleasant we always try to control it in one way, and when it's pleasant we try to control it in another. But there's still the belief that: "I am that. I have control over a feeling."

And that's where the decision is that I was talking about last night, the decision of whether you take this personally or impersonally. And that's the thing that makes Dependent Origination such an amazing process to watch because you see; because this arises, that arises; and because that arises, this arises. When feeling arises, craving arises; because of craving, clinging arises; because of clinging your habitual tendencies arise. There's no personal thing in that, its just part of an impersonal process, and it always works in the same way. It always... it has contact, it has feeling, craving, clinging, habitual tendency. But, when you make the decision to let go of the craving, then the clinging, the habitual tendency, and the rest of Dependent Origination doesn't arise. Now, you have that pure mind, now you have that clear mind, and you always bring that clear mind back to your object of meditation. That is how you develop your wisdom. That is what wisdom is all about.

I got on a web site last year I think it was, and it was with a bunch of people that were studying Abhidhamma, and they were throwing the word "wisdom" around left and right, and how you have to develop your wisdom, and I finally said: "Well, what in the world are you talking about? What's your definition of wisdom?" And one person actually wrote me back and said: "Well, wisdom is wisdom." Oh, that makes a lot of sense. Yeah, now I understand.

when feeling a worldly neither-painful-nor-pleasant feeling, he understands: 'I feel a worldly neither-painful-nor-pleasant feeling;'

What is a worldly neither-painful-nor pleasant feeling? A worldly neither painful nor pleasant feeling is indifference. This kind of indifference has no mindfulness in it. This is why it is worldly.

MN 10: The Foundations of Mindfulness

when feeling an unworldly neither-painful-nor-pleasant feeling, he understands: 'I feel an unworldly neither-painful-nor-pleasant feeling.'

What is an unworldly neither painful nor pleasant feeling? This unworldly feeling is equanimity which has very strong mindfulness in it. Each time you experience a jhana you have some equanimity in it. As you progress further and mind begins to understand more deeply the equanimity becomes stronger until you attain the 4th jhana where that is the only feeling, this is where mind has reached a very fine state of balance.

33. "In this way he abides observing feeling as feeling internally, he abides observing feeling as feeling externally, he abides observing feeling as feeling both internally or externally. He abides observing in feelings their nature of arising, he observes in feelings their nature of vanishing, he abides observing in feelings their nature of both arising and vanishing. And he abides independent, not craving and clinging to anything in the world. That is how a monk abides observing feeling as feeling.

Ok, we have the last two foundations to go through, and I think you'll find this quite interesting. This is the mindfulness of mind, cittānupassanā.

34. "And how, Monks, does a monk abide observing mind as mind? Here a monk understands mind affected by lust as mind affected by lust, and mind unaffected by lust as mind unaffected by lust. He understands mind affected by hate as mind affected by hate, and mind unaffected by hate as mind unaffected by hate. He understands mind affected by delusion as mind affected by delusion, and mind unaffected by delusion as mind unaffected by delusion.

Question. What is delusion?

It's taking everything that arises personally. A deluded mind is a mind that doesn't see the true nature of everything that arises. It's part of impermanence, it's part of thought, but it is seeing the thoughts and feeling as being me: "This is who I am. This is what I think. This is what I feel." Not seeing the true nature of existence, which is arising and passing away continually, and not seeing the impersonal nature of whatever arises. I'm going to ask you a lot of questions on this section, so...

He understands contracted mind as contracted mind,

What is a contracted mind? A contracted mind is a mind that has sloth and torpor in it. It's a mind that pulls in and gets lost in a dream world.

and distracted mind as distracted mind.

What is a distracted mind? That's a mind that has restlessness in it. Because it's distracted, it's always going away from your object of meditation.

He understands exalted mind as exalted mind,

What is an exalted mind? A mind in a rūpa jhāna. Now, this is not just any of the jhānas, this is one of the first four jhānas. These are called exalted states of mind. Now, did you ever realize that the Satipaṭṭhāna Sutta is talking about jhānas? I was always taught that it was talking about mindfulness, and it was never explained to me.

and unexalted mind as unexalted mind.

That's pretty easy. It's a mind that doesn't have any jhāna in it. Now, remember that jhāna does not mean concentration. Jhāna means a stage of development in the meditation; it's just a stage. And it's a stage of your understanding of the process of Dependent Origination.

He understands surpassed mind as surpassed mind,

What is a surpassed mind? A surpassed mind is a mind that experiences the arūpa jhānas.

Arūpa jhānas. The arūpa jhānas are different aspects of the fourth jhāna. Now, when you talk about, in the Eightfold

Path, the last part of the Eightfold Path is called sammā samādhi. Sammā samādhi is always defined as the experience of one of the four jhānas. But in that it also includes the arūpa jhānas. The arūpa jhānas are: infinite space, infinite consciousness, nothingness, neither-perception-nor-non-perception. These are exalted states, these are very, very fine states of attention where your awareness of the mind's attention becomes very, very precise and very exact, and you get to see everything very clearly. And it's just different stages of clarity when we get into the arūpa jhānas.

Now, one of the things that had always happened to me when I was practicing Vipassanā, straight Vipassanā, was I was told that you can't develop insight if you're experiencing jhāna. But then again, when you look up in the suttas the words insight or Vipassanā, and you look up the word samatha, which means tranquility, and it's always translated as jhāna. Then you look at where it tells you those references are, they're always in the suttas together. Samatha and Vipassanā work hand-in-hand. They can't be any other way, not if you're going to experience what the Buddha was talking about.

and unsurpassed mind as unsurpassed mind. He understands collected mind as collected mind, and uncollected mind as uncollected mind.

What is a collected mind? A collected mind… they have in this translation, they use the word concentrate a lot. But I found in this country, concentration always means some form of absorption, some form of deep concentration, of undistractedness. So I choose to change the definition of that a little bit because it's not very well understood that a concentrated mind can also be a very calm mind, a still mind, but a mind that's still fully alert, not just absorbed into one thing. So I choose to use the word "collected," rather than "concentrated." I've even gone so far sometimes to say that that's like one of the four letter words you don't ever say again.

He understands liberated mind as liberated mind, and unliberated mind as unliberated mind.

What is a liberated mind? This is a mind that has experienced very deeply the third noble truth, the cessation of suffering. Every time your mind gets distracted away from your object of meditation, the instructions are: let go of that distraction and relax; let go of the tension caused by that movement of mind's attention. When you let go of that tension, that tightness, your mind, it feels expanded and then it becomes calm. Right after that your mind is very clear, your mind is pure, your awareness is very sharp. And you bring that mind back to your object of meditation. You have liberated your mind from the tightness of craving; you've let go of the craving. Craving always manifests as tension and tightness in your mind and in your body. So every time you let go of that you're experiencing a liberated mind. What's an unliberated mind? That's when somebody's practicing one-pointed concentration, their mind is distracted, they let go of the distraction and immediately come back to your object of meditation. There is no letting go of the craving. Your mind is not liberated at that time.

This particular part of the Satipaṭṭhāna Sutta... I've had many discussions with Sayadaw U Silananda about this, and I always questioned him as to why he didn't explain it: because he was a Vipassanā teacher. Now, you're supposed to explain these things, but if you're a straight Vipassanā teacher you don't want your students getting into the jhānas, you want them just experiencing what they call the insight knowledges. Which actually as it turns out by the practice of straight Vipassanā, it is a form of absorption concentration. It might be moment-to-moment, it might be quick kinds of concentration, but it's still concentration. And when mind gets into what they call access concentration, what happens is the force of the concentration that they have developed suppresses, pushes down, doesn't allow hindrances to arise. And that's the main problem.

MN 10: The Foundations of Mindfulness 85

Hindrances are where your attachments are. You purify your mind for the period of time that you're in "access concentration," but you haven't completely purified your mind because when you get out of that access concentration, the hindrances come back. And by your not being able to recognize the hindrances so easily, it's very easy to get caught by them. So when you're practicing watching and relaxing, whenever the hindrance arises, your mind gets distracted and you start thinking about this or that, whatever it happens to think about. That is part of restlessness, that's a hindrance. How do you handle the hindrance? You let the thought go, you relax the craving, and now you have this pure mind that doesn't have any craving in it. Now, when you're practicing straight Vipassanā, they tell you: "When your mind gets distracted, watch that distraction until it goes away, and then immediately come back to your attention on the breath." There's no relaxing in that, so they're bringing back the craving. So there's no true purity of mind with that kind of practice.

I wrote a book called The Ānāpānasati Sutta: A Practical Guide to Mindfulness of Breathing and Tranquil Wisdom Meditation. In that book I described everything I'm talking to you right now. And after I wrote that book, I sent a copy to Sayadaw U Silananda, and he read the book, and he was impressed enough that he put it on the website. And it's fantastic the number of people that have gone to the book because he did that. He and I had a discussion about the method I was showing in the book, which is what I'm talking about right now, and he agreed that it was a very good method of meditation, and it more explained how you practice the meditation that the Buddha taught. But he said he could never teach that kind of meditation because for forty years he's been teaching the other kind of meditation. Isn't that odd?

Any practice of meditation that you do, if it does not have the letting go and release of craving, then it turns out to be one form or another of absorption concentration. And when you practice absorption concentration, there is no way to be able to see Dependent Origination in the way that it needs to be seen. Now tomorrow, in our Dhamma talk, we will have a discourse that's one of the most powerful discourses in The Middle Length Sayings; it's called "The Six Sets of Six." And I'm going to read that sutta to you with all of the repeating in it. And the reason I'm going to do that is because that will stick in your mind like you can't believe. And you will be able to see more and more clearly how the process of Dependent Origination works.

Anyway, when we're talking about observation of mind, the cittānupassanā, we're talking about being able to recognize lust, hatred, delusion, contraction of mind, distraction of mind, exalted mind, surpassed mind. You're able to see all of these different states as they arise, and they will. All of these different things will arise while you're doing your practice. What you do with them dictates what will happen in the future. If you let go of the distraction and relax, and bring that relaxed mind back to your object of meditation, you can look forward to being more and more alert to how this process works.

Now, for the last two or three Dhamma talks, I've talked quite a bit about the five aggregates. I haven't specifically said these are the aggregates, but I have talked about them quite a bit. This process is made up of five things. You have physical body. What's the first part of the Satipaṭṭhāna Sutta? Kāyānupassanā, mindfulness of body. You have feeling. What's the second part of the Satipaṭṭhāna Sutta? Vedanānupassanā, mindfulness of feeling. You have perception, and depending on your translation, the next one is, in Pāli, it's called sankhāra. Bhikkhu Bodhi, in this book, he calls it volition. I call it thoughts. And all of those are correct. So perception is the mind that puts names on things. You see this; your mind says this is a book. The perception is the mind that recognized that, and it also has memory in it. Now, when

MN 10: The Foundations of Mindfulness

we get to the third part here, this is cittānupassanā, or mindfulness of mind, that includes the sankhāras, the thoughts and the volition, and the perception. And the last part of the aggregates is consciousness. And that is very akin to dhammānupassanā, mindfulness of mind objects.

So you can see that the five aggregates and the four foundations of mindfulness are actually the same thing. Where we continually cause ourselves so much suffering is when a feeling arises, we try to think the feeling away. And the more you try to think the feeling, the bigger the feeling becomes; the more intense the feeling becomes; the more pain you are causing yourself. So what's the instructions in the meditation? When a feeling arises, it's a pleasant feeling, it's a painful feeling. I won't go with the rest of them because it doesn't matter.

There is craving that arises right after feeling. And craving is always the "I like it, I don't like it" mind. Craving always manifests as tension and tightness in your mind and in your body. Right after craving is clinging. Clinging is the thoughts, the story, the opinions, the concepts about why you like or dislike that feeling. The weak link in Dependent Origination is craving. Why? Because craving is the easiest thing to recognize when it comes up. It always comes up and it does that in your mind and in your body. There's tightness, there's tension. So when a feeling arises, we like it and don't like it, whichever one it happens to be.

And then we have thoughts and then we have our habitual tendencies about those thoughts. We always think this way when this kind of feeling arises. So the first part of the instruction says, when a feeling arises, there are thoughts about the feeling. So what you have to do is let go of the thoughts, don't get involved and caught in the story about, and relax.

Next, you see that feeling, and that's what you're seeing, just the feeling. There's a tight mental fist wrapped around the feeling. Either we like it or we don't like it. And there's always the want to control the feeling, to make it be the way we want it to be. If it's a painful feeling, we want it to disappear, we want it to stop and we try to push it away as hard as we can. If it's a pleasant feeling, we grab onto that baby and pull it in and try to hold on as tight as we can. But the truth is, when a feeling arises it's there, and it's ok for the feeling to be there. It has to be ok because that's the truth. So, you have to let go of that mental hold around the feeling. Now, this feeling can be a contracted mind, it can be a distracted mind. It can be a mind that has lust in it, has hatred in it, doesn't matter. What you do is say: "Ok, that feeling is there and it's fine for it to be there." Now, you relax that tension and tightness and come back to your object of meditation. When you treat the feeling in this way, there's no suffering. There's no: "I want it to be different that it is." There's no need to control. There's seeing what arises as it arises, as it truly is.

This is real important stuff. The more you start getting into the habit of relaxing, the more your mind becomes liberated. And that's what this part of the sutta is all about. And as you get deeper into your practice, you start to experience the candy of the meditation. The Buddha called it the pleasant abiding here and now, the jhāna. But jhāna doesn't mean concentration, it means your level of understanding, your level of your meditation, that's all. And whether you know which jhāna you're in, or not, doesn't really matter; the only person it matters to is me. So when you come and talk to me about what your experience is, I know how to talk back to you. I know how to say things that can be helpful for you. Again, whatever I say is suggestion. Don't believe what I say, try it and see if it works. If it works, keep it, if it doesn't, throw it away. I'm not attached to the things I say too much. Maybe a little.

35. "In this way he abides observing mind as mind internally, he abides observing mind as mind externally, he abides observing mind as mind both internally and

externally. He abides observing in mind its nature of arising, he abides observing in mind its nature of vanishing, he abides observing in mind its nature of both arising and vanishing.

Now, with the sutta that I gave the other night, One by One (MN-111, The Anupada Sutta), I showed you all of these different things that Sāriputta experienced while he was in the jhāna. And they all arise and pass away, arise and pass away, they didn't all gang up and come up at one time, and that's how you experience impermanence. And the more clear you become with seeing this as a process of Dependent Origination, the more you truly understand that this is an impersonal process. Everything happens because of a cause; it's dependent on the cause. So you're seeing the true nature of everything when you see it as continually moving and changing, and seeing it as being impersonal.

And he abides independent, not craving or clinging to anything in the world.

How do you not crave or cling to anything in the world? What's the definition of craving, the "I like it" or "I don't like it" mind? What's the definition of clinging? It's all of your opinions, all of your concepts, all of your thinking and story telling in your mind, and identifying with those opinions and thoughts and that sort of thing. So if you don't want to cling to anything, continually let go of the craving. Why? Because clinging doesn't arise after that. Your mind is pure, you don't have any thoughts in it, every time you let go of that craving.

That is how a monk abides observing mind as mind.

Now, we get into the observation of mind objects. And this is real interesting because the first part of this is the five hindrances; awareness of the hindrances. This particular section tells you exactly how to handle a hindrance when it arises.

36. "And how, Monks, does a monk abide observing mind-objects as mind-objects? Here a monk abides observing

mind-objects as mind-objects in terms of the five hindrances. And how does a monk abide observing mind-objects as mind-objects in terms of the five hindrances? Here, there being sensual desire in him, a monk understands: 'There is sensual desire in me;' or there being no sensual desire in him, he understands: 'There is no sensual desire in me;'

That's pretty straightforward.

and he also understands how there comes to be the arising of unarisen sensual desire,

How do you understand how there comes to be the arising of unarisen sensual desire? When your mind is on your object of meditation, and it begins to become distracted, what happens is your mind is here and all of a sudden it's there, and you didn't see that process. All you know is your mind jumped from being on the breath and relaxing to having sensual desire in it. How did that happen? What happened first; what happened after that; what happened after that; what happened after that? What you'll be able to see, when your mind is reasonably calm, is that there is more happening than just all of a sudden there's this distraction. As you let go of the distraction and relax, bringing that pure mind back to your object of meditation, it will go back to that distraction. But now you start working with the awakening factor of the investigation of your experience. So, how did your mind jump over here?

What you will see is there's something that happened before your mind got carried away and starts getting involved and really getting caught by the sensual desire. There's something that happens right before that. As you are able to see as it keeps pulling back and you relax and you come back, you'll be able to start to become familiar with how this distraction occurs. This is one of the reasons why your hindrances are your best friends, because they're showing you where your attachment is. Mind gets pulled away, you'll see this feeling arise right before you start thinking about that sensual desire, whatever that happens to be.

So as you are, quote, "wrestling with the hindrance," as you're getting caught by the hindrance, at first you might get caught for a minute or two minutes before you even notice that you are caught, and then you let go of that hindrance and relax, and bring that attention back to your object of meditation. The nature of the hindrances is they'll keep pulling you back to it, and that's good. Why? Because every time you get your mind pulled away from your object of meditation, and you notice it and you relax, and you come back to your object of meditation, you are improving your mindfulness. You're improving your observation of the movement of mind's attention. So, it's going to be bouncing back and forth. But as you become more familiar with how this process works, you start to see little things more and more clearly.

Now, what happens first? And you won't be able to notice this until, most of you until a little bit later, but you'll notice that your mind is very still on your object of meditation, and all of a sudden it starts moving, it starts wobbling. And it wobbles and it wobbles faster and faster and faster and then finally it floats away. Now, what this is talking about is how to be aware of that process; how to be aware of this movement. At first you're not going to see this at all, and sometimes you might be able to catch just as it's starting to go away, and you can let go right then and relax and come back. And you're not really caught by that hindrance, and sometimes you won't be able to. So it's letting go of the hindrance, relaxing, coming back.

You might do this a hundred times, you might do it a thousand times, depending on how strong your attachment is to believing that these thoughts and these feelings of sensual pleasure are yours. But as you start looking at this as a process instead of: "This is me, this is who I am," you start letting go of that ego belief that this is who you are, and you start seeing little parts of this distraction. As you start letting go, as you become more familiar with the distraction and how it arises, you start catching it a little bit faster. So instead of being distracted for one or two minutes, you might be distracted for thirty seconds. And then as you continue on with that, it might be fifteen seconds. And as you continue on, you start seeing the process more clearly; it might be only five seconds.

As you improve your mindfulness, you will get to the state where you see your mind starting to wobble and you let go right then and your mind doesn't even get distracted. You see this is the importance of having the hindrances because they are your teachers. I'm not your teacher. The hindrances are your teacher because they're showing you very clearly how mind's attention moves. And when you see it very clearly, you start seeing more and more clearly the little tiny pieces, and you'll start recognizing different parts of the Dependent Origination. Dependent Origination happens fast. Now, I know that there's some commentaries where they talk about Dependent Origination happening over three lifetimes. That's wishful thinking. But {BV snaps his finger} that was a million thought moments, that was a million arising and passing away of the twelve links of Dependent Origination. It happens in a thought moment. As you become more familiar with how that process works, you start educating yourself and teaching yourself how to let go of believing that anything that arises is personal. You start seeing everything as an impersonal process, and that is incredibly freeing and liberating when you're able to do that.

{repeats} and he also understands how there comes to be the arising of unarisen sensual desire,

He sees the movements. That's how you're able to see that.

and how there comes to be the future non-arising of abandoned sensual desire.

MN 10: The Foundations of Mindfulness

How does that come to be? It is staying on your object of meditation. When you stay on your object of meditation, the hindrance won't arise. So what we have is we have a distraction that you're starting to catch a little bit quicker, and little bit quicker, and little bit quicker. And you're improving your mindfulness all the time by letting this go and relaxing, coming back to your object of meditation. Eventually, that hindrance doesn't have enough energy to even arise and your mind naturally stays on your object of meditation for longer and longer periods of time. And that's how you overcome every hindrance. But the trick is you are on your object of meditation, but you're not holding on to it. If you hold on to your object of meditation, you're putting in too much energy and too much effort, and you will have one of your friends come to visit, called restlessness. Now, this is the same for all of the hindrances. How you treat all of the hindrances, you treat all of the hindrances in the same way. And I call hindrances "distractions." So any time your mind gets pulled away, it's distracted. Let go of the distraction, relax, gently come back to your object of meditation.

Every time you let go of the tension and tightness, you are experiencing Nibbāna. It's mundane, it's still a worldly kind of Nibbāna, but there is no fire in that. Nibbāna, ni - no, bāna - fire. And craving is called fire; it's heat! So every time you let go of that distraction, doesn't matter which one of the hindrances it is, when you let it go and you relax, you're bringing that pure mind back to your object of meditation. Your mindfulness, your awareness of the movements of mind becomes sharper every time you let go of the distraction, relax and come back. So you're not caught for as long a period of time, and you start staying on your object of meditation for longer periods of time, and that's where you start experiencing your jhānas. Investigating constantly improves the mindfulness. And you have to see the whole thing with the awakening factors, is they have to be in balance. So we can talk about the awakening factors in just a minute actually. Well, I'll go to it because this is just repeating the whole thing over and over again, and I've repeated it plenty of times for you, so I'll give you a break this time.

"There being ill will in him... There being sloth and torpor in him... There being restlessness and remorse in him... There being doubt in him, a monk understands: 'There is doubt in me;' or there being no doubt in him, he understands: 'There is no doubt in me;' and he understands how there comes to be the arising of unarisen doubt, and how there comes to be the abandoning of arisen doubt, and how there comes to be the future non-arising of abandoned doubt.

37. "In this way he abides observing mind-objects as mind-objects internally, he abides observing mind-objects as mind-objects externally, he abides observing mind-objects as mind-objects both internally and externally. He abides observing in mind-objects their nature of arising, he abides observing in mind-objects their nature of vanishing, he abides observing in mind-objects their nature of both arising and vanishing. And he abides independent, not craving or clinging to anything in the world. That is how a monk abides observing mind-objects as mind-objects in terms of the five hindrances.

Ok, I'm going to jump to the seven factors of awakening. We'll go back to the five aggregates and the six bases in just a minute.

42. "Again, Monks, a monk abides observing mind-objects as mind-objects in terms of the seven awakening factors. And how does a monk abide observing mind-objects as mind-objects in terms of the seven awakening factors? Here, there being the mindfulness awakening factor in him, a monk understands: 'There is the mindfulness awakening factor in me;' or there being no mindfulness awakening factor in him, he understands: 'There is no mindfulness awakening factor in me;' and he also understands...

You're going to love this.

MN 10: The Foundations of Mindfulness

how there comes to be the arising of the unarisen mindfulness awakening factor, and how the arisen mindfulness awakening factor comes to fulfillment by development.

How do you bring up that mindfulness awakening factor? The function of mindfulness is to remember. To remember what? What is your mind doing in the present moment. How is mind's attention moving from one thing to another? How does that happen? See, it always comes back to the investigation of Dependent Origination. Seeing all of these different links arising and passing away. It's remembering to look, remembering to observe. That's what mindfulness is.

{repeats} he also understands how there comes to be the arising of the unarisen mindfulness awakening factor,

How does that come to be? Remember to pay attention. Remember to observe how mind's attention is moving from one thing to another. Letting it be, relaxing, coming back to your object of meditation, is the way you strengthen that mindfulness. That's how you develop the mindfulness, and how the mindfulness awakening factor comes to be fulfilled by development.

Get good at it. Now, when I'm talking to you about doing your meditation, most people think meditation is just sitting on your cushion and that's it, and you know that I'm not talking about that, I'm talking about all the time. And this is somewhat difficult practice to do the meditation all the time. It doesn't matter what you're doing. What are you doing in the meditation? Developing that sharp awareness of what mind is doing in the present moment. Right now, mind's tight. Why? There's craving in it. Let it go and relax, smile, come back to your object of meditation. When you get into the jhānas, that doesn't mean that you're only sitting in meditation. You can be in a jhāna while you're chopping vegetables, or washing your clothes, or taking a bath. You can be in jhāna at any time. Can you have joy when you're taking a bath? Can you have joy when you're chopping vegetables?

Can you have joy when you're mowing the lawn? Whatever task there is, if your mindfulness is sharp, you can be in a jhāna. And that's where your mind is absolutely pure. No hindrances arise when these jhāna factors are present. It's when your mindfulness slips a little bit for whatever reason.

Remember I gave you that chart yesterday that had the five aggregates and the four foundations of mindfulness, and the hindrances right underneath that. When your mindfulness is weak, when your mindfulness slips a little bit, you can look forward to one of those hindrances coming, or two of those hindrances coming because they like to gang up, they don't like to come one at a time. You get restlessness and you like the restlessness if you're planning, or you don't like the restlessness when you feel like jumping out of your skin. So you not only have the restlessness to deal with, you have the aversion to it or the grabbing on to it.

Now, you have to have enough interest in having an uplifted mind to recognize this as what it is, to let it be, relax, come back to an object of meditation. For some of you, you're doing mindfulness of breathing, so you come back to your mindfulness of breathing and relaxing. On the in-breath relax, on the out-breath relax. For some of you, you're doing your mettā. Come back to that feeling of loving-kindness. With your daily activities you don't necessarily have to stay with that one spiritual friend. You can radiate loving-kindness to everybody, that's fine. But the key is to recognize that your mind is caught by a hindrance, let that hindrance be, relax, come back to your object of meditation. You do this with your daily activities. That's why I'm pushing you right now. I want to know how your daily activities are going. Are you able to stay with feeling happy when you're doing your loving-kindness? Can you be happy while you're chopping this or sweeping that, or washing this, or going to the toilet, or eating? Can you do that? Keep it going, don't let your mind just ho hum? That's what the practice is about. And the more closely you can continue on doing that, the less suffering you will experience. The more you will experience a mind that is uplifted, and happy, and very alert! Any time you see that you have repeat thoughts; you have an attachment there and your mind is caught by the craving and clinging, and that is a distraction.

You relax after you recognize... the recognition is part of the mindfulness, and it's also part of the investigation. But right after that there is the energy of letting go of that distraction. And then the joy will arise, and after the joy, there's tranquility, and your mind becomes very still, and it becomes balanced. I've just gone through all of the different factors of awakening. And that's the way it works.

And that's the very thing that changes what the Buddha's teaching, that it changes the end result of the meditation because you're able to see everything as process when you're doing this. You don't see it as being a personal thing. Now, one of the things that I try to get you to remember to do is to develop your sense of humor about yourself when you get caught, and you can laugh at being caught, then you're not caught anymore. "I'm mad. I don't like this. Ha Ha, look at that, my mind got caught again. Oh, it's only this anger. Nothing." So it changes your perspective from: "I am this" to "It's only that." It goes from being personal, big problem, "I got to fight with this." to "Well it's only this, it's only this feeling, nothing." Easy to let go of. See, that's the whole process of the seven factors of awakening.

You have joy right in the middle of that. Joy is your balancing factor. Joy helps you to have the perspective so that you don't get caught, and when you have joy, your mind is very light, and very alert, and very agile. So when your mind starts to get pulled down by a mental state, it's real easy to see that. So why do I want you to smile all the time? Why do I want you to laugh? Because it helps your mindfulness, it helps your investigation of all of your experience. The more you can smile, the more you can laugh, the easier it is to stay in balance. And the way you tell that you are progressing spiritually is that you stop laughing at things and you start laughing with them. You don't take things personally. When I hear somebody say something that's very true, the first thing that happens is I laugh. I can't help it. And I'm not laughing at anything. It's just true. "Ha ha, that was a good one."

It's joy arising.

So the whole thing with the awakening factors is they can be incredibly helpful when you have sloth and torpor. You need mindfulness, you need your investigation, you need your energy, and when you bring your energy up then joy will arise. When you have restlessness, you still need your mindfulness and your investigation, but you want to focus on tranquility, on stillness of mind, on balance. So you can call up these different awakening factors as you need them, and that again is part of mindfulness because you're remembering, you're remembering to focus with a tranquil mind, or a joyful mind, whatever.

Now, the whole thing with right effort in the Eightfold Path is really important to your practice. With your investigation, you have to be able to do this with a balanced kind of effort. Now, what is right effort? Right effort is seeing when your mind is unwholesome, letting go of that unwholesome state and relaxing, bringing up a wholesome state, and staying with that wholesome state. Now, let's look at the hindrances again. What are you doing when a hindrance arises? You're seeing your mind has an unwholesome state in it. You let go of that unwholesome state and relax. Now, you come back to your wholesome state, and you stay with your wholesome state; it's right effort. Effort and energy is not quite the same thing. You have to do it with a balanced kind of energy. If you try too hard, you're going to cause yourself to get restless. If you don't try hard enough, you're going to get sloth and torpor.

There was a student that I had in Malaysia; I'd just given a talk on how to make a determination when you're working with jhānas. So she went home and about a week later she

MN 10: The Foundations of Mindfulness 99

came back to me and she said: "I'm very familiar with getting into the jhāna," and I'd known that. And she said: "Now, I can't get into the jhānas at all. What's the problem?" And I said: "What kind of determination are you making?" And she said: "Well, I'm making a determination to get into the first jhāna." And with that kind of determination, she was trying too hard. And the more she didn't get into the jhāna like she expected, the more energy and effort she put into it, and the more restlessness she had. And she never got into that state. So I said: "Well, let's change your wording on your determination. Let's make a determination that your mind can be peaceful and calm, and then see what happens after that." And with that determination, all of a sudden she was very easily getting into the jhāna. See, it can be a subtle thing, "Ah I don't feel like meditating today, but I guess I'd better." What happens when you sit with that kind of mental state?

You know that one?

You get restless. "I don't really want to be here doing it, but I feel like I should be, so I'm going to do it anyway." You have to let go of all of those kind of ideas. The whole thing with the meditation is to make it fun, make it a game. Don't get over-serious with it. I've been to way too many retreats and some of the retreats have been very long, three months and eight months, things like that, where I didn't see any of the yogis smile, the whole time because they were trying really hard. And I appreciate very much the effort they were putting in. I was doing the same thing; I didn't smile either, but I appreciate very much the effort that was being put in. But it was not quite the right kind of energy that they were using, or we were using, and mind tended to get "heavied out" and over-serious. And then there's a subtle self criticism that happens because you feel like you're putting in the effort, you're putting in the energy, but you're not getting the progress that you think you should. So you put in a little bit more, and a little bit more, and you don't have any progress in your meditation.

Now, I was with a Vietnamese monk that had been at that meditation center a year before I got there. And he was putting in so much effort, I mean he was stale. You know, when I used to play basketball we'd get to a place where we played it so much that we needed to have a break from it. And he wouldn't take a break, even of a day or two, just to let all of the pressure go and just kind of kick back and relax for a little while. In the time I was there, he finally got to-this was the Vipassanā that I was practicing at the time-he finally got to the second insight knowledge. In a year and a half. Yeah. Because he was trying way, way too hard.

The whole thing with the meditation is learning how to adjust the amount of energy you're putting in. As you go deeper into your meditation, you have to adjust in more and more subtle, little ways. And it gets incredibly interesting, especially when your mindfulness is sharp because you see, if you put in just a taste too much effort, too much energy, your mind starts tending towards the restlessness. So you back away from that and your mindfulness says "Ok, now we're in balance again." Then you say: "Oh maybe that was… I need to take a little bit less." And you get a little bit dull, and it's always different. Every time you sit, you have to judge the amount of energy that you're using so that you can stay in balance. Gets to be a real fun experience.

And again, the real difference between people practicing meditation in Asia and people practicing meditation in this country, as I'm teaching it anyway, is in Asia the people are very light naturally, and they like to fool around, and they like to chit chat and they like to laugh, and have lots of food, and that's a wonderful existence for them. Then they get to the meditation center, the teachers there have to be tough, they're really coming down on them all the time. I saw one monk, that he was supposed to be doing a very intensive meditation, and the teacher caught him laying down sleeping in a room. And he grabbed him by the ear, and picked him up, and scolded him the whole time, and made him go sit. He had to sit in front of the teacher. But we don't need that in this country; we don't need tough teachers. We need teachers that say: "Hey, you're trying too hard, back off." Your balance has got to be good. And the way we do things with our "always trying for perfection" and "always putting as much effort in to be as successful as we can be," we have to be told: "Back off a little bit!" You need to get into your joy more. Because we're so goal oriented we'll kill ourselves to get to Nibbāna, and it just don't work that way. The awakening factors have to be in perfect balance in order to attain Nibbāna. And that means having joy in balance with all the others. Ok, we'll go back now to the five aggregates...

38. "Again, Monks, a monk abides observing mind-objects as mind-objects in terms of the five aggregates affected by craving and clinging.

Now, this is an interesting statement: "the five aggregates affected by craving and clinging." Depending on your mindfulness, the five aggregates may or may not be affected by craving and clinging. If a feeling arises and you see it right then and you let it be and relax, no clinging will arise. If your mindfulness isn't so sharp then clinging can arise. What is clinging? Again, that's where your opinions are, your concepts, your thinking about, your stories, and your strong grabbing onto the belief that these are you, the personal nature of things.

And how does a monk abide observing mind-objects as mind-objects in terms of the five aggregates affected by craving and clinging? Here a monk understands: 'Such is material form, such its origin, such its disappearance; such is feeling, such its origin, such its disappearance; such is perception, such its origin, such its disappearance; such are the formations, such their origin, such their disappearance; such is consciousness, such its origin, such its disappearance.'

39. "In this way he abides observing mind-objects as mind-objects internally, externally, and both internally and

externally... And he abides independent, not craving or clinging to anything in the world. That is how a monk abides observing mind-objects as mind-objects in terms of the five aggregates affected by craving or clinging.**

It's being aware of the aggregates as they arise and letting them be. How do you see the origin, what is the origin of feeling? Tricky question if you don't know about Dependent Origination, but if you do know about Dependent Origination, you say: "The cause of feeling is contact." With contact as condition, feeling arises. And it's that way all the way through the five aggregates. So it always comes back to the Dependent Origination and how that arises, how that changes, how it fades away.

Now, we'll get into the six sense bases...

40. "Again, Monks, a monk abides observing mind-objects as mind-objects in terms of the six internal and external bases. And how does a monk abide observing mind-objects as mind-objects in terms of the six internal and external bases? Here a monk understands the eye, he understands forms, and he understands the fetter that arises dependent on both; and he also understands how there comes to be the arising of the unarisen fetter, and how there comes to be the abandoning of the arisen fetter, and how there comes to be the future non-arising of the abandoned fetter.

Sound familiar? Not much? Hindrance. So it's when eye hits color and form, eye consciousness arises, the meeting of the three is called eye contact. With eye contact as condition, eye feeling arises; with eye feeling as condition, eye craving arises; with eye craving as condition, clinging arises. So when eye hits color and form and consciousness arises, there will be a feeling that arises; pleasant, painful, neither painful nor pleasant. If at that time you see and relax, then no fetter will arise. If your mindfulness is not sharp enough, that fetter will arise. And what happens, you start thinking about what you're seeing, and you start thinking: "Ah, I like this and this is really good." And "Oh, I remember when there was

**

another one that was just like that down the road." And all of a sudden you're out in lala land a thousand miles away. That's the way these distractions work.

One time I was in, I think it was Malaysia at the time, I'd been really starting to become familiar with Dependent Origination. And I thought that it would be real interesting to see if I could eat some mango, which I truly love, without any craving in it. So I picked up a piece of mango, and I put it in my mouth, and I noticed the taste, and I noticed how these different tastes arise, and I started chewing it, and there was a very pleasant feeling, and I went "Now, the craving," and then I saw the craving. And so I relaxed, said: "Ok, I got to do this again, I didn't see it clearly enough." So I picked another one up, and I went through this whole process again, and I said: "That craving was really fast, I didn't see the start of it, I got to do it again." And I wound up eating a whole bowl of mango, but I didn't do it from a clinging mind, I did it from an investigative mind because I wanted to see exactly where and when this craving arose and how it arose. And when I got down to the last piece: "Well ok, I might as well do it one more time," I actually saw that when that feeling arose, and I relaxed, there wasn't any craving. That was a revelation, right there! This is wonderful stuff.

And you can do this with all of the six sense bases. You can do it with the eye and form, the ear and sound, the nose and smell, the tongue and taste, the body and sensation, and mind and mind objects. You can see these things. Takes a lot of practice to be able to see them, but the thing that's most important is your interest. If you take one of the sense doors, and play with just that sense door for a day or two days, and see if you can catch the feeling arising and relaxing right then; "Wow, that's really something." It's a real interesting process to go through. Don't recommend it with food too much because you get full and you wind up getting fat. "Yeah, let me try another one of those." Ha Ha.

The fat Buddha is not the Buddha. I'll let you have this story. He was a cousin of the Buddha and he looked very similar to the Buddha, and people kept on thinking that he was the Buddha. So what he did was he started eating more so he would look differently. And the Chinese-he wound up traveling quite a bit-and he was an arahat, and the Chinese found out about him through the Mahayana that he was a fat arahat, and they started calling him the Fat Buddha. Now, anything in China, any person that's fat is considered very, very happy. Because they have all kinds of diseases and worms and stuff, and nobody is ever fat in China. So they take this-the Buddha's cousin-and they say: "He's the Buddha, and he's happy." And that's why they like him so much. And they give him, sometimes they give him just a great smile, and looks like he's laughing. That wouldn't be the deportment of the Buddha, not the kind of smiles they give him, that sort of thing.

Anyway, we get to the last part of the mind objects as mind objects.

"He understands the ear, he understands sounds... He understands the nose, he understands odors... He understands the tongue, he understands flavors... He understands the body, he understands tangibles... He understands the mind, he understands mind-objects, and he understands the fetter that arises dependent on both; and he also understands how there comes to be the arising of the unarisen fetter, and how there comes to be the abandoning of the arisen fetter, and how there comes to be the future non-arising of the abandoned fetter.

41. "In this way he abides observing mind-objects as mind-objects internally, externally, and both internally and externally... And he abides independent, not craving or clinging to anything in the world. That is how a monk abides observing mind-objects as mind-objects in terms of the six internal and external bases.

42. {repeated for continuity} "Again, Monks, a monk abides observing mind-objects as mind-objects in terms of the seven awakening factors. And how does a monk abide observing mind-objects as mind-objects in terms of the seven awakening factors? Here, there being the mindfulness awakening factor in him, a monk understands: 'There is the mindfulness awakening factor in me;' or there being no mindfulness awakening factor in him, he understands: 'There is no mindfulness awakening factor in me;' and he also understands how there comes to be the arising of the unarisen mindfulness awakening factor, and how the arisen mindfulness awakening factor comes to fulfillment by development.

"There being the investigation-of-states awakening factor in him... There being the energy awakening factor in him... There being the joy awakening factor in him... There being the tranquility awakening factor in him... There being the collectedness awakening factor in him... There being the equanimity awakening factor in him, a monk understands: 'There is the equanimity awakening factor in me;' or there being no equanimity awakening factor in him, he understands: 'There is no equanimity awakening factor in me;' and he also understands how there comes to be the arising of the unarisen equanimity awakening factor, and how the arisen equanimity awakening factor comes to fulfillment by development.

43. "In this way he abides observing mind-objects as mind-objects internally, externally, and both internally and externally... And he abides independent, not craving or clinging to anything in the world. That is how a monk abides observing mind-objects as mind-objects in terms of the seven awakening factors.

44. "Again, Monks, a monk abides observing mind-objects as mind-objects in terms of the Four Noble Truths. And how does a monk abide observing mind-objects as mind-

objects in terms of the Four Noble Truths? Here a monk understands as it actually is: 'This is suffering;'

Now, when you're looking at Dependent Origination, they don't use the word suffering. They'll use the word ignorance and then they'll go to formations, and then they'll say consciousness and then they'll say mentality and materiality. They go through all of the different links of Dependent Origination, and instead of saying suffering they will say each one of those different links.

he understands as it actually is: 'This is the origin of suffering;'

Now, you can say suffering or you can say one of those links.

he understands as it actually is: 'This is the cessation of suffering;'

suffering or the one of those links.

he understands as it actually is: 'This is the way leading to the cessation of suffering.'

That's the Eightfold Path.

45. "In this way he abides observing mind-objects as mind-objects internally, he abides observing mind-objects as mind-objects externally, he abides observing mind-objects as mind-objects both internally and externally. He abides observing in mind-objects their nature of arising, he abides observing in mind-objects their nature of vanishing, he abides observing in mind-objects their nature of both arising and vanishing. And he abides independent, not craving or clinging to anything in the world.

That is how a monk abides observing mind-objects as mind-objects in terms of the Four Noble Truths.

46. "Monks, if anyone should develop these four foundations of mindfulness in such a way for seven years, one of two fruits could be expected for him: either final

knowledge here and now, or if there is a trace of clinging left, non-return.

Now, it's final knowledge here and now, he's talking about becoming an arahat. Or if there's a trace of clinging, then becoming a non-returner, which is an anāgāmī. Well, this doesn't say anything about the first two stages of awakening does it? Why? You don't necessarily need to practice meditation in order to experience becoming the first stage or the second stage of awakening. These are stages that have to do with your understanding, and seeing Dependent Origination through your own understanding. You don't have to practice meditation at all. Sāriputta didn't practice meditation at all when he became a sotāpanna. When he became a sotāpanna, Venerable Assaji came and he said: "Tell me the essence of the teaching." And Venerable Assaji, he just said two lines: "The Tathāgata said: 'Everything that arises';" as soon as he heard that he became a sotāpanna. And then Venerable Assaji said: "Everything arises from a cause." That was the first part of the statement. The second was: "And the Tathāgata said: "Everything ceases;" I can't remember it exactly. Anyway, when Venerable Sāriputta heard just the first two lines, he became a sotāpanna because his understanding was so good, he just needed a little clue; but he heard all four lines. He goes walking around and Moggallāna sees him and he said: "Hey, you've had some kind of experience. Tell me what it is." So Sāriputta says these four lines to Moggallāna and he becomes a sotāpanna. It has to do with your understanding.

And there's a lot more experiences like that. The banker, Anāthapindika, he just went to the Buddha and the Buddha gave him a discourse, he became a sotāpanna. The chief female supporter, Visākha, when she was eight years old, she went to the Buddha, he gave a discourse, she became a sotāpanna. You don't have to practice meditation to become a sotāpanna. It depends on your understanding. And again, what you think and ponder on that's the inclination of your mind. That's the little hint I'll give you about that. And it's the same with sakadāgāmī, the second stage of awakening. Now, the only way you're going to become an anāgāmī or an arahat is through the practice of meditation; you have to be able to see much more deeply the links of Dependent Origination.

"Let alone seven years, Monks. If anyone should develop these four foundations of mindfulness in such a way for six years... for five years... for four years... for three years... for two years... for one year, one of two fruits could be expected for him: either final knowledge here and now, or if there is a trace of clinging left, non-return.

"Let alone one year, Monks. If anyone should develop these four foundations of mindfulness in such a way for seven months... for six months... for five months... for four months... for three months... for two months... for one month... for half a month, one of two fruits could be expected for him: either final knowledge here and now, or if there is a trace of clinging left, non-return.

"Let alone half a month, Monks. If anyone should develop these four foundations of mindfulness in such a way for seven days,

How long is your retreat? Still got time!

one of two fruits could be expected for him: either final knowledge here and now, or if there is a trace of clinging left, non-return.

47. "So it was with reference to this that it was said: 'Monks, this is the direct path for the purification of beings, for the surmounting of sorrow and lamentation, for the disappearance of pain and grief, for the attainment of the true way, for the realization of Nibbāna - namely, the four foundations of mindfulness.'"

That is what the Buddha said. The monks were satisfied and delighted in the Blessed One's words.

MN 10: The Foundations of Mindfulness

So, does anybody have any questions, comments, statements. Anything? Yes?

ST: What is a sotāpanna?

BV: Sotāpanna means a person has experienced the first stage of awakening. When that happens their mind becomes pure enough, that they will not break a precept for any reason, on purpose. And that's the way you test whether you become a sotāpanna or not, actually. Try to say something that's not true, your mind will not go, it won't go there, just won't do it. And according to the text in the suttas, it says that when you become a sotāpanna, the most lifetimes that you will experience in the future is seven. You come back seven times. Sakadāgāmī is the second stage of awakening; it's called a once-returner. And that means that they will come back to the human form one more time before they become an arahat and get off the wheel. An anāgāmī is someone that is reborn in a special kind of Brahma-loka; there's five or six of those. And there they will live for an incredibly long time, and become an arahat, and before they die, and they will get off the wheel of samsāra. You become an arahat, it means that there is no more returning to any realm.

Now, Nibbāna, what is it? I won't talk about it, because I can't.

Well, it's an unconditioned state, and how can you talk about an unconditioned state with conditioned words?

And I get into conversation with monks, and we might sit around for four or five hours trying to define what the word Nibbāna means, and what the experience is. And we always come up with the same answer: "I don't know."

We're trying to figure out more closely what it really... what is that? And in the Aṅguttara Nikāya there's one sutta that says: "The way to look at an arahat is this: if I go down to the beach, and I make a castle, and a wave comes and takes it all away, all of those little pieces of sand are still there, but they're not ever going to be put together in the same way again." So you can say that the glue that holds the aggregates together is ignorance and craving. When you don't have ignorance and craving. then when the body dies, there is no more holding together of these things. Where does it go, what does it do, your guess is as good as mine. I don't know. But the Buddha did describe it as a kind of happiness. But even that is kind of... I mean what a relief, not ever having to see lust arise in your mind for anything, ever again! Or what relief you have from never having to experience anger at anything, for any reason; never having those experiences again. There's real relief there-that's a kind happiness-and it's the same with all of the different fetters.

ST: What's "magga" and "phala?"

BV: That's path and fruition.

ST: What's fruition?

BV: Fruition, it's the fruit of the experience. When there is talk about the Saṅgha, and it says that there's eight different kinds of individuals that are worthy of gifts, and worthy of respect, and praise, and all of this kind of thing. When it's talking about these eight kinds of individual, it is: a sotāpanna, and a sotāpanna with fruition; a sakadāgāmī, a sakadāgāmī with fruition; an anāgāmī, an anāgāmī with fruition; an arahat, an arahat with fruition. It's a different experience than the initial experience of Nibbāna that you can experience. It happens sometime after the initial experience.

According to Abhidhamma, which I definitely do not agree with, they say that there's seventeen different parts of a thought moment, and seven of those thought moments are javana moments. You experience Nibbāna in either the first javana moment, or the second javana moment, or the third javana moment. And you experience the fruition in the fifth javana moment, or the sixth javana moment. So they're saying in a thought moment, you're going to have the experience of the path and the fruition. But who would ever be able to see something like that, or know something like that? Why would they talk about eight different kinds of individuals? That doesn't make sense. What I have seen is that people can have the initial experience of Nibbāna, of deep understanding and seeing Dependent Origination, and then sometime in the future, they will have another experience of that where there's more clarity in seeing Dependent Origination, and understanding of Dependent Origination, and that's the fruition that occurs. And that happens with every stage.

There is one sutta that it kind of confirms the fact that if you have the initial experience of Nibbāna, and you just let your mind go back and do the things that it always does in the same way, that you can actually lose that experience, and lose the benefit, and never have the fruition. So you have to be careful. You have to, once you have the experience of Nibbāna, you need to very, very closely watch all the sense doors, keep your precepts exceptional, be very careful with your awareness or you could lose that attainment. Until you have the fruition, you don't really have that personality change. When you have the fruition, the personality changes, and it is really there. But there are suttas that talk about… you have to still be careful; you still have to be careful until you have the fruition. And then you don't need to be careful any more, you already… you are careful; you don't have to think about it anymore.

Ok, let's share some merit then.

May suffering ones be suffering free
And the fear struck fearless be.
May the grieving shed all grief
And may all beings find relief.
May all beings share this merit
That we have thus acquired
For the acquisition of
All kind of happiness.
May beings inhabiting space and earth
Devas and Nagas of mighty power
Share in this merit of ours.
May they long protect
the Buddha's Dispensation.
Sādhu… Sādhu… Sādhu…

MN-111: One By One As They Occurred (Anupada Sutta)

Presented by Ven Bhante Vimalaraṁsi on 20th February 2006 at Dhamma Dena Vipassanā Center, Joshua Tree, California

BV: This particular sutta is really interesting because the Buddha is describing Sāriputta's practice in meditation, and the states that he went through and what he saw while he was in each one of the meditation states.

So…

1. THUS HAVE I HEARD. On one occasion the Blessed One was living at Sāvatthī in Jeta's Grove, Anāthanpiṇḍika's Park. There he addressed the monks thus: "Monks." - "Venerable, sir," they replied. The Blessed One said this:

2. "Monks, Sāriputta is wise; Sāriputta has great wisdom; Sāriputta has wide wisdom; Sāriputta has joyous wisdom;

I like that one.

Sāriputta has quick wisdom; Sāriputta has keen wisdom; Sāriputta has penetrative wisdom. During half a month, Monks, Sāriputta gained insight into states one by one as they occurred. Now Sāriputta's insight into states one by one as they occurred was this:

Before we get going too far: the word "wisdom" is one of those words that everybody is supposed to know what the definition is, but nobody really has a clear idea of what that word means. In Buddhism, any time the word "wisdom" is used, it is referring directly to seeing Dependent Origination. When you see Dependent Origination and how it works, you're developing your wisdom, you're developing insight into the true nature of everything that arises. So anytime you see the word "wisdom," it's actually referring to Dependent Origination.

3. "Here, Monks, quite secluded from sensual pleasures, secluded from unwholesome states,

How do you become secluded from sensual pleasures? Actually, while you're sitting in your meditation, you're sitting with your eyes closed. The sensual pleasure of seeing is not there; it's secluded. If you hear a sound, the directions are: as soon as your mind goes to that distraction, let it go, relax, and come back to your object of meditation. You don't get involved in the content of what that sound is about. If someone is talking, you don't get involved in the conversation. You just hear it as sound, let it be, relax, and come back; and taste, and smell, and touch. So when you're secluded from sensual pleasures, it means not getting involved with whatever sensual pleasure it is that arises. Not get caught about how much you like this sight, or this sound, or this touch, or taste, or smell, but seeing it for what it is. It is just... this, and it's all right for it to be there. But you allow it to be, relax, and come back to your object of meditation.

Now, "secluded from unwholesome states," what does that mean? Being secluded from unwholesome states. Being secluded from unwholesome states means letting go of all hindrances. As your mind begins to become more calm, more at ease, hindrances will not have a tendency to arise at that time.

Sāriputta entered upon and abided in the first jhāna, which is accompanied by thinking and examining thought, with joy and happiness born of seclusion.

The way jhāna occurs is: you're working with a distraction, a hindrance of one kind or another, whatever it happens to be, and as you let it go, and relax, and come back to your object of meditation, it begins to get weaker, and weaker, until finally it doesn't arise anymore. When it doesn't arise anymore, you have a real sense of relief. And right after that relief, you feel joy arising.

MN 111: One By One As They Occurred

Now, there are five different kinds of joy. The first kind of joy is like goose bumps; it's there for just a brief moment, and then it goes away. The next kind of joy is, it's like a flash of lightening; it's real intense for a very short period of time, and then that fades away. The next kind of joy is like you're standing in the ocean, and you have these waves of joy come over you; it's just wave after wave. Now, these three kinds of joy can happen to anyone for any reason. When the conditions are right, these kinds of joy will arise. The last two kinds of joy only arise through mental development. The next kind of joy is called uplifting joy, you feel very light in your mind and light in your body. You feel very happy and there's excitement in it. The last kind of joy is called all pervading joy. And it just kind of comes out of everywhere; it just kind of bubbles over and just kind of comes through your whole body.

Now, when you're looking at Buddha images, quite often you'll look at a Buddha image and you'll see that their eyes are partially open. The artist is showing the all-pervading joy. And it happens when the joy is very deep. You'll be sitting in meditation, this joy arises, it feels very good, doesn't have near as much excitement in it, but your mind is very alert and very calm; but there's a happiness about whatever you're seeing.

When you're sitting, all of a sudden this joy arises, and your eyes open up. And you think: "Well, that was strange." So you close your eyes, and your eyes open up; so you close your eyes, and your eyes open up. And you say: "Well, ok, you want to be open, stay open." But this is what the artist is trying to show with the eyes partially open in the Buddha images.

Now, in the first jhāna, and if you'll remember what I was saying about jhāna, the word "jhāna" quite often, in this country, is translated as "concentration." Actually, the word "jhāna" means a stage of your meditation. It's just a level of your understanding about Dependent Origination; it's just a level. The joy arises, right after that when it fades away, you feel very comfortable in your mind and in your body. This feeling is what the Buddha called "sukha" in Pāli, which is happiness. And your mind doesn't wander very much in your meditation; your mind doesn't wander away. It stays with your meditation; you feel very peaceful and very calm. In Pāli, the word for that is "ekaggatā." And if you look up the word in the (Pāli) dictionary, "ekagga," it means tranquility, it means peacefulness, it means stillness of mind. Ekaggatā means the act of... this stillness.

So these are the things that Sāriputta experienced in the first jhāna.

4. "And the states in the first jhāna - the thinking and examining thought, the joy, the happiness, and the unification of mind;

Those are the five factors right there. Then he says:

the contact, feeling, perception, formations and mind;

The five aggregates are present in that jhāna. Then it says:

the enthusiasm, decision, energy, mindfulness, equanimity, and attention - these states were defined by him one by one as they occurred; known to him those states arose, known they were present, known they disappeared.

What are we talking about right here? We're talking about impermanence. You're seeing impermanence while you are in the jhāna; you're seeing these things arise and pass away one by one as they occur. They don't necessarily follow the order that they're given here; they kind of come up whenever they're going to come up.

He understood thus: 'So indeed, these states, not having been, come into being; having been, they vanish.'

Impermanence again.

Regarding those states, he abided unattracted,

He didn't grab onto it, try to hold on to them.

unrepelled,

He didn't try to push them away, stop them from happening.

independent,

He saw the true nature of all of these states as being impersonal; anatta - impersonal. I don't like the definition of "anatta" being "not self" because so many people misunderstand that. When you say "impersonal," you see it as part of a process; when you see "not self," you get confused.

detached,

Again, impersonal.

free,

Again, impersonal.

dissociated, with a mind rid of barriers. He understood: 'There is an escape beyond,' and with the cultivation of that attainment, he confirmed that there is.

So he got into the first jhāna, he knew there's still more work to be done. But while he was in the jhāna, he was seeing impermanence. Anyone that sees impermanence sees a form of unsatisfactoriness because we want things to be permanent, and when it's not, there's this little dissatisfaction that arises. And we're seeing the impersonal nature of all of these different states as they arise and pass away. You don't have any control over these; they happen when the conditions are right for them to arise. There's no "me;" there's no "my;" there's no "I." So you're seeing anicca, dukkha, anatta, while you are in the jhāna. You're also seeing the five aggregates. This is very key. Seeing these things, and we'll get to see that Sāriputta saw these things all the way up to the realm of nothingness. Seeing the five aggregates... in the Saṃyutta Nikāya, there's a section on the five aggregates, and it says that the five aggregates and the four foundations of mindfulness are the same thing. So when you're practicing and getting into the jhāna, by adding that extra step of relaxing, you're practicing the four foundations of mindfulness, while you're in the jhāna.

5. "Again, Monks, with the stilling of thinking and examining thought, Sāriputta entered upon and abided in the second jhāna, which has self-confidence and stillness of mind without thinking and examining thought, with joy and happiness born of collectedness.

Now, here it says "concentration," but I don't like to use the word "concentration" because it's misunderstood. Just about everybody that practices concentration, they're practicing an absorption kind of concentration. When you're reading a book and you're really concentrated, and somebody comes up and you don't even know they're there because you're so absorbed in what you're reading, that's concentration. But what the Buddha was talking about, because you have these five aggregates, is a collected kind of mind. It's a mind that's peaceful; it's a mind that's still and tranquil, but it's alert to everything else around you.

You see, when we're talking about the five aggregates here, they use the word - instead of "body" - they use the word "contact." In order for there to be contact, you have to have a body, but you don't necessarily notice your body until there is contact. When there's a touch, then you know that body is still around. And this is one of the things that happens in absorption concentration, is your mind becomes so absorbed in your object of meditation that you lose all feeling of the body.

I've been to meditation centers where people are practicing concentration, and the way we find out whether they're really concentrated or not, just come up and touch them, they don't know. Make loud noises right beside them, they don't know. They don't have full awareness. They have a deeply concentrated mind, but they don't have awareness around them. They can't feel the contact. The contact with the ear, the contact with the body, they can't feel that when they get to deep stages of concentration. But as you'll see here, even when you get into the arūpa jhānas, you still have that contact. And if you're in an arūpa jhāna, and I walk up to you and I say: "I need to talk to you right now," you will hear that. And then you make a decision of whether you're going to break your sitting or not. So this particular sutta is very important because it's showing that there is full awareness while you're in a jhāna. And what's the difference between absorption concentration and the samatha-vipassanā? The samatha-vipassanā has that one extra step of relaxing. When you put that in, that changes the entire meditation. And this is the thing that made the Buddha's teaching so unique from whatever was being taught by other teachers at that time.

6. "And the states in the second jhāna - the self-confidence,

Now, why do you have self confidence when you're starting to develop your deeper stages of meditation? Because you're really starting to understand the process of Dependent Origination and you're starting to see it as being an impersonal process; you're starting to see. Now, yesterday I was telling everyone I want you to see how your minds movement works. What happens; how does it happen? As you start seeing that, you start seeing individual parts of Dependent Origination, and you see that there is a cause and effect; when this arises, then that arises. When you let go of the craving, when you let go of that tension and tightness caused by that mind's attention and its movement, there's no clinging. There's no habitual tendency arising. At that moment, you have a very clear mind. It's alert, there are no thoughts, and you bring that mind's attention back to your object of meditation. So you can see that Sāriputta's experience, while he was in each one of these jhānas, is a lot different than the ones that are being described as absorption concentration.

6. {repeats} "And the states in the second jhāna - the self-confidence,

You start actually seeing it and you start believing that this stuff is real, and you get a lot of confidence when you do that.

the joy,

The joy that arises in the second jhāna is stronger; you feel much lighter in your mind; you feel much lighter in your body. I've had students that they say they feel so light when they come to give me an interview; they feel so light that they had to open up their eyes because they thought they were going to hit the ceiling. That's how light they felt.

the happiness,

The happiness you experience: more comfort, very, very nice, peaceful, calm feeling in your mind and in your body. You don't have a lot of... you don't have pains arising because of this sublime comfort.

and the unification of mind; the contact, feeling, perception, formations and mind;

Five aggregates again.

the enthusiasm, decision, energy, mindfulness, equanimity, and attention - these states were defined by him one by one as they occurred; known to him those states arose, known they were present, known they disappeared.

He's seeing anicca, dukkha, anatta, in every one of the jhānas.

Now, the enthusiasm as you begin to see how the Dependent Origination works; how, when craving arises, it always manifests as a tension and tightness in your body and mind, and that you can let go of that, and relax, and come back to your object of meditation, you start to get a little bit of enthusiasm about that; this stuff works. And I don't want you to believe me, and I don't want you to believe the Buddha. See it for yourself, see whether it works or not.

{repeats} the decision

Now, this is always an interesting aspect of the meditation. You have a choice, while you're meditating, you can either get caught by thoughts or feelings, sensations, emotions, or not; it's up to you. What arises in the present moment dictates what happens in the future. Your choice is what will happen in the future. If you decide to stay with that emotion, that sadness, dissatisfaction, or whatever, you grab onto it; you can look forward to that happening over and over again; you can look forward to suffering. Or you can see it for what it really is, and you let it go, and relax, and come back to your object of meditation. When you do that, you can look forward to the release from the suffering. That's the third noble truth.

I've always been amazed at the use of the word "enlightenment." If I tell you something you don't know, then I've enlightened you. If you let go of craving and come back to your object of meditation with that clear mind, that moment is an enlightening moment because there's no craving, there's only this pure unadulterated mind that you're bringing back to your object of meditation. So they talk about the Buddha being enlightened; well in a lot of ways he was truly enlightened. But the word "Buddha" doesn't mean the enlightened one, it means the awakened one. When you let go of craving, and you do it enough so that a hindrance fades away, you become more and more awake as to how the process works. So when it comes to the word "enlightenment," I kind of back away from that.

But the Buddha teaches us how to be more and more awake, more and more alert to how we cause our own suffering. There's not another person in this world that causes your suffering. You cause your own suffering by the decision of when that feeling arises, and it's a painful feeling, and you don't like it, of grabbing on to that and trying to control it and fight with it. And then you wind up saying things and doing things that cause suffering for yourself and other people around you. But it's your choice, it's your decision. When you become more and more awake as to how this process works, you start seeing and becoming more aware of how you cause your own suffering, and you start letting that go, more, and more, and more. And then your mind starts to get into a state of equanimity. And with that there's no more reactions; act like you always act when this particular feeling arises. You start letting go of the old reactions and you start responding in a new way, in a way that has happiness and leads to happiness for yourself and everybody else around you.

Now, the next part of this - the energy - is real interesting. Now, when people first start meditating and they finally get it, and they get some joy, and they get into the first jhāna, they get real enthusiastic. But it's time to break it for one reason or another, and then you come back, and you sit down and you say: "I'm going to have that one again." Well actually, you wind up putting too much energy into it and you wind up getting restless, and then you have to work with the restlessness. The energy is really interesting because it's not always the same every time. You have to nudge it a little bit this way or a little bit that way. It's like being on a tightrope. If you have too much energy, you fall off one way, if you don't have enough, you fall off the other way, and it's a constant adjustment with your energy so that you can stay in balance. "Well, I had this mental state come up before, I'm going to put this much energy and make it go away." Sometimes, sometimes not. It depends on how you apply the energy and how you're able to adjust in the appropriate way. As you go deeper into the jhānas, it's a finer and finer adjustment with your energy.

Now, the next word in here is "mindfulness." Now, mindfulness is another one of those words; everybody's supposed to know what mindfulness is, right? What's the definition of mindfulness?

ST: Seeing before the doing?

BV: In a very general way, yes, that's right. But when you're sitting in meditation and you're getting into these deeper

MN 111: One By One As They Occurred

states, it's observing the mind's attention... the movement of mind's attention from one thing to another, and seeing it impersonally, seeing it as a process.

Now, you're sitting in meditation, you have a pain arise in your knee. How do you handle the pain arising in your knee? When you're practicing the way that I'm showing you right now, you notice the first thing is that your mind begins to think about the sensation: "I wish it would stop, I wish it would go away, I hate it when it's there." All of those thoughts cause the sensation to get bigger and more intense. So the first thing we have to do is make the decision to let go of the thoughts about the pain, and relax because that has caused tension and tightness to arise. The next thing you'll notice is there is a tight mental fist around that sensation. The truth is, when a sensation arises, it's there; that is the Dhamma; that's the truth. What you do with the truth, right here, right now, dictates what happens in the future. If you resist the truth, if you try to control the truth, if you try to make the truth be the way you want it to be, you can look forward to a lot of suffering. Continually, over, and over, and over again, until you learn that you have to accept the truth that it's there. Relax and allow that truth to do whatever it wants to do. If it wants to bounce around, it can bounce around, if it wants to go to another place in your body, it can go to another place in your body, it doesn't matter. Allow that feeling to be, relax, and come back to your object of meditation.

Now, the sensation we call pain, and if you'll remember, I was telling you that pain is a concept. It's made up of a lot of tiny little things that arise and pass away. How does pain arise? When you look at Dependent Origination, you will see that there is a feeling that arises, and that feeling is unpleasant; it's painful. The next thing you'll see is that mind, it grabs onto that and says: "I don't like that;" that is craving. And then you'll have thoughts, the story about how you don't like it and how you want it to disappear; that's clinging.

And this process happens over, and over, and over again. So when you let go of the thoughts and relax, you let the feeling be, and relax, you're letting go of the attachment to that sensation.

The nature of these kind of sensations is they don't go away right away. So it's going to be bouncing back and forth. You let it go, you relax, you come back to your object of meditation; you might get one wish in, you might not, before it goes back. And then the same thing happens all over again. How did that happen? Right before that pain became so incredibly tense and tight, what happened right before that; and what happened right before that; what happened before that? As you start to see how this sensation arose, you will start to see, through very strong mindfulness, that this is part of a process. And as you let go of different parts of the process, there's balance in your mind and the emergency disappears. The one that says: "I have to get up and move, I can't stand this anymore;" it will disappear. Now, sometimes the pain goes away, and sometimes it doesn't. But if it doesn't go away, there is very strong balance of mind, so that it doesn't even pull your attention to it; then you don't pay attention to it.

So mindfulness is the observation power of the mind that sees mind's attention move from one thing, to another thing, to another thing. As your mindfulness gets deeper, you start to see more and more clearly all of the little parts of the distraction. As you start to understand and let go of that distraction, eventually the distraction doesn't pull your mind to it anymore; there's a sense of relief and you get into a jhāna. Now, I say that with pain, but it doesn't matter whether it's physical or mental, you treat all of these in the same way.

One of the things that I've noticed happening in this country is when you start talking about the five aggregates, you say there's body, there's feelings, there's perception, there's formations, there's consciousness. Feelings: they're trying to make it just a mental definition. And then they say: "Well, you have these feelings come up; we need to work with these feelings so that you can get rid of these feelings. And that's not what the Buddha was teaching at all. He was teaching that feeling is pleasant and painful. It doesn't matter if it's sadness, if it's anger, if it's fear, if it's anxiety, if it's depression, it doesn't matter what kind of mental feeling that is, you need to see it for what it truly is, and how that process works. As you start letting go of the craving, the feeling loses a lot of its energy, and stops pulling your attention to it. You start gaining more and more a sense of balance in your mind, which happens to be the next part of this, which is equanimity.

Equanimity is always balance in your mind. It's not the mind that goes on the roller coaster of: "I like this, I don't like that, I like this, I don't like that." It's the mind that says: "Ok, this is here right now, so what." It's not indifference; indifference has... it has aversion in it. Equanimity is extreme clarity of being able to see things with this balance. The equanimity helps very much with being able to see everything as being part of an impersonal process. Why is that important? If you take whatever arises personally, in your mind you're saying: "This is me. This is who I am." And you're not seeing the four noble truths the way they truly are, and this is really important. If you don't see the four noble truths that means you have ignorance. Now, what's the base word of "ignorance:" "to ignore." That means you're ignoring the truth of how things arise and how they work, you're ignoring that there's suffering, there's a cause of suffering, there's a way to let go of that suffering; there is letting go of the suffering and a way of letting go of the suffering. There is that, but you're ignoring that by taking this feeling and saying: "This is me. This is who I am." And because you ignore it, you cause yourself more and more suffering, more and more pain, more and more anxiety, depression, whatever it happens to be.

He understood thus: 'So indeed, these states, not having been, come into being; having been they vanish.' Regarding those states he abided unattracted, unrepelled, independent, detached, free, dissociated, with a mind rid of barriers. He understood: 'There is an escape beyond,' and with the cultivation of that attainment, he confirmed that there is.

So you're in the second jhāna, you still have a feeling there's more work to do.

7. "Again, Monks, with the fading away as well of joy, Sāriputta abided in equanimity, and mindful, and fully aware, still feeling pleasure with the body, still feeling happiness with the body, he entered upon and abided in the third jhāna, on account of which noble ones announce: 'He has a pleasant abiding who has equanimity and is mindful'.

8. "And the states in the third jhāna - the equanimity,

When you get into the third jhāna... well let's go back a little bit. When you're in the first jhāna, you can still have distracting thoughts and you still have some thinking mind. When you get into the second jhāna, this is where true noble silence begins to take hold. You can't make a wish, when you're practicing loving-kindness, because it causes your head to get tightness in it. You let go of making the wish and you just feel the wish. If you try to verbalize when you're in the second jhāna, it causes a lot of tightness; so you let go of that; so now there's true noble silence. When you get into the third jhāna, the joy doesn't arise anymore.

Now, one of the things that I do when I teach is I don't talk to you about which jhāna you're in, I let you figure that out for yourself, doesn't matter. These are just stages, but certain things will happen. That they're like signposts for me, so I know how to talk to you about what your experience is. They help me to be able to help you. Now, when you get into the third jhāna, it's always kind of comical, especially when this is the first time you've ever experienced getting into the third jhāna, because you're so used to having this joy, that all of a sudden it disappears, and you come into the interview and we started: "How's your meditation going?" - "Well, it's ok, but I don't have any more joy." I say: "Yeah, ok." - "But you don't understand, I don't have any more joy. It's always there!" And I say: "Yeah, yeah, ok. Do you feel more balance in your mind than you've ever felt before?" - "Well yeah, but there's no joy!" - "Ok, do you feel really, truly, happy? Do you feel comfortable in your mind and in your body like you've never felt before?" - "Yes." And I say: "Good, continue. You don't have to have joy." So when you get into the third jhāna, the joy disappears, but there's other things that take its place. The highest feeling that you can experience is equanimity, that balance. And the balance starts to get real good.

When you get into the third jhāna, as you go deeper into that jhāna, you start losing body parts; you'll be sitting and all of a sudden: "I don't feel my hands," or "I don't feel my leg," or "my shoulder disappeared." When you get into the third jhāna, you let go of a lot of mental tension. When you let go of a lot of mental tension, you start letting go of a lot of physical tension, and that's what you feel in your body. When you're sitting in meditation and you feel something in your body, it's because there's mental tension that caused that physical tension to arise. As you go deeper into your third jhāna, you're letting go of all of this; all of a sudden you start losing feeling, unless there's contact; I can come up and I can touch you, and you'll know that it happened, but you have a balanced mind, you have this equanimity. So it doesn't make your mind shake; it doesn't make your mind flutter; it just says: "Ok, there was a touch." Never mind, relax, come back to your object of meditation. There is this very strong balance that occurs. And you feel more comfortable than you've ever felt, very much at ease in your body. Your mind is very, very calm, like looking out on a pond that doesn't have any ripples in it; very peaceful.

"And the states in the third jhāna - the equanimity, the happiness, the mindfulness, the full awareness,

Now, you see you still have mindfulness, you're still able to see movements that arise, and you have full awareness at all of the sense doors. You still hear sounds, you open up your eyes, you will be able to see things, but you have this equanimity that doesn't run to them and grab onto them anymore.

and the unification of mind;

Your mind becomes very tranquil, very unified. It's not so one-pointed that it just stays on one object. That means there's not mindfulness there, that's absorption concentration. It's seeing with a very still mind. And you're able to watch when movements first start to arise. And you can let them go and relax. You'll start to see that mind starts to flutter a little bit, and then it flutters faster and faster, and then it can get distracted. You'll see how that process works. And when you start to see this fluttering, if you relax right then, then your mind stays on your object of meditation.

the contact, feeling, perception, formations and mind;

Still we have the five aggregates here.

the enthusiasm, decision, energy, mindfulness, equanimity, and attention - these states were defined by him one by one as they occurred;

Again, one of the things that I noticed when I came to this country is everybody that talked about jhāna, they had the idea that all of these different states in the jhāna all happened at the same time. But right here you can see these were defined by Sāriputta one by one as they occurred. They don't all happen at the same time. So that's another slight difference between the absorption concentration and the samatha-vipassanā that I'm talking about.

known to him those states arose, known they were present, known they disappeared. He understood thus: 'So indeed,

these states, not having been, come into being; having been they vanish.'

Anicca.

Regarding those states, he abided unattracted, unrepelled, independent, detached, free, dissociated, with a mind rid of barriers. He understood: 'There is an escape beyond,' and with the cultivation of that attainment, he confirmed that there is.

9. "Again, Monks, with the abandoning of pleasure...

Now, even the happiness gets to be too coarse a feeling.

{repeats} with the abandoning of pleasure and pain, and with the previous disappearance of joy and grief, Sāriputta entered upon and abided in the fourth jhāna, which has neither-pain-nor-pleasure and purity of mindfulness due to equanimity.

It doesn't mean that there cannot be a pain arising, or a pleasurable feeling arising, it means that it doesn't make your mind shake. You see it for what it is, and you have this balance towards it. Now, you don't really have any sensations arising in your body. But again, if an ant walks on you, you know it. But you have such equanimity that it doesn't bother you, or a mosquito comes around and he bites you, it's ok, so what, no big deal.

Now, one of the mistakes that an awful lot of people have, when they are talking about jhāna is they think that the jhāna only arises while you're doing your sitting meditation. And you can take any one of these jhānas and stay with the jhāna while you get up and do your walking meditation. You can have equanimity when you're washing the dishes; you can have equanimity while you're taking a bath, or going to the bathroom, but it takes staying with your object of meditation and really being focused on your object of meditation. In any one of the jhānas, you can have them during your daily activities. This is one of the reasons why I'm real adamant, I guess you might say, about keeping your meditation going all the time. I don't care what you're doing; it's part of the practice. Everything that you do is a part of the practice, if you practice that way, if you do that. Our habit is to kind of forget and get caught up in our daily stuff, and forget about the meditation, and then come back and sit, and then it takes a little while to get back into your meditation; that's our habit. But I want you to be very aware of what your mind is doing all the time. Stay in that meditation state as much as you possibly can remember to do it.

Now, one of the functions of mindfulness is to remember. To remember what? To remember to stay with watching mind's attention and how it moves from one thing to another. How to let things go, relax, and come back to your object of meditation. Very important!

Now, when you get in the fourth jhāna, because there is contact when you're walking, you will feel sensation on your feet. You don't feel anything in between your head and your feet, unless it happens to be windy, then you start feeling that, but that's because there is contact.

Try to develop the mind that is alert all the time. Takes practice, not easy, but it's definitely worthwhile. As you become more aware with your daily activities, how your mindfulness slips, and the hindrance arises, then the hindrances will be let go of more quickly if you're alert to how the process works, and you can have happiness with you all of the time. And the happiness is not a giddy kind of happiness; this is a happiness of not having the suffering, not identifying with the thoughts and feelings that arise, seeing them for what they are. Just thoughts, just feelings, let them be, relax, come back.

Now, one of the interesting things that I ran across in the Saṃyutta Nikāya was a section on Loving-Kindness Meditation that had to do with the factors of enlightenment.

And this particular sutta was a real revelation to me because it starts talking about practicing loving-kindness in the fourth jhāna... Now, the reason that it's a revelation to me was because I had always heard and definitely believed that loving-kindness can only take you to the third jhāna. But there it is, in the sutta talking about it being in the fourth jhāna. And this is talking about the Brahma Vihāras.

Now, I was always told that the Brahma Vihāras, that is, loving-kindness, compassion, sympathetic joy or altruistic joy, and equanimity; that compassion only goes to the third jhāna, the joy goes to the third jhāna, equanimity goes to the fourth jhāna. But when I was reading this sutta, I was truly amazed because it says: loving-kindness goes to the fourth jhāna, compassion goes to the realm of infinite space, the fifth jhāna - the first arūpa jhāna - joy goes to the realm of infinite consciousness, and equanimity goes to the realm of nothingness. The practice that I'm actually teaching you, when you're practicing loving-kindness is not just loving-kindness; it is the practice of the Brahma Vihāras.

10. "And the states in the fourth jhāna - the equanimity, the neither-painful-nor-pleasant feeling, the mental unconcern due to tranquility,

Isn't that an interesting statement?

the purity of mindfulness, and the unification of mind; the contact, feeling, perception, formations and mind;

The five aggregates are still here. Now, too many times, I've run across an awful lot of teachers that are very adamant about: "If you're doing Mindfulness of Breathing, when you get to the fourth jhāna, you don't breath through your lungs anymore." And that's not necessarily true. You still have body; you still have contact; that means you're still breathing. It's not breathing through the skin, it's breathing. What they're talking about is when you get to the fourth absorption jhāna, but that's not the same jhāna as we're talking about here.

the enthusiasm, decision, energy, mindfulness, equanimity, and attention - these states were defined by him one by one as they occurred;

Still has his mindfulness, still has his full awareness of what's happening as it arises. Mind is not glued to one particular thing. There are still movements that need to be observed.

known to him those states arose, known they were present, known they disappeared. He understood thus: ... and with the cultivation of that attainment he confirmed that there is still more.

When the meditator gets to the fourth jhāna, they give up their rookie status; you're not a rookie anymore; now you've become an advanced meditator.

11. "Again, Monks, with the complete surmounting of perceptions of form, with the disappearance of perceptions of sensory impact, with non-attention to perceptions of diversity,

That's kind of a bad translation. It's not non-attention, it's knowing that there is change, but mind isn't shaking, mind isn't going to that change.

aware that 'space is infinite,' Sāriputta entered upon and abided in the base of infinite space.

Now, what's that experience all about? You have very strong equanimity, and all of a sudden you start feeling an expansion that arises. If you're practicing Loving-Kindness Meditation, this is where the loving-kindness turns into compassion, which is a very different kind of feeling, I won't describe it to you, you have to describe it to me, and I'll confirm whether that's really it or not. But it is a different kind of feeling, and with that feeling there is a continual expansion in all directions at the same time, but there's no center-point. There's just an expansion feeling, and that's what infinite space is. It's a feeling of space being infinite; it just keeps going, and going, and going. Very pleasant. And this is the state that so many people, when they talk about the Buddha's infinite compassion, this is the state that he was actually experiencing. He did this every morning, of getting into the realm of infinite space with the compassion as his object of meditation.

12. "And the states in the base of infinite space - the perception of the base of infinite space and the unification of mind; the contact, feeling, perception, formations and mind;

Still have the five aggregates, even though you're in an arūpa jhāna. This says that you're still practicing the four foundations of mindfulness even while you are in an arūpa jhāna state.

the enthusiasm, decision, energy, mindfulness, equanimity, and attention - these states were defined by him one by one as they occurred; known to him those states arose, known they were present, known they disappeared. He understood thus: . . . and with the cultivation of that attainment, he confirmed that there is still more.

13. "Again, Monks, by completely surmounting the base of infinite space, aware that 'consciousness is infinite,' Sāriputta entered upon and abided in the base of infinite consciousness.

This is a real interesting state. For one thing, the compassion of feeling changes again to a feeling of altruistic joy, but that's not really a good definition; I haven't run across one yet. But it is a feeling that's very different from the compassion. Now what happens is, your awareness starts to be so good and so sharp that you start to see individual consciousnesses arise and pass away, arise and pass away, arise and pass away. You are seeing firsthand how truly impermanent everything is. There's no doubt in your mind anymore that everything really is impermanent. And after you sit with that for a little while, it's kind of comical because people will come to me and they'll say: "Well yeah, I'm seeing all these consciousnesses: the eye, the ear, the nose, the tongue, the body, and mind." You're seeing all of these consciousnesses arise and pass away and it's really tiresome. What you're seeing now is not only impermanence, but you're seeing suffering. And you're seeing there's nobody home, there's no control over this stuff, it happens all by itself. You're seeing up close and personal anicca, dukkha, anatta, while you're in the arūpa jhānas, and this is really an amazing state. It answers a lot of questions that you ever had before, and everybody talks about things happening so fast; now your awareness is so sharp you're seeing them. And it really is interesting, if not a little tiresome after awhile because they keep on arising and passing away. It doesn't matter whether you're doing your walking meditation, and you're eating, or anything, you're seeing all these consciousnesses continually.

14. "And the states in the base of infinite consciousness - the perception of the base of infinite consciousness and the unification of mind; the contact, feeling, perception, formations and mind;

Still have the five aggregates here.

the enthusiasm, decision, energy, mindfulness, equanimity, and attention - these states were defined by him one by one as they occurred; known to him those states arose, known they were present, known they disappeared. He understood thus... and with the cultivation of that attainment, he confirmed that there is still more.

As you go deeper into your meditation, you begin to realize these things for yourself. This is called direct knowledge and vision.

15. "Again, Monks, by completely surmounting the base of infinite consciousness, aware that 'there is nothing,' Sāriputta entered upon and abided in the base of nothingness.

This is an incredibly interesting thing. Where before you were seeing everything outside of the body, now you're not seeing anything. But you're still seeing different movements of mind, but it's not outside of mind.

16. "And the states in the base of nothingness

Oh, by the way, where you were feeling joy before, now you're feeling equanimity that is very, very strong, and you have this balance of mind. This particular state of mind is by far the most interesting state that you can experience in the meditation. You still have the energy things, and the energy becomes really, really subtle. If you don't put quite enough energy into watching that equanimity, your mind gets dull. You don't have sleepiness, but there's a dullness that occurs. If you put a little bit too much energy in, your mind gets restless. And because of the way the hindrances work, they don't just come one at a time. If you have restlessness arise, because you put in too much energy, you're not in that jhāna anymore; you're caught by the hindrance. But it's not just say, the restlessness, but it's the restlessness and the dislike of the restlessness. So you have two hindrances that you get to work with. But it's quite easy to let that go and balance your energy by this time. But it's like walking the finest rope you've ever seen, you know, it's like walking on a spider web; it's that fine. And the balance, it just takes a little twip, a little twerp, and psssst, you're knocked off balance. And then you have to work with that, relax, and come back. And then, not quite enough. And this is where working with the energy is incredibly interesting.

Now, this is an interesting part of this particular state of mind.

16. "And the states in the base of nothingness - the perception of the base of nothingness and the unification of mind; the contact, feeling, perception, formations and mind,

Still have the five aggregates; still practicing the four foundations of mindfulness.

the enthusiasm, decision, energy, mindfulness, equanimity, and attention - these states were defined by him one by one

as they occurred; known to him those states arose, known they were present, known they disappeared. He understood thus… and with the cultivation of that attainment, he confirmed that there is still more.

Now, this is the state that when he was a Bodhisatta, he got to this state in absorption concentration, and went to the teacher and said: "Is there more?" And the teacher said: "No, that's it. You can teach right along beside me. Come, help." The Bodhisatta said: "No, not satisfied with that." He still saw that there's more; there's more to this.

17. "Again, Monks, by completely surmounting the base of nothingness, Sāriputta entered upon and abided in the base of neither-perception-nor-non-perception.

Now, if you look at it this way, when you start meditating your mind has these kinds of movements. As you get deeper in your meditation, the movements become less and less. When you get into the arūpa jhānas, it starts turning into vibration. As you go higher into the jhānas, the vibration becomes faster and finer. When you get to the state of neither-perception-nor-non-perception, there's slight movement, but it's really hard to tell. Mind is there, but it's hard to perceive. When you're practicing the Brahma Vihāras, they will take you to the realm of nothingness, and that's as high as you can go, with the Brahma Vihāras, because…

18. "He emerged mindful from that attainment.

Mind is so subtle, it's hard to tell whether it's there or not, and the only way you know that you've experienced that experience is, when you come out, you start reflecting on what you saw. Feeling is still there although it's subtle, and perception is kind of there and kind of not. So the only way you know that you've experienced this is by reflecting on what you've done while you were sitting. Now, this is the time when I'll come to somebody and I'll say: "I really want you to make sure that you've developed that habit of relaxing, continually, all the time." So when you get into this

MN 111: One By One As They Occurred 137

state, you're doing this as an automatic. Now, what is the relaxing doing? When you relax, the movement becomes less and less, until you finally get to a state that you can't really see it, but it's still vibrating a bit.

Having done so, he contemplated the states that had passed, ceased, and changed, thus:

So you still have that, even though you get into the neither-perception-nor-non-perception.

'So indeed, these states, not having been, come into being; having been, they vanish. Regarding those states, he abided unattracted, unrepelled, independent, detached, free, dissociated, with a mind rid of barriers. He understood: 'There is an escape beyond,' and with the cultivation of that attainment, he confirmed that there is.

So he still knows that there's some more work to do. As he keeps relaxing more and more, that vibration becomes so still that all of a sudden it stops.

19. "Again, Monks, by completely surmounting the base of neither-perception-nor-non-perception, Sāriputta entered upon and abided in the cessation of perception, feeling and consciousness.

Just like somebody turned the lights off. Click! There's nothing there; there's no perception; there's no feeling; there's no consciousness.

And his taints were destroyed by his seeing with wisdom.

You remember that word that I talked about at the start of this, "wisdom." So what is it saying? What happens is, the state of the cessation of perception, feeling and consciousness occurs, and it's going to last as long as it's going to last. When perception, feeling and consciousness return, you have a chance of seeing exactly, clearly, with very sharp mindfulness, every one of the steps of Dependent Origination. And you will see how: when this doesn't arise, that doesn't arise. You'll see the cessation, and with the final letting go of ignorance, of seeing the four noble truths and applying it to everything; that's when Nibbāna occurs; that's when all the taints are destroyed; that's how the end of this process works.

20. "**He emerged mindful from that attainment. Having done so, he recalled the states that had passed, ceased, and changed, thus: 'So indeed, these states, not having been, come into being; having been, they vanish.'**

He saw all of the states of Dependent Origination and how they cease to be.

Regarding those states, he abided unattracted, unrepelled, independent, detached, free, dissociated, with a mind rid of barriers. He understood: 'There is no escape beyond,' and with the cultivation of that attainment, he confirmed that there is not.'

That's it, it can't go any further. Now, when this happened, his mind became so incredibly clear, his understanding of Dependent Origination, as a true process, his understanding was absolutely unshakable. And with that he let go of everything that would possibly cause his mind to become unwholesome. He only had wholesome thoughts arise.

21. "**Monks, rightly speaking, were it to be said of anyone: 'He has attained mastery and perfection in noble virtue, attained mastery and perfection in noble collectedness, attained mastery and perfection in noble wisdom, attained mastery and perfection in noble deliverance,' it is of Sāriputta indeed that rightly speaking this should be said.**

22. "**Monks, rightly speaking, were it to be said of anyone: 'He is the son of the Blessed One, born of his breast, born of his mouth, born of the Dhamma, created by the Dhamma, an heir in the Dhamma, not an heir in material things,' it is of Sāriputta indeed that rightly speaking this should be said.**

23. "Monks, the matchless Wheel of the Dhamma set rolling by the Tathāgata is kept rolling rightly by Sāriputta."

That is what the Blessed One said. The monks were satisfied and delighted in the Blessed One's words.

And now we'll hear, from all the devas that are listening, the Hallelujah Chorus, ha-ha. I know that this has been a long talk again, sorry. But this particular sutta, it shows exactly that vipassanā and samatha, they're strung together, they're yoked together, just like two oxen that are pulling a cart. They're tied together and they will take the cart wherever you want it to go. And we need to practice them, not singly, but we need to practice them together, as Sāriputta showed in his experience of the meditation. What I'm showing you is that slight difference in the meditation about letting go of the distraction, and relaxing; that one extra step put into your practice changes the entire practice, so you'll be able to see everything that Sāriputta saw. You can, it does happen, I promise! And one of the things that's real amazing is, I've run across too many monks that have this idea that it's impossible to obtain Nibbāna in this lifetime, so why even try? But, I'm here to tell you, it is attainable. Simple instructions: let go of any distraction, relax, and come back to your object of meditation. Too simple. We like things to be complicated.

See how mind's attention moves. I have students that have all of these things that they're talking about here. I won't claim that any of them are arahats, but they have seen Dependent Origination for real, and they understand it very deeply. So I know that these things are possible, and a lot of people have this idea that it takes a long time to be able to experience all of these things.

I had one student that she was ready to meditate. She'd ask other people how to meditate. She was going to Thai temples and they only spoke Thai, but she was still trying to follow what they were saying. She came to an eight day retreat and in eight days she did experience the state of nothingness, in eight days. And that goes along with what the Buddha was talking about, that this Dhamma is immediately effective. You can see it right here, right now. Practice! Doesn't matter what you're doing; watch what mind is up to. If you start identifying with your dissatisfaction of this or your like of that, as soon as you're aware that mind is doing that, let it go, relax, come back to an object of meditation.

Now, most of you I'm teaching loving-kindness. Why? There are certain advantages for practicing Loving-Kindness Meditation. And one of those advantages is that your progress in the meditation is faster with loving-kindness than it is with any other kind of meditation. And because I'm teaching you that there are the four foundations of mindfulness in this, it is working towards that end goal. It really does work, I promise. The only thing is, don't add anything, don't subtract anything, just... when your mind becomes distracted, let go of the distraction, relax, and come back. It goes back to that distraction, pay attention to how did that happen; what happened first; what happened after that; what happened after that?

When you start seeing that, you are starting to see Dependent Origination. You're starting to see how you cause your own pain by having an opinion or a concept that's contrary to what's happening right here, right now. And you're causing your own pain. It's not someone else doing something that's causing your pain. It's your own attachments to the pain. What is the attachment? The attachment is: "This is my pain and this is who I am. It's me, and I don't like it, and I want it to be different." See how much pain you cause yourself. The hindrances are incredibly important because they're showing you where your attachments are. When you start seeing how the hindrance arises, how it pulls your mind away and you start letting go little by little, then you will be able to experience the jhānas. And the jhānas again, they're not some pie in the sky thing to talk about. Jhānas can happen very easily in a short period of time depending on your doing the practice in the correct way.

MN 111: One By One As They Occurred

Now, I want to stress that this is not my practice. I am reading these things to you from the Buddha's teaching. I don't have anything to do with this stuff. I practice it, but it's not me; it's not, quote, "my method;" it's the Buddha's method.

So the more you can closely observe how the Buddha was teaching, the more you'll see for yourself that the Buddha was right. I don't have any doubt at all whether he was right or not. You might be able to tell, by the way that I give Dhamma talks, because I have a lot of confidence in the Buddha's teaching. I don't have any doubt in his teaching at all. I would like that for you. So that when you're practicing you can actually see and confirm these things for yourself. You know, in the Kālāma Sutta, it talks very much about: don't believe what's written, and don't believe what's traditional, and don't believe anything. The Buddha said: "Don't even believe me." Go out and do it on your own, confirm it for yourself.

Ok. So I've been talking for a really long time, does anybody have any questions?

ST: "He establishes mindfulness in front of him." What does that mean?

BV: It means that he's watching what arises in his mind. That's an English kind of expression. But establishing mindfulness in front of you means what's in front of you right now, what kind of thoughts are you experiencing right now? Observing what's in front of you right at that moment means seeing what's happening at that moment.

ST: How does what you are saying change from what the Burmese Vipassanā Practice that I did says happens?

BV: It changed everything because it is a form of absorption concentration that was developed, and these insight knowledges, the way that they have occurred. Mahasi Sayadaw was really amazing because he took nine insight knowledges out of the Visuddhimagga and made it sixteen. It's a kind of absorption, yes. Because even moment-to-moment concentration... it's not the seeing how that process works, it's just seeing one part of the process and then putting a label on it…

ST: So Vipassanā says that there is the Magga Phala path moment but what you are saying sounds different but is it the same?

BV: Yeah, I know, and I was hoping nobody was going to ask me that question because it's tough. You get to places where there is, it's kind of like a blackout. There's a stop, but it's not the same as the cessation of perception and feeling. There is still a slight feeling in the blackout; it's still there. Now, what's real different is what happens after that, and that is, when you're practicing insight knowledges, you have the reviewing of all of the insight knowledges. When you're practicing the way it said in the sutta, what you see after the cessation of perception and feeling is Dependent Origination. This is the core teaching of the Buddha. And that's where our wisdom is developed, by seeing that.

Well, another thing that they talk about is right before this blackout occurs, you see… the importance in the insight knowledges is seeing impermanence, suffering and not self. And right before that occurs, according to Mahasi Sayadaw, you see the impermanence, three or four times very quickly in a row, or you see the suffering three or four times quickly in a row, or you see the anatta three or four times quickly in a row, and then there's this blackout.

That doesn't occur in the suttas ever, and I confirmed that with the Mingun Sayadaw, the monk that was so incredibly bright. He was telling me that there were a lot of differences between the commentaries and the suttas. And I ask him to confirm a lot of things that I had studied because I'd practiced straight Vipassanā for twenty years. After I had this experience, I wanted some confirmation, so I was going to these monks that, while I was in Burma that were very advanced in their understanding, and I wanted to find out. And when I go to someone like him and I say: "Is there such a thing as "access concentration" or "moment-to-moment concentration" in the suttas?" And he says: "No." It makes me wonder whether I'd been practicing the right practice after twenty years.

What was that experience? So then I started going to the suttas, but because I was still taking the commentary as the main source, I couldn't understand the suttas, until I had somebody tell me to take the commentaries, just leave them alone, and just delve into the suttas. And then it all became very clear.

ST: How do you feel about anatta as being defined as "uncontrollable?"

BV: In a way you could look at anatta and you could say: "Yes, it is uncontrollable," but impersonal is a much better translation. Because every time you take something personally, that means there's "was talking about," there's that belief. And it's a false belief, but it's still there; "I am that." When you say: "Impersonal" it means there are just these things rolling along. They're not personal at all; they're impersonal. I worked a long time coming up with that word, actually. One of my favorite books is a thesaurus, and I don't just go to one. I might go to three or four thesauruses with the same word to come up with a word that's easy to understand and simple, but precise. And I even got a, somebody, a student of mine got me an etymology of English. So now I can go and look up all of the different things about the word to help me as to whether it's the right word to use or not.

Ok, does anybody else have a question?

Is everybody going to be happy? Is everybody going to smile? That's the important part too. I mean the absolutely most important part is: seeing, letting go, relaxing, coming back, but put a smile in with that. So you can do it lightly, so you can have fun with the meditation. For almost twenty years, I was way too serious with my meditation, and then when I found out you can have fun and actually do better in your meditation, that was another revelation that was quite good.

Ok, let's share some merit then.

> May suffering ones be suffering free
> And the fear struck fearless be.
> May the grieving shed all grief
> And may all beings find relief.
> May all beings share this merit
> That we have thus acquired
> For the acquisition of
> All kind of happiness.
> May beings inhabiting space and earth
> Devas and Nagas of mighty power
> Share in this merit of ours.
> May they long protect
> the Buddha's Dispensation.
> Sādhu... Sādhu... Sādhu...

MN-38: The Greater Discourse on the Destruction of Craving (Mahātaṇhāsankhaya Sutta)

The Bhikkhu Sàti states the wrong view that consciousness passes on from life to life independent of conditions. The Buddha proves this wrong by Dependent Arising. The whole discourse is consequently an exposition of the conditionality in all components of conscious existence. To drive this home, Dependent Arising (or the structure of conditionality) is approached and converged upon from several different successive points. [2]

Presented by Ven Bhante Vimalaraṁsi on 24th February 2006 at Dhamma Dena Vipassanā Center, Joshua Tree, California

This is a real interesting sutta, so please listen attentively and all will become clear.

1. THUS HAVE I HEARD. On one occasion the Blessed One was living at Sāvatthī in Jeta's Grove, Anāthanpiṇḍika's Park.

2. Now on that occasion a pernicious view had arisen in a monk named Sāti, son of a fisherman, thus: "As I understand the Dhamma taught by the Blessed One, it is this same consciousness that runs and wanders through the round of rebirths, not another."

3. Several monks, having heard about this, went to the monk Sāti and asked him: "Friend Sāti, is it true that such a pernicious view has arisen in you?"

You know what a question like that implies? It's like me walking up to you and say: "You know this view that you have that's so incredibly stupid? Are you really saying that?"

And his reply was...

---

[2] *Ibid.*

"Exactly so, friends. As I understand the Dhamma taught by the Blessed One, it is this same consciousness that runs and wanders through the round of rebirths, not another." Then those monks, desiring to detach him from that pernicious view, pressed and questioned and cross-questioned him thus: "Friend Sāti, do not say so. Do not misrepresent the Blessed One; it is not good to misrepresent the Blessed One. The Blessed One would not speak thus. For in many ways the Blessed One has stated consciousness to be dependently arisen, since without a condition there is no origination of consciousness." Yet although pressed and questioned and cross-questioned by those monks in this way, the monk Sāti, son of a fisherman, still obstinately adhered to that pernicious view and continued to insist upon it.

Now, this view is a brahmin view. When you get right down to it there's no such religion as Hinduism; it's Brahmanism. And if you go to India and you talk to them about Hinduism, they'll look at you, wondering what you're talking about. So this is a brahmin view.

4. Since the monks were unable to detach him from that pernicious view, they went to the Blessed One, and after paying homage to him, they sat down at one side and told him all that had occurred, adding: "Venerable sir, since we could not detach the monk Sāti, son of a fisherman, from this pernicious view, we have reported this matter to the Blessed One."

5. Then the Blessed One addressed a certain monk thus: "Come, Monk, tell the monk Sāti, son of a fisherman, in my name that the Teacher calls him." - "Yes, venerable sir," he replied, and he went to the monk Sāti and told him: "The Teacher calls you, friend Sāti." - "Yes, friend," he replied, and he went to the Blessed One, and after paying homage to him, sat down at one side. The Blessed One then asked him: "Sāti, is it true that the following pernicious view has arisen in you: 'As I understand the Dhamma taught by the Blessed One, it is this same consciousness that runs and wanders

through the round of rebirths, not another'?" - "Exactly so, venerable sir. As I understand the Dhamma taught by the Blessed One, it is the same consciousness that runs and wanders through the round of rebirths, not another." - "What is that consciousness, Sāti?" - "Venerable sir, it is that which speaks and feels and experiences here and there the result of good and bad actions." - "Misguided man,

This is a real heavy censure, whenever the Buddha would say that.

to whom have you ever known me to teach the Dhamma in that way? Misguided man, have I not stated in many ways consciousness to be dependently arisen, since without a condition there is no origination of consciousness? But you, misguided man, have misrepresented us by your wrong grasp and injured yourself and stored up much demerit; for this will lead to your harm and suffering for a long time."

And we're still talking about Sāti, the son of a fisherman twenty-five hundred years later, so it's really true, isn't it?

6. Then the Blessed One addressed the monks thus: "Monks, what do you think? Has this monk Sāti, son of a fisherman, kindled even a spark of wisdom in this Dhamma and Discipline?" - "How could he, venerable sir? No, venerable sir." When this was said, the monk Sāti, son of a fisherman, sat silent, dismayed, with shoulders drooping and head down, glum, and without response. Then, knowing this, the Blessed One told him: "Misguided man, you will be recognized by your own pernicious view. I shall question the monks on this matter."

7. Then the Blessed One addressed the monks thus: "Monks, do you understand the Dhamma taught by me as this monk Sāti, son of a fisherman, does when he misrepresents us by his wrong grasp and injures himself and stores up much demerit?" - "No, venerable sir. For in many discourses the Blessed One has stated consciousness to be dependently arisen, since without a condition there is

no origination of consciousness." - "Good, Monks. It is good that you understand the Dhamma taught by me thus. For in many ways I have stated consciousness to be dependently arisen, since without a condition there is no origination of consciousness. But this monk Sāti, son of a fisherman, misrepresents us by his wrong grasp and injures himself and stores up much demerit; for this will lead to the harm and suffering of this misguided man for a long time.

What happened with Sāti, the son of the fisherman, was right after this he disrobed, and he started heavily criticizing the Buddha for what he considered was wrong view.

8. "Monks, consciousness is reckoned by the particular condition dependent upon which it arises. When consciousness arises dependent on the eye and forms, it is reckoned as eye-consciousness; when consciousness arises dependent on the ear and sounds, it is reckoned as ear-consciousness; when consciousness arises dependent on the nose and odors, it is reckoned as nose-consciousness; when consciousness arises dependent on the tongue and flavors, it is reckoned as tongue-consciousness; when consciousness arises dependent on the body and tangibles, it is reckoned as body consciousness; when consciousness arises dependent on the mind and mind-objects, it is reckoned as mind-consciousness. Just as fire is reckoned by the particular condition dependent on which it burns - when fire burns dependent on logs, it is reckoned as a log fire; when fire burns dependent on faggots, it is reckoned as a faggot fire; when fire burns dependent on grass, it is reckoned as a grass fire; when fire burns dependent on cow-dung, it is reckoned as a cow-dung fire; when fire burns dependent on chaff, it is reckoned as a chaff fire; when fire burns dependent on rubbish, it is reckoned as a rubbish fire - so too, consciousness is reckoned by the particular condition dependent on which it arises. When consciousness arises dependent on the eye and forms, it is reckoned as eye-consciousness; when consciousness arises

dependent on the ear and sounds, it is reckoned as ear-consciousness; when consciousness arises dependent on the nose and odors, it is reckoned as nose-consciousness; when consciousness arises dependent on the tongue and flavors, it is reckoned as tongue-consciousness; when consciousness arises dependent on the body and tangibles, it is reckoned as body consciousness; when consciousness arises dependent on the mind and mind-objects, it is reckoned as mind-consciousness.

9. "Monks, do you see: 'This has come to be'?" - "Yes venerable sir." - "Monks, do you see: 'Its origination occurs with that as nutriment'?" - " , venerable sir." - "Monks, do you see: 'With the cessation of that nutriment, what has come to be is subject to cessation'?" - "Yes, venerable sir."

What is the nutriment? For the eye, it's the color and form, for the ear, it's sound, that's what the nutriment is.

10. "Monks, does doubt arise when one is uncertain thus: 'Has this come to be'?" - "Yes, venerable sir."- "Monks, does doubt arise when one is uncertain thus: 'Does its origination occur with that as nutriment'?" - "Yes, venerable sir." - "Monks, does doubt arise when one is uncertain thus: 'With the cessation of that nutriment, is what has come to be subject to cessation'?" - "Yes, venerable sir."

11. "Monks, is doubt abandoned in one who sees as it actually is with proper wisdom thus: 'This has come to be'?" - "Yes, venerable sir." - "Monks, is doubt abandoned in one who sees as it actually is with proper wisdom thus: 'Its origination occurs with that as nutriment'?" - "Yes, venerable sir." - "Monks, is doubt abandoned in one who sees as it actually is with proper wisdom thus: 'With the cessation of that nutriment, what has come to be is subject to cessation'?" - "Yes, venerable sir."

12. "Monks, are you thus free from doubt here: 'This has come to be'?" - "Yes, venerable sir." - "Monks, are you thus free from doubt here: 'Its origination occurs with that as

nutriment'?" - "Yes, venerable sir." - "Monks, are you thus free from doubt here: 'With the cessation of that nutriment, what has come to be is subject to cessation'?" - "Yes, venerable sir."

13. "Monks, has it been seen well by you as it actually is with proper wisdom thus: 'This has come to be'?" -

Now, what he's doing is he's asking if they have the direct experience.

"Yes, venerable sir." - "Monks, has it been seen well by you as it actually is with proper wisdom thus; 'Its origination occurs with that as nutriment'?" - "Yes, venerable sir." - "Monks, has it been seen well by you as it actually is with proper wisdom thus: 'With the cessation of that nutriment, what has come to be is subject to cessation'?" - "Yes, venerable sir."

14. "Monks, purified and bright as this view is, if you adhere to it, cherish it, treasure it, and treat it as a possession, would you then understand that the Dhamma has been taught as similar to a raft, being for the purpose of crossing over, not for the purpose of grasping?" - "No, venerable sir." -

If you hold on to this view, you're not following what the Buddha's teaching is - it's just seeing, allowing, letting it be.

"Monks, purified and bright as this view is, if you do not adhere to it, cherish it, treasure it, and treat it as a possession, would you then understand that the Dhamma has been taught as similar to a raft, being for the purpose of crossing over, not for the purpose of grasping?" - "Yes, venerable sir."

15. "Monks, there are these four kinds of nutriment for the maintenance of beings that already have come to be and for the support of those about to come to be. What four? They are: physical food as nutriment, gross or subtle; contact as

the second; mental formations as the third; and consciousness as the fourth.

16. "Now, Monks, these four kinds of nutriment have what as their source, what as their origin, from what are they born and produced? These four kinds of nutriment have craving as their source, craving as their origin; they are born and produced from craving.

And how does craving manifest itself? Tension and tightness in mind and body. That's always how you recognize it. This is why craving is the weak link in Dependent Origination because it's not something that's easy to observe and relax. Craving is not particularly strong but it's particularly persistent, but it's not particularly hard to let go of by recognizing it and relaxing.

And this craving has what as its source...? Craving has feeling as its source... And this feeling has what as its source...? Feeling has contact as its source... And this contact has what as its source...? Contact has the six-fold base as its source... And this six-fold base has what as its source...? The six-fold base has mentality/materiality as its source... And this mentality/materiality has what as its source...? Mentality/materiality has consciousness as its source... And this consciousness has what as its source...? Consciousness has formations as its source... And these formations have what as their source, what as their origin; from what are they born and produced? Formations have ignorance as their source, ignorance as their origin; they are born and produced from ignorance.

What is ignorance? Ignorance is not seeing the four noble truths. Ignorance is always not seeing the four noble truths. In other words, there is an ignoring that happens. Why does it happen? Because we take these things personally and think they are ours. And we ignore the fact that there is suffering, there is a cause of suffering, there is cessation of suffering, and the way to the cessation.

17. "So, Monks, with ignorance as condition, formations come to be; with formations as condition, consciousness comes to be; with consciousness as condition, mentality/materiality comes to be; with mentality/materiality as condition, the six-fold base comes to be; with the six-fold base as condition, contact comes to be; with contact as condition, feeling comes to be; with feeling as condition, craving comes to be; with craving as condition, clinging comes to be; with clinging as condition, being comes to be;

Now, the "being," this translation, we'll call it "habitual tendency" comes to be.

with habitual tendency as condition, birth comes to be; with birth as condition, aging and death, sorrow, lamentation, pain, grief, and despair come to be. Such is the origin of this whole mass of suffering.

18. "'With birth as condition, aging and death': so it was said. Now, Monks, do aging and death have birth as condition or not, or how do you take it in this case?" - "Aging and death have birth as condition, venerable sir. Thus we take it in this case: 'with birth as condition, aging and death comes to be." - "'With habitual tendency as condition, birth': so it was said. Now, Monks, does birth have habitual tendency as condition or not, or how do you take it in this case?" - "Birth has habitual tendency as condition, venerable sir. Thus we take it in this case: 'With habitual tendency as condition, birth comes to be.'" - "'With clinging as condition, habitual tendency': so it was said. Now, Monks, does habitual tendency have clinging as condition or not, or how do you take it in this case?" - "Habitual tendency has clinging as condition, venerable sir. Thus we take it in this case: 'With clinging as condition, habitual tendency comes to be.'" - "'With craving as condition, clinging': so it was said. Now, Monks, does clinging have craving as condition or not, or how do you take it in this case?" - "Clinging has craving as condition,

venerable sir. Thus we take it in this case: 'With craving as condition, clinging comes to be.'" - "'With feeling as condition, craving': so it was said. Now, Monks, does craving have feeling as condition or not, or how do you take it in this case?" - "Craving has feeling as condition, venerable sir. Thus we take it in this case: 'With feeling as condition, craving comes to be.'" - "'With contact as condition, feeling': so it was said. Now, Monks, does feeling have contact as condition or not, or how do you take it in this case?" - "Feeling has contact as condition, venerable sir. Thus we take it in this case: 'With contact as condition, feeling comes to be.'" - "'With the sixfold base as condition, contact': so it was said. Now, Monks, does contact have the six-fold base as condition or not, or how do you take it in this case?" - "Contact has the six-fold base as condition, venerable sir. Thus we take it in this case: 'With the six-fold base as condition, contact comes to be.'" - "'With the mentality/materiality as condition, the six-fold base': so it was said. Now, Monks, does the six-fold base have mentality/materiality as condition or not, or how do you take it in this case?" - "The six-fold base has mentality/materiality as condition, venerable sir. Thus we take it in this case: 'With mentality/materiality as condition, the six-fold base comes to be.'"

The mentality/materiality, in Pāli it's called nāma-rūpa, and it's most often translated as name and form. And that's incredibly difficult to understand. When you say mentality and materiality, it makes it a lot different. I'll go into the definitions of each one of these in just a minute.

"'With consciousness as condition, mentality/materiality': so it was said. Now, Monks, does mentality/materiality have consciousness as condition or not, or how do you take it in this case?" - "Mentality/materiality has consciousness as condition, venerable sir. Thus we take it in this case: 'With consciousness as condition, mentality/materiality comes to be.'" - "'With formations as condition, consciousness': so it was said. Now, Monks, does consciousness have formations as condition or not, or how do you take it in this case?" - "Consciousness has formations as condition, venerable sir. Thus we take it in this case: 'With formations as condition, consciousness comes to be.'" - "'With ignorance as condition, formations': so it was said. Now, Monks, do formations have ignorance as condition or not, or how do you take it in this case?" - "Formations have ignorance as condition, venerable sir. Thus we take it in this case: 'With ignorance as condition, formations come to be.'"

19. Good, Monks. So you say thus, and I also say thus: 'When this exists, that comes to be; with the arising of this, that arises.' That is, with ignorance as condition, formations come to be; with formations as condition, consciousness comes to be; with consciousness as condition, mentality/materiality comes to be; with mentality/materiality as condition, the six-fold base comes to be; with the six-fold base as condition, contact comes to be; with contact as condition, feeling comes to be; with feeling as condition, craving comes to be; with craving as condition, clinging comes to be; with clinging as condition, habitual tendency comes to be; with habitual tendency as condition, birth comes to be; with birth as condition, aging and death, sorrow, lamentation, pain, grief and despair come to be. Such is the origin of this whole mass of suffering.

Now, get into the definitions. Huh?

Well, it's actually the link between feeling and craving. Ah, page #534. Ok. This is called the Analysis of Dependent Origination, in the Saṃyutta Nikāya.[3]

---

[3] The Connected Discourses of the Buddha: A Translation of the Saṃyutta Nikāya, by Bhikkhu Bodhi, Part II: The Book of Causation (Nidānavagga),

MN 38: Discourse on the Destruction of Craving 155

At Sāvatthi. "Monks, I will teach you Dependent Origination and I will analyze it for you. Listen to that and attend closely. I will speak." - "Yes, venerable sir," those monks replied. The Blessed one said this: "And what, Monks, is Dependent Origination? With ignorance as condition, formations [come to be]; with formations, consciousness...

... and we go through the whole thing.

"Such is the origin of this whole mass of suffering.

"And what, Monks, is aging-and-death? The aging of the various beings in the various orders of beings, their growing old, brokenness of teeth, grayness of hair, wrinkling of skin, decline of vitality, degeneration of the faculties: this is called aging.

And I feel every one of those. Ha ha!

"The passing away of the various beings from the various orders of beings, their perishing, breakup, disappearance, mortality, death, completion of time, the breakup of the aggregates, the laying down of the carcass: this is called death. Thus this aging and this death are together called aging-and-death.

"And what, Monks, is birth? The birth of the various beings into the various orders of beings, their being born, descent [into the womb], production, the manifestation of the aggregates, the obtaining of the sense bases. This is called birth.

"And what, Monks, is existence?

This is your habitual tendency again, but this... when I'm talking about the habitual tendency that is in the sense-sphere

---

Chapter I (12 Nidānasamyutta, Connected Discourses on Causation), I The Buddhas, 2(2) Analysis of Dependent Origination, Page 534 existence, because that's the practical application for seeing it. But there is more to this.

There are these three kinds of existence: sense-sphere existence, form-sphere existence, formless-sphere existence. This is called existence.

The form-sphere existence is the lower jhānas. First jhāna, second jhāna, third jhāna, and the fourth jhāna. And the formless-sphere existence is the arūpa jhānas: infinite space; infinite consciousness; nothingness; neither-perception-nor-non-perception.

"And what, Monks, is clinging? There are these four kinds of clinging: clinging to sensual pleasures, clinging to views, clinging to rules and vows,

Rites and rituals, believing that rites and rituals will lead you to Nibbāna, or take you to Nibbāna.

clinging to a doctrine of self. This is called clinging.

Now, in this clinging, you've heard me talk about thinking, and that has to do with the views. And also I talk about concepts, and that has to do with the views. I also talk about when you let go of the craving, there is no clinging. That means you've let go of the views for that brief moment. You've let go of concepts for that brief moment. You've let go of the belief that there is a personal self for that moment. As you do this over and over, it starts to sink in.

This is one of the reasons why when restlessness arises, it is your best friend because when you have these thoughts, and concepts, and ideas of what you like and what you don't like, and all of this stuff, when you let go of that and relax, you're letting go of the belief that these thoughts and feelings are yours personally. You're starting to see that this is an impersonal process. The beginning of the "I" belief is in craving, but the building up of that belief and really taking good strong hold of it is in clinging. Now, one of the things that's happening in this country right now, is that a lot of people are putting craving and clinging together and they say: "Well, that's grasping." And on a surface level, they're right. But when you start looking more and more closely, you start to see that they are two separate things, and you can't put them together.

"**And what, Monks, is craving? There are these six classes of craving: craving for forms, craving for sounds, craving for odors, craving for tastes, craving for tactile objects, craving for mental phenomena. This is called craving.**"

It's the "I like it, I don't like it" at each one of the sense doors. Each one of the sense doors has the feeling and the craving right behind it. So this is why being able to recognize the feeling that arises at each one of the sense doors is incredibly important. And as soon as you recognize a feeling, then you relax right then, you don't have the craving or the rest of... the end of the Dependent Origination arising. That is why your mind becomes pure. That's why your mind becomes clean. Because you've let go of all concepts, and you're seeing this process as a process. It's not personal. These things all arise because of conditions. And there is no "me," there is no "I" in any of this, when you let go at craving.

"**And what, Monks, is feeling? There are these six classes of feeling: feeling born of eye-contact, feeling born of ear-contact, feeling born of nose-contact, feeling born of tongue-contact, feeling born of body-contact, feeling born of mind-contact. This is called feeling.**"

"**And what, Monks, is contact? There are these six classes of contact: eye-contact, ear-contact, nose-contact, tongue-contact, body-contact, mind-contact. This is called contact.**"

"**And what, Monks, are the six sense bases? The eye base, the ear base, the nose base, the tongue base, the body base, and mind base. These are called the six sense bases.**"

"**And what, Monks, is mentality/materiality? Feeling, perception, volition, contact, attention: this is called mentality. The four great elements and the form derived**"

from the four great elements: this is called... materiality. Thus this mentality and this materiality are together called mentality/materiality.

Now, when you have a feeling arise, it always seems like that's part of materiality, doesn't it? But it's not, it's mentality. It's a mental feeling, even though it's at each one of the sense doors. That's why these two things are together. You have to have the four elements, in all of their different forms, the earth element, the water element, the fire element, the air element. You have to have these four elements; that's what makes up the physical body; that's what makes up the physical universe. It's just the different degrees of these elements that come together. And this is one of the things that made the Buddha so incredibly unique. He saw that there is a dependence on mentality and materiality. They depend on each other for existence.

When you're practicing meditation, and you are doing absorption concentration, you lose sensation in your body completely. Now, you remember a few nights ago, we went through the "One by One as it Occurred" (MN-111, The Anupada Sutta), and all of the way up to the realm of nothingness there was contact. In other words, you had your physical body, and if there was contact, there was feeling arising. When you get up into your arūpa jhānas, you won't necessarily feel your body until there would be contact. You would feel the wind blow on your face, or you would feel an ant walk across you. But your equanimity is strong enough that it doesn't make your mind wobble and shake. That's a major difference between what the Buddha is teaching, and what was taught before the time of the Buddha.

When practicing absorption concentration - the concentration gets so deep that you don't even know that there is a body present, because you're focused so deeply on one thing. And when you practice absorption concentration - and I've run across this many, many, many times - people practicing different forms of absorption concentration, they wind up getting a lot of tension and tightness in their head. And it gets so intense, it's like a hot needle that's sticking right in the head. And the instructions are always: "Well, don't pay any attention to it, just keep going, it will disappear," and it does. But that is not what we would call full awareness. You keep on focusing on one point until you don't have any sensation in your body at all, even if I were to come up and hit you on the head, you wouldn't feel it. If I take a gun and put it right by your ear, you wouldn't hear it. That is not full awareness. That is what was practiced before the time of the Buddha. Now, with this one extra step that the Buddha put in the meditation, it does not allow your mind to get so incredibly one-pointed. There's still full awareness, you still have the five aggregates in the jhānas; they're still there. So when he started talking about mind and body, he was talking about that connection that's always there. You don't have one without the other, not in the way the Buddha taught us to practice.

"And what, Monks, is consciousness? There are these six classes of consciousness: eye-consciousness, ear-consciousness, nose-consciousness, tongue-consciousness, body-consciousness, mind-consciousness. This is called consciousness.

"And what, Monks, are the formations? There are these three kinds of formations: the bodily formation, the verbal formation, the mental formation. These are called the formations.

By the way, when Bhikkhu Bodhi wrote this book, he added the word "volitional" to the formations. And you could say that's ok, and you could say it's not ok. The Pāli word is sankhāra. Sankhāra is one of the biggest words in the Pāli language because it covers so much; there's so many different kinds of definitions you can give to sankhāra. So in a way "volitional" formations is good, in a way it's a little bit misleading. I think it's better to leave the word "volitional" out with this definition.

"And what, Monks, is ignorance?

I bet we know what that one is...

Not knowing suffering, not knowing the origin of suffering, not knowing the cessation of suffering, not knowing the way leading to the cessation of suffering. This is called ignorance.

Thus, Monks, with ignorance as condition, formations come to be; with formations as condition, consciousness comes to be; with consciousness as condition, mentality/materiality comes to be; with mentality/materiality as condition, the six sense doors come to be; with the six sense doors as condition, contact comes to be; with contact as condition, feeling comes to be; with feeling as condition, craving comes to be; with craving as condition, clinging comes to be; with clinging as condition, habitual tendency comes to be; with habitual tendency as condition, birth comes to be; with birth as condition, aging-and-death, sorrow, lamentation, pain, grief, and despair comes to be. Such is the origin of this whole mass of suffering. But with the remainderless fading away and cessation of ignorance comes the cessation of formations;

And we'll let that go right now because we're going to go back to... oh. This is an interesting thing too, this is the next sutta in the Saṃyutta Nikāya, it's number three, it's called "The Two Ways."

At Sāvatthi. "Monks, I will teach you the wrong way and the right way. Listen to that and attend closely, I will speak." - "Yes venerable sir." those monks replied. The Blessed One said this: "And what, Monks, is the wrong way? With ignorance as condition, formations come to be; with formations as condition, consciousness comes to be...

Why is that the wrong way?

This, Monks, is called the wrong way. "And what, Monks, is the right way? With the remainderless fading away and cessation of ignorance comes cessation of formations; with the cessation of formations, cessation of consciousness... Such is the cessation of this whole mass of suffering. This, Monks, is called the right way."

The one way is talking about the arising of these conditions, one way is talking about the cessation of these conditions. He says the proper way to practice is with the cessation of these conditions.

Now, when you're sitting in meditation and you have a wandering thought and you let go, and you relax, and you come back, and your mind does that again, the last thing right before getting caught with those thoughts is you'll notice that there's something right before that. And when you see that, then you let that go, and then you go along a little bit more and you'll see something right before that. You're seeing the cessation of these different things. Oh, wow!

So when we're practicing seeing how these things arise, and we become familiar, more and more familiar with the process, and we start letting go, a little bit, and a little bit, and a little bit, you are practicing the cessation, and that's the right way.

20. "But with the remainderless fading away and cessation of ignorance comes cessation of formations; with the cessation of formations, cessation of consciousness; with the cessation of consciousness, cessation of mentality/materiality; with the cessation of mentality/materiality, cessation of the six-fold base; with the cessation of the six-fold base, cessation of contact; with the cessation of contact, cessation of feeling; with the cessation of feeling, cessation of craving; with the cessation of craving, cessation of clinging; with the cessation of clinging, cessation of habitual tendency; with the cessation of habitual tendency, cessation of birth; with the cessation of birth, aging and death, sorrow, lamentation, pain, grief and despair cease. Such is the cessation of this whole mass of suffering.

So you get to hear this a lot.

21. "'With the cessation of birth, cessation of aging and death': so it was said. Now, Monks, do aging and death cease with the cessation of birth or not, or how do you take it in this case?" - "Ageing and death cease with the cessation of birth, venerable sir. Thus we take it in this case: 'With the cessation of birth, cessation of aging and death.'"

"'With the cessation of habitual tendency, cessation of birth'…'With the cessation of clinging, cessation of habitual tendency'… 'With the cessation of craving, cessation of clinging.'… 'With the cessation of feeling, cessation of craving'… 'With the cessation of contact, cessation of feeling'… 'With the cessation of the sixfold base, cessation of contact'… 'With the cessation of mentality-materiality, cessation of the sixfold base'… 'With the cessation of consciousness, cessation of mentality-materiality'… 'With the cessation of formations, cessation of consciousness'… 'With the cessation of ignorance, cessation of formations': so it was said. Now, Monks, do formations cease with the cessation of ignorance or not, or how do you take it in this case?" - "Formations cease with the cessation of ignorance, venerable sir. Thus we take it in this case: 'With the cessation of ignorance, cessation of formations.'"

22. "Good, Monks. So you say thus, and I also say thus: 'When this does not exist, that does not come to be; with the cessation of this, that ceases.' That is, with the cessation of ignorance comes cessation of formations; with the cessation of formations, cessation of consciousness; with the cessation of consciousness, cessation of mentality-materiality; with the cessation of mentality-materiality, cessation of the sixfold base; with the cessation of the sixfold base, cessation of contact; with the cessation of contact, cessation of feeling; with the cessation of feeling, cessation of craving; with the cessation of craving, cessation of clinging; with the cessation of clinging, cessation of habitual tendency; with the cessation of habitual tendency, cessation of birth; with

MN 38: Discourse on the Destruction of Craving

the cessation of birth, aging and death, sorrow, lamentation, pain, grief, and despair cease. Such is the cessation of this whole mass of suffering.

When you are doing your meditation, and this can happen any time when you are coming out of a jhāna, there can be the cessation of perception and feeling. When that happens, it's like somebody turns the lights out, it's just "click." There's no perception, there's no feeling at all in this state. When the perception and feeling arise again, you will see all of these different links of Dependent Origination. You will see it forwards, and then you'll see it, the arising, and then you'll see the cessation. And when you finally let go of ignorance, completely, there is the experience of Nibbāna at that time. That is how you experience Nibbāna. It is the deep, true, not only understanding, but also realization of Dependent Origination. When you realize it, everything changes. The fetters don't arise anymore, ever again. Doesn't that sound nice? Think about it. I mean your five lower fetters at least are going to disappear. And this is why you need to do the meditation, so that you can see very clearly how this process works.

You can just by mentally understanding Dependent Origination, you can become a sotāpanna, the first stage of awakening, or a sakadāgāmī, the second stage of awakening. You will never get any deeper than that if you do not do the meditation, and you can also realize these first two states through meditation. And that's what a very interesting sutta, number seventy (MN-70, The Kiṭāgiri Sutta) in the Majjhima Nikāya is all about. And I'm currently writing a book about this and how the fruition occurs, which is basically the same way. But when fruition occurs, say you become an anāgāmī, then at some time later, it can happen the next day, it can happen the next sitting, it just depends on you personally. What will happen is, you'll be, say it happens the next day, and you're in and you're preparing a meal and you're cutting vegetables, and you start feeling your mind become very,

very clear and very, very alert, and you know it's time to sit. So you go down and you sit and all of a sudden there's the cessation of perception and feeling again. When that fades away and the perception and feeling comes back, you will see the Dependent Origination, the arising and the ceasing, three times, very quickly. And then you will have another experience of the Nibbāna, and that is called the fruition of that state.

If you've only gotten to the first stage, you will only see that one time. When you sit a second time, you will only see Dependent Origination arise and pass away that one time, and then you'll have another experience which is the fruition of the Nibbāna. With the fruition at that stage, you forever leave alone doubt, it will never come up in your mind again, doubt that this is the right path. You will never have any belief that rites and rituals will lead to Nibbāna. That means chanting and all that other sort of thing too. And you will never again truly believe that there is a permanent self anywhere, you'll see things as being impermanent.

If it happens that you get to the second stage, when the fruition occurs, there is the cessation of perception and feeling, and then you will see Dependent Origination two times. You'll see the arising and the cessation, and the arising and cessation. It happens very quickly. And then that second experience of Nibbāna. When that happens, lust and hatred are very much weakened.

When you have that happen a third time, you see it three times, then not only these first three fetters have disappeared, but lust and hatred never arise in your mind again. Yeah, think about that, I mean that's really something. I've only met one person that was like that.

When you have the experience of arahatship, the fruition happens in the same way, but you see everything four times. And with that the last five fetters disappear. Pride, restlessness, desire for realms of form, desire for immaterial realms, and ignorance. Now, think about that one, no more,

MN 38: Discourse on the Destruction of Craving

ever again, will ignorance arise. You'll see everything so clearly, and that's one of the reasons that it was so nice being around the time of the Buddha because you could go and talk to these men and these women that had that experience. And their mind was so clear, that when you talk to them, you would be able to have deep experiences, because they were so clear without having any fetter arise in their mind again. That's worth working for, to my way of thinking. You think so?

ST: Did you say there is still restlessness in the non-returner?

BV: Yes, little bit, and there's still a taste of dullness. You're still learning that super fine balance. That's what we're doing here. Got one more day guys. Couple of you got a shot at it, more than that, actually.

ST: Is there any way to tell somebody is an arahat?

BV: In every country that has Buddhism, you have a lot of people that talk about this monk or that monk being arahats. I spent a lot of time looking for one. And it's very difficult to know when someone is an arahat; you have to spend time with them.

Now, there's a story about these two monks, that they went out on alms round and the senior monk, somebody gave him some hot rice soup in his bowl, that was the first thing that was put in his bowl, and he sat down and he started drinking it. And the junior monk started criticizing him pretty heavily, because you're not supposed to do that, but the senior monk said: "I have a problem with my stomach, and taking this while it's hot will help settle my stomach. That's why I'm doing it." And then the senior monk looked at him and said: "Friend, have you ever had any attainment in your spiritual path?" And the junior monk said: "Yes, I am a sotāpanna." And the senior monk said: "Don't look forward to any more progress in your meditation in this lifetime." And the junior monk was shocked, and he said: "Why?" And the senior monk said: "Because you criticized an arahat."

ST: But isn't that pride on the senior monk's part?

BV: No, it's stating a fact.

ST: Isn't that from commentaries?

BV: Now, now, now. Not all commentaries are bad or wrong, because I'm giving you commentary all the time here. Ok? And you can take it or leave it, it's up to you, it's just whether it agrees with most of the suttas that you've run across. That's the way you tell.

But I don't think that I've run across an arahat yet. I know that there was a lot of talk about Taungpulu Sayadaw being an arahat. When I was with U Silananda, there were people that when he was giving a retreat they were going around talking to the other Burmese saying: "You got to go practice with him, he's an arahat." And U Silananda took me aside and he said: "It's impossible for him to be an arahat." And I said: "How do you know that?" He said that Taungpulu Sayadaw, in one of his talks, said that he had taken a Bodhisatta vow.

Now, when you take a Bodhisatta vow, that will stop you from attaining Nibbāna in this lifetime. That's how strong this vow is. And if you have taken the Bodhisatta vow and you want to obtain Nibbāna in this lifetime, I strongly recommend that you renounce that vow. The Tibetans and a lot of Mahayana rather insist that everybody that practices with them, they take the Bodhisatta vow. And they're going to be of service and not attain Nibbāna until everybody attains Nibbāna. Which really sounds great, but the Buddha couldn't do it. If he could, we wouldn't be here. So it's not a realistic kind of vow.

And that's the vow that the Bodhisatta took to become the Bodhisatta. He had the potential, when he saw the Buddha that was around at that time; he had the potential to become an arahat in seven days. If he would have stayed without that Bodhisatta vow, he would have become an arahat in that dispensation. But in front of a Buddha, he took that vow, and said: "I want to become a future Buddha." And that Buddha looked into the future with his divine eye, and saw that, yes, in fact he will become a Buddha. So he confirmed that this Bodhisatta vow is very good and it will happen.

Now, what happens when people on their own take a Bodhisatta vow, is after five hundred, or a thousand, or five thousand, or twenty five thousand lifetimes, they start realizing: "Hey, this is tough." And they'll renounce the Bodhisatta vow. And when they renounce the Bodhisatta vow, it cannot be in a Buddha era, so they're losing the chance of attaining Nibbāna until they happen to run across another Buddha sometime in the future. How long will that take to happen? Who knows? I mean with the Bodhisatta vow, it took the Buddha four mahakappas and a hundred thousand lifetimes.

Now, a mahakappa is a big span of time. There's four parts to the mahakappa; they're called asankheyya. Each one of these asankheyyas lasts ten to the hundred and sixtieth power in years. So you've got to figure, it's really long time. But you think of it this way: there's four asankheyyas, and during that asankheyya, there's the expansion of the universe, for one asankheyya, it stops for one asankheyya. There's the contraction of the universe for one asankheyya, and that's when everything gets bound to a little tiny black hole, for one asankheyya. And then there's an expansion of an asankheyya. The only time that beings are in this universe is when we're in the expansion. Now, you think about four mahakappas; you're talking about a lot of lifetimes. You're talking about more than a million; you're talking about a lot of lifetimes!

And each one of those lifetimes he had some pretty heavy-duty lessons to let go of. He had a lot to learn; he suffered a lot. There was one time he was reborn as a nāga, a snake, and he was very powerful. And if he got angry and he looked at you, you would turn into a cinder. Ok, this is the way the story goes. And in that lifetime he was practicing two of the pāramīs. The pāramīs are the perfections. He was practicing loving-kindness, and he was practicing patience. There were some boys in a village that saw this big snake, and they took sharp sticks and they stabbed him a bunch of times all the way through, and then carried him into the village. Now, because he was practicing his patience and his loving-kindness, he didn't do anything to these boys. He used that as his lesson, learning through his direct experience this lesson. That's just one lifetime.

Another lifetime - he was born as a young prince, and his mother loved him very much. He was about a year, year and a half old, and the mother was playing with the young prince and really having a great time with him. And the king walked into the room and said something to the mother, and the mother, the queen, didn't respond at all. And the king got jealous. And he started thinking: "Ah, what's going to happen in the future? She's so attached to this prince that they're going to conspire against me in the future and they're going to assassinate me, and I'm not going to allow that to happen, so the prince can become king. So I'm not going to allow that to happen." So he called the executioner. And he went and he picked up the young boy, and of course the mother is crying and all of this sort of stuff, and he tells the executioner: "Cut off his hands." So the executioner lopped off his hands. The Bodhisatta at that time realized that this was his challenge for learning how to protect his loving-kindness. He looked around the room; he saw that there were four different kinds of beings. There was himself, there was his mother that he loved very dearly, there was a neutral person, that was the executioner, he didn't know him that well. And there was his enemy, the father. So he started focusing his loving-kindness on these four different beings, and he didn't cry. And the king got furious with that, and he said: "Cut off his legs." So the executioner cut his legs off. And still he didn't give into that pain, he didn't cry out. He was practicing his loving-kindness very much. And finally the king said: "He's so disgusting, just cut off his head!," and he cut off the prince's head.

The prince was immediately born in a heavenly realm because his mind was very pure, he didn't entertain one thought of dissatisfaction, which is something you might think about when a hindrance arises. He just focused on his object of meditation and he was reborn in a heavenly realm. Right after the prince had his head cut off - his mother was holding the hands and feet - she died right then of a broken heart, and she was reborn in a heavenly realm right alongside the prince because of her deep love for her son. And the king took one step and died. He had a heart attack, and he was reborn in one of the hell realms. The only one that got out without dying that day was the executioner. Why? He wasn't doing it out of hatred; he was just doing what he was told to be doing. Of course, that's not a good profession to be in, I would think. He eventually died and went to a nasty place, one of the hell realms.

But when you take a Bodhisatta vow, these are the kind of tests that happen all along the way. So if you haven't had the assurance from a living Buddha, that you're going to be reborn as a Buddha, it's very hard to keep that vow. During the time of Buddha, there were people that tried to take the Bodhisatta vow and they were told not to. So even today there are people that take a Bodhisatta vow that are Theravādan, but they don't go advertising it. It's a very personal thing. And they feel like they have the strong enough faith in the Buddha that they will go ahead and take that. But to me, personally, it doesn't make sense to take a Bodhisatta vow and stop from having the attainment of Nibbāna. Even if you only get to the first stage of Nibbāna, at least you're assured that you're going to get off the wheel of samsāra; you don't have to put up with all of this dukkha.

On of the biggest incentives for me to get off the wheel of samsāra is so that I don't have to be a teenager again. I mean, think about all the emotional ups and downs, and the craziness that happens, and the hard lessons. Falling in love and out of love every other week, and finding out you have a body and wondering: "What is this thing?" All of this, it's real suffering. So to me it makes more sense while we're in a Buddha era, and the Buddha's teaching is in relatively good shape, that we should go ahead and try to follow what he says and get off the wheel as fast as we can. That's what would make him the happiest. The more people that can experience Nibbāna, the happier the Buddha would be if he were still here teaching.

And the interesting thing about taking the Bodhisatta vow is the next time you're reborn as a human being, when you're fairly young, you can be eight or ten or a young teenager, you will have a dream. And in that dream you will see an image of the Buddha. And you will see yourself enter into the Buddha, into that Buddha image, and that way you know that you've taken the vow. And it's a very personal thing and there's no doubt in your mind that you've taken that vow. And if you enter into his feet, he's sitting right here, and you enter into either his knee or his feet, then that means that you're just beginning. If you enter into the navel, that means you've gone along, but you still got a long ways to go. If you enter into the heart, this is like… you still got a long ways to go but you're really getting there and you're starting to understand very deeply. When you enter into the third eye, that means you've only got a few hundred thousand lifetimes to go. They will have a dream and they know beyond the shadow of a doubt that that's what they're doing, they're working towards the final stage. And they will not be reborn in a Buddha era again. They do it all on their own.

There are lots of stories about the adversity that the Buddha went through; that's what the Jātaka tales were all about. They were the challenging lifetimes that he went through and that's why the Jātaka tales, each one of them is like: "And the moral of the story is he perfected this part of the pāramīs," whatever that happened to be; his determination, or his patience, or his honesty, or whatever it happened to be. Consciously working on something, on one of the pāramīs, sometimes he works on two at one time. Like the last Jātaka tale - it's quite long - it's about seventy pages or something like that, is a story about how he knew that he was working on his final perfection of generosity. And he was a king and he started giving away everything, and he gave away the white elephant and it got everybody upset with him, and they took his throne away and they threw him out. And then somebody came along and said: "Well, I like your wife," so he gave his wife away. And then somebody came along and said: "I like your kids," and he gave the kids away. And the kids didn't like that, so they came back to him, and then he forced them to go back because he was practicing his generosity. And in the end, they all came back together and they lived happily ever after.

Anyway, let's get back to some Dependent Origination.

23. "Monks, knowing and seeing in this way, would you run back to the past thus: 'Were we in the past? Were we not in the past? What were we in the past? How were we in the past? Having been what, what did we become in the past'?" - "No venerable sir." - "Knowing and seeing Dependent Origination in this way, would you run forward to the future thus: 'Shall we be in the future? Shall we not be in the future? What shall we be in the future? How shall we be in the future? Having been what, what shall we become in the future'?" - "No, venerable sir." - "Knowing and seeing in this way, would you now be inwardly perplexed about the present thus: 'Am I? Am I not? What am I? How am I? Where has this being come from? Where will it go'?" - "No, venerable sir."

When you see Dependent Origination these questions won't even arise.

24. "Monks, knowing and seeing in this way, would you speak thus: 'The Teacher is respected by us. We speak as we do out of respect for the Teacher'?" -"No, venerable sir." -

No, they wouldn't say that. Why? Because they know and see it for themselves what Dependent Origination is and how it is. They wouldn't merely say something out of respect; they're taught from direct knowledge.

"Knowing and seeing in this way, would you speak thus: 'The Recluse says this, and we speak thus at the bidding of the Recluse'?" - "No, venerable sir." - "Knowing and seeing in this way, would you acknowledge another teacher?" - "No, venerable sir." - "Knowing and seeing in this way, would you return to the observances, tumultuous debates, and auspicious signs of ordinary recluses and brahmins, taking them as the core [of the holy life]?" -

Of course not.

"No, venerable sir." - "Do you speak only of what you have known, seen, and understood for yourselves?" - "Yes, venerable sir."

25. "Good, Monks. So you have been guided by me with this Dhamma, which is visible here and now, immediately effective, inviting inspection, onward leading, to be experienced by the wise for themselves. For it was with reference to this that it has been said: 'Monks, this Dhamma is visible here and now, immediately effective, inviting inspection, onward leading, to be experienced by the wise for themselves.'

26. "Monks, the descent of the embryo takes place through the union of three things. Here, there is the union of the mother and father, but the mother is not in season, and the coming being is not present - in this case no descent of an embryo takes place. Here, there is the union of the mother and father, and the mother is in season, but the coming being is not present - in this case too no descent of the embryo takes place. But when there is the union of the mother and father, and the mother is in season, and the coming being is present, through the union of these three things the descent of the embryo takes place.

MN 38: Discourse on the Destruction of Craving 173

27. "The mother then carries the embryo in her womb for nine or ten months with much anxiety, as a heavy burden. Then, at the end of nine or ten months, the mother gives birth with much anxiety, as a heavy burden. Then, when the child is born, she nourishes it with her own blood; for the mother's breast-milk is called blood in the Noble One's Discipline.

28. "When he grows up and his faculties mature, the child plays at such games as toy ploughs, tipcat, somersaults, toy windmills, toy measures, toy cars, and a toy bow and arrow.

29. "When he grows up and his faculties mature [still further], the youth enjoys himself provided and endowed with the five cords of sensual pleasure, with forms cognizable by the eye... sounds cognizable by the ear... odors cognizable by the nose... flavors cognizable by the tongue... tangibles cognizable by the body that are wished for, desired, agreeable, and likable, connected with sensual desire, and provocative of lust.

30. "On seeing a form with the eye, he lusts after it if it is pleasing; he dislikes it if it is unpleasing. He abides with mindfulness of the body unestablished, with a limited mind, and he does not understand, as it actually is the deliverance of mind and deliverance by wisdom wherein those evil unwholesome states cease without remainder. Engaged as he is in favoring and opposing, whatever the feeling he feels - whether pleasant or painful or neither-painful-nor-pleasant - he delights in that feeling, welcomes it, and remains holding to it. As he does so, delight arises in him. Now, delight in feelings is clinging. With his clinging as condition, habitual tendency [comes to be]; with habitual tendency as condition, birth comes to be; with birth as condition aging and death, sorrow, lamentation, pain, grief, and despair come to be. Such is the origin of this whole mass of suffering.

"On hearing a sound with the ear... On smelling an odor with the nose... On tasting a flavor with the tongue... On touching a tangible with the body... On cognizing a mind object with the mind, he lusts after it if it is pleasing; he dislikes it if it is unpleasing... Now, delight in feelings is clinging. With his clinging as condition, habitual tendency [comes to be]; with habitual tendency as condition, birth; with birth as condition, aging and death, sorrow, lamentation, pain, grief, and despair come to be. Such is the origin of this whole mass of suffering.

31. "Here, Monks, a Tathāgata appears in the world, accomplished, fully enlightened, perfect in true knowledge and conduct, sublime, knower of worlds, incomparable leader of persons to be tamed, teacher of gods and humans, enlightened, blessed. He declares this world with its gods, its Māras and its Brahmās, this generation with its recluses and brahmins, its princes and its people, which he has himself realized with direct knowledge. He teaches the Dhamma good in the beginning, good in the middle, good in the end, with the right meaning and phrasing, and he reveals a holy life that is utterly perfect and pure.

32. "A householder or householder's son or one born in some other clan hears that Dhamma. On hearing the Dhamma he acquires faith in the Tathāgata. Possessing that faith, he considers thus: 'Household life is crowded and dusty; life gone forth is wide open. It is not easy, while living in a home, to lead the holy life utterly perfect and pure as a polished shell. Suppose I shave off my hair and beard, put on the yellow robe, and go forth from the home life into homelessness.' On a later occasion, abandoning a small or a large fortune, abandoning a small or a large circle of relatives, he shaves off his hair and beard, puts on the yellow robe, and goes forth from the home life into homelessness.

33. "Having thus gone forth and possessing the monk's training and way of life, abandoning the killing of living beings, he abstains from killing living beings; with rod and weapon laid aside, conscientious and merciful, he abides

compassionate to all living beings. Abandoning the taking of what is not given, he abstains from taking what is not given, taking only what is given, expecting only what is given, by not stealing he abides in purity. Abandoning incelibacy, he observes celibacy, living apart, abstaining from the vulgar practice of sexual intercourse. Abandoning false speech, he abstains from false speech; he speaks truth, adheres to truth, is trustworthy and reliable, one who is no deceiver of the world. Abandoning malicious speech, he abstains from malicious speech; he does not repeat elsewhere what he has heard here in order to divide [those people] from these, nor does he repeat to these people what he has heard elsewhere in order to divide [these people] from those;

That's called slander.

thus he remains one who reunites those who are divided, a promoter of friendships, who enjoys concord, rejoices in concord, delights in concord, a speaker of words that promote concord. Abandoning harsh speech, he abstains from harsh speech; he speaks such words as are gentle, pleasing to the ear and lovable, as go to the heart, are courteous, desired by many and agreeable to many. Abandoning gossip, he abstains from gossip; he speaks at the right time, speaks what is fact, speaks on what is good, speaks on the Dhamma and the Discipline; at the right time he speaks such words as are worth recording, reasonable, moderate and beneficial. He abstains from injuring seeds and plants. He practices eating only one meal a day, abstaining from eating at night and outside the proper time. He abstains from dancing, singing, music, and theatrical shows. He abstains from wearing garlands, smartening himself with scent, and embellishing himself with unguents. He abstains from high and large couches. He abstains from accepting gold and silver. He abstains from accepting raw grain. He abstains from accepting raw meat. He abstains from accepting women and girls. He abstains from accepting men and women slaves. He abstains from accepting goats and sheep. He abstains from accepting fowl and pigs. He abstains from accepting elephants, cattle, horses, and mares. He abstains from accepting fields and land. He abstains from going on errands and running messages. He abstains from buying and selling. He abstains from false weights, false metals, and false measures. He abstains from accepting bribes, deceiving, defrauding, and trickery. He abstains from wounding, murdering, binding, brigandage, plunder and violence.

34. "He becomes content with robes to protect his body and with alms food to maintain his stomach, and wherever he goes, he sets out taking only these with him. Just as a bird, wherever it goes, flies with its wings as its only burden, so too the monk becomes content with robes to protect his body and with alms food to maintain his stomach, and wherever he goes, he sets out taking only these with him. Possessing...

And a pickup truck for all of the other stuff that needs to come along. The library, the library, yeah. That used to be the hardest thing for me when I was in Asia because I was traveling a lot and I always had at least fifty kilos of books. It's hard to travel without the books, because there were so few English books over there that when I got them, I didn't want to let them go.

Possessing this aggregate of noble virtue, he experiences within himself a bliss that is blameless.

35. "On seeing a form with the eye, he does not grasp at its signs and features.

What are the signs and features?

ST: Identifying what it is.

BV: That's it. Identifying what it is and then getting involved with it.

Since, if he left the eye faculty unguarded, evil unwholesome states of covetousness and grief might invade him, he practices the way of its restraint, he guards the eye faculty, he undertakes the restraint of the eye faculty.

How do you restrain the eye faculty?

ST: Close your eyes?

BV: No, when you're sitting, you close your eyes.

ST: Don't look at it?

BV: But, it's ok to look, but let it be without the craving, no clinging (thinking), that's the key.

On hearing a sound with the ear... On smelling an odor with the nose... On tasting a flavor with the tongue... On touching a tangible with the body... On cognizing a mind-object with the mind, he does not grasp at its signs and features.

Getting involved in the story when we're talking about mind.

Since, if he left the mind faculty unguarded, evil unwholesome states of covetousness and grief might invade him, he practices the way of its restraint, he guards the mind faculty, he undertakes the restraint of the mind faculty. Possessing this noble restraint of the faculties, he experiences within himself a bliss that is unsullied.

36. "He becomes one who acts in full awareness when going forward and returning; who acts in full awareness when looking ahead and looking away; who acts in full awareness when flexing and extending his limbs; who acts in full awareness when wearing his robes and carrying his outer robe and bowl; who acts in full awareness when eating, drinking, consuming food, and tasting; who acts in full awareness when defecating and urinating; who acts in full awareness when walking, standing, sitting, falling asleep, waking up, talking, and keeping silent.

Full awareness of what?

ST: Your object of meditation?

BV: And how mind's attention moves.

37. "Possessing this aggregate of noble virtue, and this noble restraint of the faculties, and possessing this noble mindfulness and full awareness, he resorts to a secluded resting place: the forest, the root of a tree, a mountain, a ravine, a hillside cave, a charnel ground, a jungle thicket, an open space, a heap of straw.

38. "On returning from his alms round, after his meal he sits down, folding his legs crosswise, setting his body erect, and establishing mindfulness before him. Abandoning covetousness for the world he abides with a mind free from covetousness; he purifies his mind from covetousness. Abandoning ill-will and hatred, he abides with a mind free from ill-will, compassionate for the welfare of all living beings; he purifies his mind from ill-will and hatred. Abandoning sloth and torpor, he abides free from sloth and torpor, percipient of light, mindful and fully aware; he purifies his mind from sloth and torpor. Abandoning restlessness and remorse, he abides unagitated with a mind inwardly peaceful; he purifies his mind from restlessness and remorse. Abandoning doubt, he abides having gone beyond doubt, unperplexed about wholesome states; he purifies his mind of doubt.

39. "Having thus abandoned these five hindrances, imperfections of the mind that weaken wisdom, quite secluded from sensual pleasures, secluded from unwholesome states, he enters upon and abides in the first jhāna... With the stilling of thinking and examining thought, he enters upon and abides in the second jhāna... With the fading away as well of joy... he enters upon and abides in the third jhāna... With the abandoning of pleasure and pain... he enters upon and abides in the fourth jhāna... which has neither-pain-nor-pleasure and purity of mindfulness due to equanimity.

40. "On seeing a form with the eye, he does not lust after it if it is pleasing; he does not dislike it if it is unpleasing. He abides with mindfulness of the body established, with an immeasurable mind...

What is an immeasurable mind?

{repeats} with an immeasurable mind, and he understands as it actually is the deliverance of mind...

Immeasurable mind is the Brahma Vihāras.

{repeats} he understands as it actually is the deliverance of mind and deliverance by wisdom

How do you have deliverance by wisdom?

ST: Dependent Origination.

BV: Seeing Dependent Origination.

wherein those evil unwholesome states cease without remainder. Having thus abandoned favoring and opposing, whatever feeling he feels, whether pleasant or painful, or neither-painful-nor-pleasant, he does not delight in that feeling, welcome it, or remain holding to it. As he does not do so, delight in feelings ceases in him. With the cessation of his delight comes cessation of clinging; with the cessation of clinging, cessation of habitual tendency; with the cessation of habitual tendency, cessation of birth; with the cessation of birth, aging and death, sorrow, lamentation, pain, grief, and despair cease. Such is the cessation of this whole mass of suffering.

On hearing a sound with the ear... On smelling an odor with the nose... On tasting a flavor with the tongue... On touching a tangible with the body... On cognizing a mind-object with the mind, he does not lust after it if it is pleasing; he does not dislike it if it is unpleasing. ... With the cessation of his delight comes cessation of clinging; with the cessation of clinging, cessation of habitual tendency; with the cessation of habitual tendency, cessation of birth; with the cessation of birth, aging and death, sorrow, lamentation, pain, grief, and despair cease. Such is the cessation of this whole mass of suffering.

41. "Monks, remember this [discourse] of mine briefly as deliverance in the destruction of craving, (as taught in brief by me) but [remember] the monk Sāti, son of a fisherman, as caught up in a vast net of craving, in the trammel of craving."

That is what the Blessed One said. The monks were satisfied and delighted in the Blessed One's words.

Ok. Any questions?

Now, tomorrow is going to be the last full day of the retreat. Please let go of the planning mind. That is part of restlessness. And you can plan, and plan, and plan, and figure it out exactly, and it ain't going to happen that way anyway, so just a waste of time. And I'll tell you first hand this story: when I was in Burma, I knew that the government was going to be kicking me out of the country because of the social unrest; all the foreigners had to leave. And I knew about a week and a half before that was going to happen. So I sat down and I started planning. And I had this monk friend in Thailand - he was an Englishman - and I had devised in my mind this great idea of how we could get a body and film it as it was decaying. And I pictured that and I knew exactly that the first thing I was going to do when I got to Thailand, was I was going to look him up and we were going to arrange this, and it was really going to be helpful for a lot of monks, to have a time-exposure of body decay. And I spent a week and a half planning that. And I left Burma, and I went to Thailand, and the monk had disrobed and married somebody! Spent a week and a half with this great plan, and it was all a waste of time. So beware of the planning mind. Ok? Let it go, it's not worth it, I promise.

Ok, let's share some merit then.

May suffering ones be suffering free
And the fear struck fearless be.
May the grieving shed all grief
And may all beings find relief.
May all beings share this merit
That we have thus acquired
For the acquisition of
All kind of happiness.
May beings inhabiting space and earth
Devas and Nagas of mighty power
Share in this merit of ours.
May they long protect
the Buddha's Dispensation.
Sādhu… Sādhu… Sādhu…

MN-135: The Shorter Discourse of Action (Cūḷakammavibhanga Sutta)

You want long life, health, beauty, power, riches, high birth, wisdom? Or even some of these things? They do not appear by chance. It is not someone's luck that they are healthy, or another's lack of it that he is stupid. Though it may not be clear to us now, all such inequalities among human beings (and all sorts of beings) come about because of the kamma they have made individually. Each person reaps his own fruits. So if one is touched by short life, sickliness, ugliness, insignificance, poverty, low birth or stupidity and one does not like these things, no need to just accept that that is the way it is. The future need not be like that provided that you make the right kind of kamma now. Knowing what kamma to make and what not to make is the mark of a wise man. It is also the mark of one who is no longer drifting aimlessly but has some direction in life and some control over the sort of events that will occur. [4]

Presented on 31st March 2007 at the Seattle Retreat

BV: Ok, this is "The Shorter Exposition on Action;" this is about karma.

1. THUS HAVE I HEARD. On one occasion the Blessed One was living at Sāvatthi in Jeta's Grove, Anāthapiṇḍika's Park.

2. Then the brahmin student Subha, Todeyya's son, went to the Blessed One and exchanged greetings with him.

Now, Subha, he was only fifteen or sixteen years old when he went to the Buddha. And he would ask questions, but he had a very, very intelligent mind. So, he could ask questions directly to the Buddha and the Buddha would treat him like he was an elder.

When this courteous and amiable talk was finished, he sat down at one side and asked the Blessed One:

---

[4] *Ibid.*

3. "Master Gotama, what is the cause and condition why human beings are seen to be inferior and superior? For people are seen to be short-lived and long-lived, sickly and healthy, ugly and beautiful, uninfluential and influential, poor and wealthy, low-born and high-born, stupid and wise. What is the cause and condition, Master Gotama, why human beings are seen to be inferior and superior?"

4. "Student, beings are owners of their actions, heirs of their actions; they originate from their actions, are bound to their actions, have their actions as their refuge. It is action that distinguishes beings as inferior and superior." - "I do not understand in detail the meaning of Master Gotama's statement, which he spoke in brief without expounding the meaning in detail. It would be good if Master Gotama would teach me the Dhamma so that I might understand in detail the meaning of Master Gotama's statement." - "Then, Student, listen and attend closely to what I shall say." - "Yes, sir," the brahmin student Subha replied. The Blessed One said this:

5. "Here, Student, some man or woman kills living beings and is murderous, bloody-handed, given to blows and violence, merciless to living beings. Because of performing and undertaking such action, on the dissolution of the body, after death, he reappears in a state of deprivation, in an unhappy destination, in perdition, even in hell. But if on the dissolution of the body, after death, he does not reappear in a state of deprivation, in an unhappy destination, in perdition, in hell, but instead comes back to the human state, then wherever he is reborn he is short-lived. This is the way, Student, that leads to short life, namely, one kills living beings and is murderous, bloody-handed, given to blows and violence, merciless to living beings.

So, a person that practices being a butcher, they generally are not very healthy people, and they generally do not live very long. But it's kind of an interesting thing because sometimes women can have a baby, and the baby only lives for a very short time and then dies. And they wonder "Why, why, why?" It's not the woman's fault that the baby died very young. It's that being. In their past life they killed other beings, so they didn't live very long.

So, one of the things that I've taught people for a long time is that when you practice the meditation, it's good to practice your generosity. And when you practice your generosity there are different kinds of generosity that you can practice. One of the things that is very good to do is to go out and buy some animal that is going to be killed, like lobster or crab or fish or chickens, and they're still alive, and then you take them and you let them go free. When you let them go free, your mind becomes very happy. Now, giving life is a very, very important gift to give. I know people that are very sick and they practice giving, and giving life, and letting go of worrying about their sickness. When they let that animal go free they let go of the worry, their body becomes healthy again. So, when you practice giving life, it's one of the most powerful gifts that you can give.

Now, the animals, let's say the lobsters or crabs, they're in a restaurant and people go up and they say "I want that one" or "I want that one," and then somebody takes and kills them and prepares the meat. When you ask for this one or that one, you are taking part in that being's death, and that is bad karma for you. But if you say "I want this one, but I want you to keep him alive. I want to take him home" and then you let him go free. What is happening in that lobster's mind? The lobster knows that it's caught; the lobster knows that it's going to be killed. Why? Because he sees other lobsters being put in the same thing and they get taken away, and they're killed, and they know that. So, the lobster has a lot of fear and is very much afraid, and then somebody comes in and they grab them. Oh, they're very, very sad. And then they come out, if not killed right away, but he still has fear of death. Then you take that lobster out to the ocean and you let that lobster go back in the ocean. What have you done? That lobster has gone from the worst day in their life - they knew they were going to be killed, they had a lot of fear, they had a lot of anxiety - and now you let them go free. They went from the worst day in their life to the best day. Now, they can continue living.

All beings want to continue living. So, when you let them go free, in your mind you say: "I let go of worry, I let go of pain, I let go of whatever it is that you have an attachment to like fear of dying." I know some people that have cancer and they want to let go of the cancer. So, you want to be healthy, they don't want to die. So, they let these animals go and let go of the worry and anxiety about the cancer. And the merit that they make for giving life comes back to them.

Now, there was one lady in Malaysia who came to me and she told me that she was going to die in about one month. The doctors said that there was nothing they could do. The cancer was so bad that she was going to die painfully. And she asked what she could do so that she could be happy for that one month. I told her to buy an animal, let it go free, and focus on happiness coming into her mind. I told her that she needed to smile and laugh more, too! She went out to the fishing boats and they have little fish that they use as bait. She bought one hundred fish, and then she would take them out and let them go free in the ocean, and she became very happy and began smiling a lot. She did this every day. After about six weeks, she went to the doctor because she felt good; she didn't feel sick. And the doctor examined her and said "What have you been doing? What kind of medicine are you taking? I want to know about this." And she said "I quit taking medicine. I went down to some fishing boats and I bought fish, then I let them go free, every day. That's all I've done different plus I began to smile and laugh more, in other words, I began to be more in the present moment with a truly happy mind." She didn't have any cancer; the cancer went away.

The gift of life is very, very powerful. Anything that you're very much worried about, you buy some animals that are going to be killed; let them go free and let go of that worry. And then everything starts working so that you don't have that worry come up any more. So, this is a very good thing to do.

ST: I have a question.

BV: Yes.

ST: Animals at the pound, where can you let them go? Like dogs and cats.

BV: Well, you don't get those kind of animals unless you take them home and take care of them yourself. Now, there's one lady that - I give retreats at Joshua Tree in California every year - and she goes to the pound and she finds animals that are going to be killed, and she brings them home with her. And she loves them and she gives them food, and then they die naturally. So, that's one way of doing it. Or you get lobster, you get crabs, you know you have to buy them alive, and then you take them out to the ocean, let them go. And you can take the mice and you can let them go in the forest, but not close to your house.

ST: You have little black and white mice running around the house. Ha Ha!

ST: I want to buy birds, but sometimes I think, you know, some of these birds have never been out in the wild and I'm afraid they won't make it.

BV: Buy birds? But what you do is you keep them in the cage and you show them where you're putting food. And then you feed them and you put some in this place, and then you let the bird go free and you keep putting food there. And they're smart, they'll stay around. So, you can do it that way. Or if you want to buy a snake, you can buy a snake, but let the snake go a long way into the forest where there's not a lot of people. They know how to take care of themselves.

In Burma, there was a monk that walked around every day in the morning to get food and this one water buffalo saw him. And the farmer that owned the water buffalo was going to have that water buffalo butchered. Now, the water buffalo was pregnant. The night before the water buffalo was going to be killed, it sent a very, very strong thought to this monk, and said: "I am very much afraid that I'm going to be killed. When I'm killed, my baby will die too. I don't want my baby to die." So, the next morning the monk went around and he found the butcher who going to kill the water buffalo and said: "Please wait." And he went around to all the villagers and he collected money, however much money this farmer was going to sell the cow for, and gave it to the farmer, and then he let the water buffalo go into the forest and go live. And the water buffalo was so thankful that she came up to the monk and she got down on her knees and bowed to the monk; and there's pictures of it. So, that monk, he saved two lives that day. A wonderful gift!

6. "But here, Student, some man or woman, abandoning the killing of living beings, abstains from killing living beings; with rod and weapon laid aside, gentle and kindly, he abides compassionate to all living beings. Because of performing and undertaking such action, on the dissolution of the body, after death, he reappears in a happy destination, even in the heavenly world. But if on the dissolution of the body, after death, he does not reappear in a happy destination, in the heavenly world, but instead comes back to the human state, then wherever he is reborn he is long-lived. This is the way, Student, that leads to long life, namely, abandoning the killing of living beings, one abstains from killing living beings; with rod and weapon laid aside, gentle and kindly, one abides compassionate to all living beings.

So, if you want to have long life, practice giving life, not taking life.

7. "Here, Student, some man or woman is given to injuring beings with the hand, with a clod, with a stick, or with a knife. Because of performing and undertaking such action, on the dissolution of the body, after death, he reappears in a state of deprivation... But if instead he comes back to the human state, then wherever he is reborn he is sickly. This is the way, Student, that leads to sickliness, namely, one is given to injuring beings with the hand, with a clod, with a stick, or with a knife.

So, quite often you'll see that butchers, they do not live very long. And as odd as it sounds, there's a lot of doctors that do not live very long because they cut people. Ok, they're doing it with good intention, hopefully, but still you don't see many doctors that are eighty, ninety, a hundred years old. They die when they're fifty, sixty, seventy years old.

8. "But here, Student, some man or woman is not given to injuring beings with the hand, with a clod, with a stick, or with a knife. Because of performing and undertaking such action, on the dissolution of the body, after death, he reappears in a happy destination... But if instead he comes back to the human state, then wherever he is reborn he is healthy. This is the way, Student, that leads to health, namely, one is not given to injuring beings with the hand, with a clod, with a stick, or with a knife.

So, you don't cause pain to other beings, and you stay more healthy. So, as you practice being more and more compassionate and kind, not only to human beings or big animals, but also small beings: insects, mosquitoes. What do you do when a mosquito bites you? And you don't even think about it. But that leads to a body that is not very healthy. So, you don't kill the mosquitoes. A mosquito lands on you, you blow it away.

I used to live in Thailand; I lived by a wasp nest. And this kind of wasp is very, very deadly. If you get stung by six or seven of these at the same time you die, and I lived right beside it, and I had to walk by every day. I go out, get food, I have to walk by the nest. The wasps come down, they start hovering around me. The first day I saw the wasp and I thought: "Ah, this is my test." So, I said "Hello friend, how are you? I hope you're having a nice day," and they left me alone. People that came to visit me, they would run into my hut because a wasp would be after them and try to sting them. I never got stung because I wasn't afraid of the wasp. I didn't try to run away, but I practiced loving-kindness. I wished that wasp a good day, a happy day, and he would be there for a little while and then he would fly away. And I'd go out and then I'd come back, I have all this food and then he would come back again. So, I say "Well, this has been a good day. I hope it's a good day for you." And then he'd fly away again. I never got stung. Many people that came to see me did because they didn't like the wasp, they tried to hit him and make him go away. That made them angry.

ST: What did you advise us... last Sunday, I remember last summer we had a green nest in front of our house, right in the door, the entrance. So, I can't suddenly not go and then tell them "You have a good day. Yes, come into the house and fly in the house" So, but...

BV: Well, you can do a couple of things. Ah, you can hire someone that takes care of bees, and they will come with a big box and put over it, and they will take it away. But there are people that... they raise bees. And they like it because they get the honey. And they know how to handle without harming. So, that's what you do. Now, if you have cockroaches, so many people: "Oh, I hate cockroaches," and kill. If you want cockroaches to leave you then you take cucumber, cut up very small, put in a dish where the cockroaches are, they leave. They don't like the smell. You don't have to kill.

ST: What about mice?

BV: Well, you can have an understanding with mice. You can tell them that you don't want them to come around. Speak to them. What you can do if your friend has a cat, you take some of the fur and put it around, and they go away. But they're smart enough to understand and they know that the scent of a cat, they need to stay away from it, and they will go away.

With rats, as odd as it sounds, is you write them a letter. Yeah, they read; they do. I've done this more than one time. I write them a letter telling them that it's not good that they are here and if they stay here I'm going to have to hurt them. Please move away, and I put it on the floor. One day they leave. See it does work, it really does.

If you have ants around your house, you want to get rid of the ants - you take water, cayenne pepper, put in the water, spray; ants go away.

Well, if you put cayenne pepper around your plants, just sprinkle it around so you can see the red pepper, they will leave that alone. They don't like that. You know how you take red peppers and if you don't have rubber gloves how it hurts? Well, it hurts them too. It doesn't kill them. Huh?

ST: Chili powder.

BV: Chili powder works.

ST: But the rain washes it away.

BV: Well, you have to keep doing it. But it will start to get into the soil a little bit and then they'll stay away. One of the things that we used to do, so that the dogs would not come onto the lawn, was we'd take a plastic bottle that's clear, fill it with water and put it on the lawn. Why that works I don't know, but they left, they never came in our yard. I don't know if that will work. We did it one time, it did work, but I don't know if it works every time or not. So, but it's worth a try.

So, if you want to stay healthy, you don't kill animals on purpose. Now, there are times when you're walking and you don't see and you step on an ant. That is not intentional, so there's no harm. In order to kill, there has to be five things: 1) There has to be a living being; 2) You have to have the intention to kill; 3) You need a weapon; 4) You use the weapon; and 5) The being dies. Ok? If one of those five things isn't present, then there is no bad karma, there's no wrongdoing. So, you're walking and you don't notice a line of ants and you step on the ants. You didn't do that with intention to kill, so there is no wrongdoing.

ST: What about when people kill an animal that is suffering out of compassion for that animal?

BV: No.

ST: No killing in that way?

BV: No. Why would you kill an animal if it were suffering?

ST: I just think of like the cow that's wrapped up in the barbed wire, there's no chance of him to get out, and just in so much pain, and people see that, and that seems like a nicer thing to do than to let it die slowly.

BV: That's that being's karma, and now you're interfering with the karma and creating bad karma for yourself. I really do not go along with taking: "Oh, my little cat or my dog is so sick. I'm going to take it to the veterinarian and they're going to 'kill' it for me." I don't go along with that. Every being wants to live as long as it possibly can, even when it's suffering. Human beings are like that, right?

ST: Let's talk about living wills, you know when you create a Health directive that says "Do Not Resuscitate." Is that suicidal intention?

BV: No that's not. That's letting nature take its course.

ST: But if a machine is keeping me alive and I tell someone else to unplug that machine so I can die won't that be bad karma for me and them?

BV: Well, then if your karma is not ended when they turn off the machine, you will not die. Right? But the way the machines are right now, they make money for the hospital and the doctors, and that's about all the good that comes from that. I do not agree with extending life in an artificial way. It's unnatural. We're here for a period of time and we're going to die. Why extend it for two weeks because a machine is keeping my organs going? That means I can't carry on; I can't get on with what's coming next.

ST: My father-in-law is in coma right now and my husband is there with him, and I know tomorrow I have to go and see him...

BV: Well, you let him know that there is no bad karma for anyone if they take him off of that machine, that's keeping him alive, and letting your father die naturally is the most humane thing you can do.

I spent a lot of time in hospitals, I spent a lot of time in nursing homes, and I was always trying to encourage people to let nature be nature. It's ok for people to die. The only reason you put them on a machine is because: "I want them to live longer," but they don't have any quality of life. So, it's better just to let them go.

ST: So, if we do that, that means we're not killing?

BV: No, you're not killing.

ST: Because we just honor their wish?

BV: Yes.

See, one of the things that's happened, especially in this country, is an awful lot of people, they are in the city so much that they don't see the real way life is. And everybody thinks that they're young and they're going to stay young forever, and they're going to last forever. And when you don't see the natural process of animals living and then dying, and you don't accept that, then you cause yourself a lot more pain than is necessary. So, it's really better to let nature be nature. I mean if you were in Vietnam, they don't have those kind of machines there. People live, they die all of the time, and that's the natural way of things. And you honor that person until they die. You make them comfortable as you can. You spend time wishing them happiness, but you allow nature to be nature.

ST: Is the person eating the meat have the same karma as the butcher?

BV: No. In order to kill there's these five things: 1) It has to be a living being. Now, if you go to the store and you buy meat, is it alive? 2) Did you intend to kill it? No, you didn't intend to kill it. What you intend to do is take that meat, cook it, put it in your body so that you have energy, so you can continue. 3) Did you have a weapon? 4) Did you use the weapon? 5) Did the being die? No. So, all five of these things that make up killing don't occur when you go to the store and you buy the meat - for you. The butcher has not got very good karma because it is a living being, they intend to kill it, they take a weapon, they use the weapon, and the being dies, but you don't get any of that karma.

ST: So, if I want to help the butcher and I don't eat meat, then he has no reason to kill?

BV: Do you think that eating vegetables means that beings don't die? Weren't you just talking about slugs in your vegetable garden?

ST: They still die, but I, you know...

BV: Ah well, but they still die. How do they die? Even if it's just their hand, that is the weapon, and they use that weapon, and the being died. You can't live in this world without beings dying because you are alive. There's eighty different kind of beings in your body that are living and dying continually.

There's a story about one monk, he became an arahat, and he was walking and he saw that he was killing living beings because he was walking. So, he stood in one spot and then he noticed that by his breathing he was killing living beings, so he stopped breathing. And the Buddha came along and said "Monk, what are you doing?" And he told the Buddha, and the Buddha said: "That is why you work to get off of the wheel of saṃsāra. That's why you want to attain Nibbāna. So, after this lifetime there will be no more beings dying because of you having a body."

So, even though you say: "Well, I'm a vegetarian" there are beings that die. Just digging in the soil kills beings. I can be at the beach and I have a knife, and a man just catches a fish, and he wants to use the knife to kill the fish and cut it open so he can cook it. I give him the knife, he can do whatever he wants with it. I get no bad karma from that, right? Because I didn't intend to kill and I didn't kill, so I'd have no bad karma from that. Believe me, I have been around a lot of vegetarians that argue with me a lot. But the whole thing comes down to: "What are you doing with your mind in the present moment?" Now, if I take a piece of meat, it's just a piece of meat, now this turns into energy for my body. I can continue living and then somebody says "Well, you paid the butcher for the meat, so if you didn't pay the butcher for the meat, then that being would still be alive," but that's not true. That being is already dead. I didn't have anything to do with it. I get no bad karma from that.

Yes...

ST: But it is true if everybody would keep their precepts there wouldn't be a lot of meat eating.

BV: There's still going to be vegetable eating and there's still going to be beings that die.

See, that's the thing. Having a human body means beings die. That's just the way it is. Actually there are a lot more beings that die when you pull it out of the dirt than if there's one cow. It's just one being. But when you disturb the soil like that, many different kinds of being die because of that. So, actually there's more beings that die from eating vegetables than from eating meat.

ST: The Buddha ate vegetables.

BV: The Buddha ate meat, too.

ST: But, that was before he became the Buddha?

BV: No, no. He ate meat. He ate whatever was offered to him. See, right before the Buddha died, Devadatta came to the Buddha and he wanted to take over the saṅgha, and the Buddha said: "No." So, Devadatta said: "Well, I want you to make the rules for the monks, so that they would always have to live in the forest - they could not live in the city," and the Buddha said: "No." He said: "I want you to make sure that all monks are vegetarian," and the Buddha said: "No. I will not make those kind of rules."

ST: That's why the Tibetan monks, I understand they eat meat?

BV: Yeah, you know why they eat meat? Because they can't grow anything: "We're up so high in the mountain." They have to eat meat in order live.

ST: There's no dirt, a lot of rock.

ST: So, who killed the meat for them?

ST: Do they go to market?

BV: No, they don't buy it, but it's given to them. It's offered to them.

ST: The Theravada monks eat meat, too?

BV: Most Theravada monks eat meat, and Tibetan monks eat meat. Now, I've known a lot of Vietnamese monks that eat meat. I have, I've known a lot of them that do eat meat. And Korean monks will eat meat, but Chinese monks, no. And let me also say I've been around a lot of vegetarian Vietnamese monks too. I've been around both.

SK: Well, when you come to the Center, if you're vegetarian, we don't make you eat meat.

BV: No. Whatever kind of food you're most comfortable with, that's what we want to make for you when you come to visit.

If you're used to eating meat then we'll fix a meat dish. If you're not used to eating meat then we'll fix vegetarian for you.

ST: Do you eat meat?

BV: Yes, I eat everything but only some seafood. Some seafood I have an allergy to. I have allergy to crab; I have allergy to lobster; I have allergy to shrimp. I still accept whatever anybody gives me, but I don't eat it.

ST: Like the Theravada monks, like they do not eat after twelve?

BV: Yes. That's one of the rules that the Buddha said was very good. It's good for the health. I only eat one time per day and it's good for my health. I don't get colds very often. I don't get sickness because I eat one time per day. The rest of the time, fast.

ST: Do you drink water or tea after lunch?

BV: Yeah. Yeah. There are some things that I can take after the meal, but it's more like sweets, which is not good for us anymore, really. But I can take ghee; I can take honey; I can take sugar; I can take salt.

ST: Can you drink wine?

BV: No, no alcohol. That's against the rules. And I know that some Tibetan monks they drink their Yak-butter beer, and that is not a good thing. Somebody asked if I wanted to taste it, so I tasted - I took one sip - oh, I would never consider drinking anything like that. It smells bad and it tastes bad.

Ok, let's see...

9. "Here, Student, some man or woman is of an angry and irritable character; even when criticized a little, he is offended, becomes angry, hostile, and resentful, and displays anger, hate, and bitterness. Because of performing and undertaking such action he reappears in a state of deprivation. But if instead he comes back to the human

state, then wherever he is reborn he is ugly. This is the way, Student, that leads to ugliness, namely, one is of an angry and irritable character and displays anger, hate, and bitterness.

Have you ever seen somebody that's very angry, and seen their face, and their face gets black? Eh, they look very ugly. They're displaying what's in their mind at that time. So, that's another reason that I want people to carry a mirror around with them; to look at your face when you become angry, and see if you want to continue on looking like that. It's the fastest way to say: "No, no, no, no, no. I don't want to do that; I want to smile; I have a beautiful face when I smile."

10. "But here, Student, some man or woman is not of an angry and irritable character; even when criticized a lot, he is not offended, does not become angry, hostile, and resentful, and does not display anger, hate, and bitterness. Because of performing and undertaking such action he reappears in a happy destination, But if instead he comes back to the human state, then wherever he is reborn he is beautiful. This is the way, Student, that leads to being beautiful, namely, one is not of an angry and irritable character and does not display anger, hate, and bitterness.

That's one of the advantages of practicing loving-kindness. Now, the Buddha talked about eleven advantages for practicing loving-kindness and one of them is that your progress in the meditation is faster with loving-kindness than any other kind of meditation. And another advantage is, your face becomes very beautiful, your face becomes radiant. So, the more you can smile, the more beautiful you become. And you will notice that other people will notice that, and they will mention it to you. So, that's one of the advantages of practicing loving-kindness.

11. "Here, Student, some man or woman is envious, one who envies, resents, and begrudges the gains, honor, respect, reverence, salutations, and veneration received by others. Because of performing and undertaking such action

he reappears in a state of deprivation. But if instead he comes back to the human state, then wherever he is reborn he is uninfluential. This is the way, Student, that leads to being uninfluential, namely, one is envious towards the gains, honor, respect, reverence, salutations, and veneration received by others.

12. "But here, Student, some man or woman is not envious, one who does not envy, resent, and begrudge the gains, honor, respect, reverence, salutations, and veneration received by others. Because of performing and undertaking such action, he reappears in a happy destination. But if instead he comes back to the human state, then wherever he is reborn he is influential.

Haven't you ever wondered why some person can say something and everybody agrees with them right away. And some people can say the same thing, in the same way, and nobody pays attention. It's because in the past they didn't like to see other people prosper. They didn't like to see other people get respect. So, they held that hard mind. So, when they're in this lifetime, they don't have much influence. Even the best idea, they can't convince anyone that this is a good thing. Now, you want to change that in this lifetime, then you start giving respect to everyone, and you become happy when you see they have gain, and they get a job promotion, you become happy for them: "Ah, this is wonderful. You're going to be great at this." And eventually after doing that for a period of time, then you start to gain more influence. Other people start paying attention to what you say.

ST: Does it have to be sincere?

BV: It has to be sincere; it cannot be fake.

This is the way, Student, that leads to being influential, namely, one is not envious towards the gains, honor, respect, reverence, salutations, and veneration received by others.

So, the more you cultivate the mind that is happy when you see other people doing well, the more positive your influence will become over time.

13. "Here, Student, some man or woman does not give food, drink, clothing, carriages, garlands, scents, unguents, beds, dwelling, and lamps to recluses or brahmins. Because of performing and undertaking such action he reappears in a state of deprivation. But if instead he comes back to the human state, then wherever he is reborn he is poor. This is the way, Student, that leads to poverty, namely, one does not give food, drink, clothing, resting places, medicines, and lamps to recluses or brahmins or the requisites for monks.

14. "But here, Student, some man or woman gives food, drink, clothing, resting places, medicines, and lamps the requisites to recluses or brahmins. Because of performing and undertaking such action he reappears in a happy destination. But if instead he comes back to the human state, then wherever he is reborn he is wealthy. This is the way, Student, that leads to wealth, namely, one gives food, drink, clothing, resting places, medicines, and lamps and other requisites to recluses or brahmins.

ST: Bill Gates must have done that.

BV: Ah, he was generous, very generous. And you can be generous in a lot of different ways. One of the things that the Buddha said was that if you saw the benefit of giving food, you would never eat alone. You would always share your food with someone around you.

Now, giving food to monks, there's a way of doing this. When you're preparing the food, you prepare with a lot of mettā, with a lot of love, with a lot of kindness, and happiness in your heart. And then while you're giving the food, you give the food with a lot of mettā, with a lot of love. After you have given the food and you go away, you remember giving the food with a happy mind: "I really did something good. I feel happy."

Being a monk, I am very used to eating food that is prepared by someone that has a happy mind. I can eat a little and it lasts all day. Occasionally someone will fix food and they don't really want to. I can hardly eat that food.

ST: How do you know?

BV: You can feel the difference. If the food does not have love in it, one bite and it's like: "Oh no, eat something else this time, I don't want that." It can make your stomach hurt.

Whenever someone wants to give something, I cannot refuse; I have to accept. And that was a hard lesson for me. It's very easy to give; it's very difficult to receive. But as a monk I had to learn that I take everything. I might not use it, but I will accept it because I want to make you happy.

When I was in Burma, I was staying for a period of time in a very small village. But because I was a big and American monk, everybody wanted to give me food. I always had enough food for five people. So, when I got back to the monastery, I would take everything and then put in what I could eat or what I wanted, but I kept all of the other food on a tray. And then I would go to the poorest family in the village, and I would give that to them, so that they could have food to eat. And I asked them to share the food with anyone that came to visit them.

I know that in some countries, monks when they're done eating they just throw the food away. I can't do that, especially in a poor country like Burma. In Burma, some people, they thought that it was a very special thing to give me one potato chip or one peanut. That was a big gift to them. How can I say no? Of course, I accept, but if I didn't happen to see that and eat it myself, I made sure someone else got to eat it.

ST: Yeah, but if the food went bad, you would...

BV: Well, if the food goes bad, but every morning they make it fresh. And in Burma I would go out for alms round not real early in the morning. I would go out around eight o'clock because that gave them time to prepare the food, and then when I was done eating, which was right around ten o'clock, I would immediately take that food and go give it back to them.

15. "Here, Student, some man or woman is obstinate and arrogant; he does not pay homage to one who should receive homage, does not rise up for one in whose presence he should rise up, does not offer a seat to one who deserves a seat, does not make way for one for whom he should make way, and does not honor, respect, revere, and venerate one who should be honored, respected, revered, and venerated. Because of performing and undertaking such action he reappears in a state of deprivation. But if instead he comes back to the human state, then wherever he is reborn he is low-born. This is the way, Student, that leads to low birth, namely, one is obstinate and arrogant and does not honor, respect, revere, and venerate one who should be honored, respected, revered, and venerated.

16. "But here, Student, some man or woman is not obstinate and arrogant; he pays homage to one who should receive homage, rises up for one in whose presence he should rise up, offers a seat to one who deserves a seat, makes way for one for whom he should make way, and honors, respects, reveres, and venerates one who should be honored, respected, revered, and venerated. Because of performing and undertaking such action he reappears in a happy destination. But if instead he comes back to the human state, then wherever he is reborn he is high-born. This is the way, Student, that leads to high birth, namely, one is not obstinate and arrogant and honors, respects, reveres, and venerates one who should be honored, respected, revered, and venerated.

Born into a wealthy family, an influential family, a family that is a Buddhist family. A low-born is someone that's born in a very poor situation and they always stay in that poor situation, and their family doesn't have any influence with other people, things like that.

17. "Here, Student, some man or woman does not visit a recluse or a brahmin and ask: 'Venerable sir, what is wholesome? What is unwholesome? What is blamable? What is blameless? What should be cultivated? What should not be cultivated? What kind of action will lead to my harm and suffering for a long time? What kind of action will lead to my welfare and happiness for a long time?' Because of performing and undertaking such action he reappears in a state of deprivation. But if instead he comes back to the human state, then wherever he is reborn he is stupid. This is the way, Student, that leads to stupidity, namely, one does not visit a recluse or brahmin and ask such questions.

Now, when I was in Asia, the Chinese will not ask questions. They have many questions, but they will never ask a question. So, I told them that if you do not ask me questions when I ask you to ask me questions, then you will be reborn stupid. And all of a sudden hands started coming up. Nobody wants to be reborn stupid.

ST: Is that because of their culture?

BV: Yeah. Yeah, their culture is such that the teacher, whatever he says, is always right, and you never ask a question because the teacher might not know the answer. But I am not Chinese, and I asked many, many, many questions when I first became a Buddhist. So much so, I lived with a monk, very, very scholarly-monk, very intelligent, and I was always asking questions, questions, questions, questions. And he said: "When you die from this world and you're reborn, you are going to be reborn smarter than Einstein," because I asked so many questions. But I also encourage everyone to ask me questions, and if I do not know the answer, I will tell you I don't know the answer, but I will try to find out the answer. So, that way we can both gain benefit because certainly I do not know everything.

Well, you know the thing with the Buddha's teaching that is so different is it does not fight with other religions. In Christianity you have belief, you have to believe in Jesus Christ and all of this other thing, but with Buddhism it's not about belief, it's about how mind works. So, it's a little bit different and it does not fight with Christianity.

ST: Well, I keep praying every night and I pray that maybe.

BV: Well, when you're practicing loving-kindness, what do you think you're doing?

Well, but that's ok for right now. As your mind goes deeper into your meditation, you will get to a place where I will come and tell you: "Now I want you to do family members," and then you can start sending loving-kindness to your husband and your sons and all of that. But this doesn't mean that you can't, during the day, think loving and kind thoughts to them. You can! It's just when you sit, when you're doing your quiet meditation, you use your spiritual friend. But during the day, if you have a thought of them, then smile and send that smile to them, feel that in your heart.

ST: I do, I do. I thought about that, but I just kind of have to get my thought back into my spiritual friend that the teacher has suggested.

BV: Well, that's just for sitting. The rest of the day you can do it to whomever you want. Ok?

ST: Thank you.

BV: Ok...

18. "But here, Student, some man or woman visits a recluse or a brahmin and asks: 'Venerable sir, what is wholesome? What kind of action will lead to my welfare and happiness for a long time?' Because of performing and undertaking

such action he reappears in a happy destination. But if instead he comes back to the human state, then wherever he is reborn he is wise. This is the way, Student, that leads to wisdom, namely, one visits a recluse or brahmin and asks such questions.

See, that's what my teacher was telling me. I'm going to be the wisest man in the world because I ask so many questions. And I have students that are going to be very, very, very wise. As a matter of fact one student, I told them that on their gravestone after they die I'm going to put: "I have a question. Can I ask you?"

19. "Thus, Student, the way that leads to short life makes people short-lived; the way that leads to long life makes people long-lived; the way that leads to sickliness makes people sickly; the way that leads to health makes people healthy; the way that leads to ugliness makes people ugly; the way that leads to beauty makes people beautiful; the way that leads to being uninfluential makes people uninfluential; the way that leads to being influential makes people influential; the way that leads to poverty makes people poor; the way that leads to wealth makes people wealthy; the way that leads to low birth makes people low-born; the way that leads to high birth makes people high-born; the way that leads to stupidity makes people stupid; the way that leads to wisdom makes people wise.

20. "Beings are owners of their actions, Student, heirs of their actions; they originate from their actions, are bound to their actions, have their actions as their refuge. It is action that distinguishes beings as inferior and superior."

21. When this was said, the brahmin student Subha, Todeyya's son, said to the Blessed One: "Magnificent, Master Gotama! Magnificent, Master Gotama! Master Gotama has made the Dhamma clear in many ways, as though he were turning upright what had been overturned, revealing what was hidden, showing the way to one who was lost, or holding up a lamp in the dark for those with

eyesight to see forms. I go to Master Gotama for refuge and to the Dhamma and to the Saṅgha of Monks. Let Master Gotama remember me as a lay follower who has gone to him for refuge for life."

Now, this was a very big statement, because Subha was very much a scholar brahmin. He had memorized all of the Vedas, and because of this clear explanation, he stopped being a brahmin, and became a Buddhist.

Ok, any other questions?

ST: What's the difference between the brahmin and the Buddha?

BV: The brahmins follow the Vedas. Basically they teach one-pointed concentration, and they teach reincarnation. They have permanent self, permanent soul, going from one lifetime to the next, to the next, to the next. But in Buddhism, we believe in rebirth. But rebirth is something like this, do you remember what happened yesterday? It's gone, it's not here now. What happened yesterday is dead. What happens right now is in the present moment, but that will die, and then a new present moment will be reborn.

Everything that arises is part of an impersonal process. With the meditation you'll be able to see that more and more clearly as you go deeper into the meditation. You'll see it much better. You're sitting and all of a sudden pain arises. Whose pain is that? Who said: "I haven't felt pain for a long time. I want pain to arise, right here." No. That doesn't work that way. You can't control the pain. The pain arises because conditions are right for pain to be there. As you let go and relax, that pain will either go away or it won't. But if it doesn't go away after you keep allowing it to be, your mind will become so balanced that it doesn't even go to that. And you will see that this is an impersonal process; it's not a personal process. And that's the one of the main differences between the brahmins and the Buddhists.

Right now it will sound like a lot of words. But as you practice the meditation more, it will become clearer, and you will understand it. So, just be patient.

ST: Buddhism is not based on reincarnation?

BV: Reincarnation means that there's a permanent self or a soul that goes from one lifetime to the next lifetime, to the next lifetime, and it doesn't work like that. And you will be able to see that when you get deep enough in your meditation. It goes out of the realm of philosophy and it comes into the realm of reality. You see things arise and pass away, arise and pass away. There's a continuum that happens, but it's not a personal continuum.

ST: I want to share an experience with you about my mom. A long time ago, she doesn't do it anymore, she did meditation, and she went really deep. She was able to see her past family in a past life, and she told us about it. Is that possible?

BV: Yes. Do you remember what happened yesterday?

ST: I went to work.

BV: Ok, that's a past life isn't it?

ST: Yes.

BV: Learning how to develop your memory, you can go deeper and deeper and you can get into past life.

ST: And then she got scared because she saw herself, she saw her spirit lift off of her body when she was sitting.

BV: That's why she needed to be around a teacher. She didn't need to be scared of something like that. These kind of things are very easy to explain. I know what she was experiencing and it's nothing to be afraid of. See, that's the advantage of being around a teacher instead of just doing the practice on your own.

Ok, let's share some merit.

May suffering ones be suffering free
And the fear struck fearless be.
May the grieving shed all grief
And may all beings find relief.
May all beings share this merit
That we have thus acquired
For the acquisition of
All kind of happiness.
May beings inhabiting space and earth
Devas and Nagas of mighty power
Share in this merit of ours.
May they long protect
the Buddha's Dispensation.
Sādhu... Sādhu... Sādhu...

MN-95: With Cankī (Cankī Sutta)

Dogmatism and Truth are the subjects of this discourse. The dogmatist, now as in the Buddha's days, says 'only this is true, anything else is wrong.' Here the dogmatist is a young brahmin who is affirming the traditional brahminical lore without himself having any basis for 'knowing and seeing' the truth of it for himself. So the dogmatists of all religions and pseudo-religious political creeds are just like blind men--they do not see (with insight-vipassanà) for themselves, they only follow along.

But. the young brahmin says, we don't only believe out of faith but also because of a divinely inspired tradition. The Buddha then gives five factors on which beliefs are based:

- *faith*
- *preference,*
- *(oral) tradition,*
- *arguing upon evidence, and*
- *liking to ponder upon views,*

which beliefs may be either true or false. That is, these five factors are no guarantee of the truth of the things believed though they do guarantee a rigid and dogmatic attitude.

The young brahmin, who evidently has a very keen mind, is stimulated by this discussion to ask: 'how does one guard the truth?'--that is, not make statements which go beyond what is legitimate. Satisfied with the reply he asks further: 'How does one discover the truth?--which is answered by the Buddha with reference to a person who sees the conduct of an enlightened bhikkhu and then gains faith in him. The way of discovering truth is then mapped out step by step from faith to the penetration of ultimate truth with wisdom. 'How is there final arrival at truth?' is the brahmin's last main question and the Buddha shows how one factor is the basis of another. finally the young brahmin declares his love and reverence for monks, which before he had despised.[5]

---

[5] *Ibid.*

Presented on 5th October 2006 at the Dhamma Sukha Meditation Center

BV: I think you will find this very interesting.

1. THUS HAVE I HEARD. On one occasion the Blessed One was wandering in the Kosalan country with a large Saṅgha of Monks, and eventually he arrived at a Kosalan brahmin village named Opasāda. There the Blessed One stayed in the Gods' Grove, the Sāla-tree Grove to the north of Opasāda.

2. Now on that occasion the brahmin Cankī was ruling over Opasāda, a crown property abounding in living beings, rich in grasslands, woodlands, waterways, grain, a royal endowment, a sacred grant given to him by King Pasenadi of Kosala.

They had a lot of divisions. If somebody did something that made the ruler of an entire area, made him happy, then he would give him this area or that area to take care of, with this many villages, and this many towns, and this many cities in it. So he was one of those kind of people.

3. The brahmin householders of Opasāda heard: "The recluse Gotama, the son of the Sakyans who went forth from a Sakyan clan, has been wandering in the country of the Videhans with a large Saṅgha of Monks, with five hundred monks. Now a good report of Master Gotama has been spread to this effect: 'The Blessed One is accomplished, fully enlightened, perfect in true knowledge and conduct, sublime, knower of worlds, incomparable leader of persons to be tamed, teacher of gods and humans, enlightened, blessed. He declares this world with its gods, its Māras and its Brahmas, this generation with its recluses and brahmins, with its princes and its people, which he has himself realized with direct knowledge. He teaches the Dhamma that is good in the beginning, good in the middle, and good in the end, with the right meaning and phrasing,

and he reveals a holy life that is utterly perfect and pure.' Now it is good to see such arahants."

4. Then the brahmin householders of Opasāda set forth from Opasāda in groups and bands and headed northwards to the Gods' Grove, the Sāla-tree Grove.

5. Now on that occasion the brahmin Cankī had retired to the upper story of his palace for his midday rest. Then he saw the brahmin householders of Opasāda setting forth from Opasāda in groups and bands and heading northwards to the Gods' Grove, the Sāla-tree Grove. When he saw them, he asked his minister: "Good minister, why are the brahmin householders of Opasāda setting forth from Opasāda in groups and bands and heading northwards to the Gods' Grove, the Sāla-tree Grove?"

6. "Sir, there is the recluse Gotama, the son of the Sakyans who went forth from a Sakyan clan, who has been wandering in the Kosalan country. They are going to see that Master Gotama." - "Then, good minister, go to the brahmin householders of Opasāda and tell them: 'Sirs, the brahmin Cankī says this: "Please wait, sirs. The brahmin Cankī will also go to see the recluse Gotama." - "Yes, sir," the minister replied, and he went to the brahmin householders of Opasāda and gave them the message.

7. Now on that occasion five hundred brahmins from various states were staying at Opasāda for some business or other. They heard: "The brahmin Cankī, it is said, is going to see the recluse Gotama." Then they went to the brahmin Cankī and asked him: "Sir, is it true that you are going to see the recluse Gotama?" - "So it is, sirs. I am going to see the recluse Gotama."

8. "Sir, do not go to see the recluse Gotama. It is not proper, Master Cankī, for you to go to see the recluse Gotama; rather, it is proper for the recluse Gotama to come to see you. For you, sir, are well born on both sides, of pure maternal and paternal descent seven generations back,

unassailable and impeccable in respect of birth. Since that is so, Master Cankī, it is not proper for you to go to see the recluse Gotama; rather, it is proper for the recluse Gotama to come to see you. You, sir, are rich, with great wealth and great possessions. You, sir, are a master of the Three Vedas with their vocabularies, liturgy, phonology, and etymology, and the histories as a fifth; skilled in philology and grammar, you are fully versed in natural philosophy and in the marks of a Great Man. You, sir, are handsome, comely, and graceful, possessing supreme beauty of complexion, with sublime beauty and sublime presence, remarkable to behold. You, sir, are virtuous, mature in virtue, possessing mature virtue. You, sir, are a good speaker with a good delivery; you speak words that are courteous, distinct, flawless, and communicate the meaning. You, sir, teach the teachers of many, and you teach the recitation of the hymns to three hundred brahmin students. You, sir, are honored, respected, revered, venerated, and esteemed by King Pasenadi of Kosala. You, sir, are honored, respected, revered, venerated, and esteemed by the brahmin Pokkharasati. You, sir, rule over Opasāda, a crown property abounding in living beings... a sacred grant given to you by King Pasenadi of Kosala. Since this is so, Master Cankī, it is not proper for you to go to see the recluse Gotama; rather, it is proper for the recluse Gotama to come to see you."

9. When this was said, the brahmin Cankī told those brahmins: "Now, sirs, hear from me why it is proper for me to go to see Master Gotama, and why it is not proper for Master Gotama to come to see me. Sirs, the recluse Gotama is well born on both sides, of pure maternal and paternal descent seven generations back, unassailable and impeccable in respect of birth. Since this is so, sirs, it is not proper for Master Gotama to come to see me; rather, it is proper for me to go to see Master Gotama. Sirs, the recluse Gotama went forth abandoning much gold and bullion stored away in vaults and depositories. Sirs, the recluse Gotama went forth from the home life into homelessness

while still young, a black-haired young man endowed with the blessing of youth, in the prime of life. Sirs, the recluse Gotama shaved off his hair and beard, put on the yellow robe, and went forth from the home life into homelessness though his mother and father wished otherwise and wept with tearful faces. Sirs, the recluse Gotama is handsome, comely, and graceful, possessing supreme beauty of complexion, with sublime beauty and sublime presence, remarkable to behold. Sirs, the recluse Gotama is virtuous, with noble virtue, with wholesome virtue, possessing wholesome virtue. Sirs, the recluse Gotama is a good speaker with a good delivery; he speaks words that are courteous, distinct, flawless, and communicate the meaning. Sirs, the recluse Gotama is a teacher of the teachers of many. Sirs, the recluse Gotama is free from sensual lust and without personal vanity. Sirs, the recluse Gotama holds the doctrine of the moral efficacy of action, the doctrine of the moral efficacy of deeds; he does not seek any harm for the line of brahmins. Sirs, the recluse Gotama went forth from an aristocratic family, from one of the original noble families. Sirs, the recluse Gotama went forth from a rich family, from a family of great wealth and great possessions. Sirs, people come from remote kingdoms and remote districts to question the recluse Gotama. Sirs, many thousands of deities have gone for refuge for life to the recluse Gotama. Sirs, a good report of the recluse Gotama has been spread to this effect: 'That Blessed One is accomplished, fully enlightened, perfect in true knowledge and conduct, sublime, knower of worlds, incomparable leader of persons to be tamed, teacher of gods and humans, enlightened, blessed.' Sirs, the recluse Gotama possesses the thirty-two marks of a Great Man. Sirs, King Seniya Bimbisara of Magadha and his wife and children have gone for refuge for life to the recluse Gotama. Sirs, King Pasenadi of Kosala and his wife and children have gone for refuge for life to the recluse Gotama. Sirs, the brahmin Pokkharasati and his wife and children have gone for refuge for life to the recluse Gotama. Sirs, the recluse Gotama has arrived at Opasāda and is living at Opasāda in the Gods' Grove, the Sāla-tree Grove to the north of Opasāda. Now any recluses or brahmins that come to our town are our guests, and guests should be honored, respected, revered, and venerated by us. Since the recluse Gotama has arrived at Opasāda, he is our guest, and as our guest should be honored, respected, revered, and venerated by us. Since this is so, sirs, it is not proper for Master Gotama to come to see me; rather, it is proper for me to go to see Master Gotama.

Sirs, this much is the praise of Master Gotama that I have learned, but the praise of Master Gotama is not limited to that for the praise of Master Gotama is immeasurable. Since Master Gotama possesses each one of these factors, it is not proper for him to come to see me; rather, it is proper for me to go to see Master Gotama. Therefore, sirs, let all of us go to see the recluse Gotama."

10. Then the brahmin Cankī, together with a large company of brahmins, went to the Blessed One and exchanged greetings with him. When this courteous and amiable talk was finished, he sat down at one side.

11. Now on that occasion the Blessed One was seated finishing some amiable talk with some very senior brahmins. At the time, sitting in the assembly, was a brahmin student named Kāpaṭhika. Young, shaven-headed, sixteen years old, he was a master of the Three Vedas with their vocabularies, liturgy, phonology, and etymology, and the histories as a fifth; skilled in philology and grammar, he was fully versed in natural philosophy and in the marks of a Great Man. While the very senior brahmins were conversing with the Blessed One, he often broke in and interrupted their talk. Then the Blessed One rebuked the brahmin student Kāpaṭhika thus: "Let not the venerable Bhāradvāja break in and interrupt the talk of the very

senior brahmins while they are conversing. Let the venerable Bhāradvāja wait until the talk is finished."

When this was said, the brahmin Cankī said to the Blessed One: "Let not Master Gotama rebuke the brahmin student Kāpaṭhika. The brahmin student Kāpaṭhika is a clansman, he is very learned, he has a good delivery, he is wise; he is capable of taking part in this discussion with Master Gotama."

12. Then the Blessed One thought: "Surely, since the brahmins honor him thus, the brahmin student Kāpaṭhika must be accomplished in the scriptures of the Three Vedas." Then the brahmin student Kāpaṭhika thought: "When the recluse Gotama catches my eye, I shall ask him a question." Then, knowing with his own mind the thought in the brahmin student Kāpaṭhika's mind, the Blessed One turned his eye towards him. Then the brahmin student Kāpaṭhika thought: "The recluse Gotama has turned towards me. Suppose I ask him a question." Then he said to the Blessed One: "Master Gotama, in regard to the ancient Brahmanic hymns that have come down through oral transmission and in the scriptural collections, the brahmins come to the definite conclusion: 'Only this is true, anything else is wrong.' What does Master Gotama say about this?"

13. "How then, Bhāradvāja, among the brahmins is there even a single brahmin who says thus: 'I know this, I see this: only this is true, anything else is wrong'?" - "No, Master Gotama." - "How then, Bhāradvāja, among the brahmins is there even a single teacher or a single teacher's teacher back to the seventh generation of teachers who says thus: 'I know this, I see this: only this is true, anything else is wrong'?" - "No, Master Gotama." - "How then, Bhāradvāja, the ancient brahmin seers, the creators of the hymns, the composers of the hymns, whose ancient hymns that were formerly chanted, uttered, and compiled, the brahmins nowadays still chant and repeat, repeating what

was spoken and reciting what was recited - that is, Atthaka, Vamaka, Vamadeva, Vessamitta, Yamataggi, Angirasa, Bhāradvāja, Vasettha, Kassapa, and Bhagu - did even these ancient brahmin seers say thus: 'We know this, we see this: only this is true, anything else is wrong'?" - "No, Master Gotama." - "So, Bhāradvāja, it seems that among the brahmins there is not even a single brahmin who says thus: 'I know this, I see this: only this is true, anything else is wrong.' And among the brahmins there is not even a single teacher or a single teacher's teacher back to the seventh generation of teachers, who says thus: 'I know this, I see this: only this is true, anything else is wrong.' And the ancient brahmin seers, the creators of the hymns, the composers of the hymns... even these ancient brahmin seers did not say thus: 'We know this, we see this: only this is true, anything else is wrong.' Suppose there were a file of blind men each in touch with the next: the first one does not see, the middle one does not see, and the last one does not see. So too, Bhāradvāja, in regard to their statement the brahmins seem to be like a file of blind men: the first one does not see, the middle one does not see, and the last one does not see. What do you think, Bhāradvāja, that being so, does not the faith of the brahmins turn out to be groundless?"

14. "The brahmins honor this not only out of faith, Master Gotama. They also honor it as oral tradition." - "Bhāradvāja, first you took your stand on faith, now you speak of oral tradition. There are five things, Bhāradvāja, that may turn out in two different ways here and now. What five? Faith, approval, oral tradition, reasoned cogitation, and reflective acceptance of a view. These five things may turn out in two different ways here and now. Now something may be fully accepted out of faith, yet it may be empty, hollow, and false; but something else may not be fully accepted out of faith, yet it may be factual, true, and unmistaken. Again, something may be fully approved of... well transmitted... well cogitated... well reflected upon, yet it may be empty,

hollow, and false; but something else may not be well reflected upon, yet it may be factual, true, and unmistaken. [Under these conditions] it is not proper for a wise man who preserves truth to come to the definite conclusion: 'Only this is true, anything else is wrong.'"

15. "But, Master Gotama, in what way is there the preservation of truth? How does one preserve truth? We ask Master Gotama about the preservation of truth." - "If a person has faith, Bhāradvāja, he preserves truth when he says: 'My faith is thus;' but he does not yet come to the definite conclusion: 'Only this is true, anything else is wrong.' In this way, Bhāradvāja, there is the preservation of truth; in this way he preserves truth; in this way we describe the preservation of truth. But as yet there is no discovery of truth. "If a person approves of something... if he receives an oral tradition... if he [reaches a conclusion based on] reasoned cogitation... if he gains a reflective acceptance of a view, he preserves truth when he says: 'My reflective acceptance of a view is thus;' but he does not yet come to the definite conclusion: 'Only this is true, anything else is wrong.' In this way too, Bhāradvāja, there is the preservation of truth; in this way he preserves truth; in this way we describe the preservation of truth. But as yet there is no discovery of truth."

16. "In that way, Master Gotama, there is the preservation of truth; in that way one preserves truth; in that way we recognize the preservation of truth. But in what way, Master Gotama, is there the discovery of truth? In what way does one discover truth? We ask Master Gotama about the discovery of truth."

17. "Here, Bhāradvāja, a monk may be living in dependence on some village or town. Then a householder or a householder's son goes to him and investigates him in regard to three kinds of states: in regard to states based on greed, in regard to states based on hate, and in regard to states based on delusion: 'Are there in this venerable one

any states based on greed such that, with his mind obsessed by those states, while not knowing he might say, "I know," or while not seeing he might say, "I see," or he might urge others to act in a way that would lead to their harm and suffering for a long time?' As he investigates him he comes to know: 'There are no such states based on greed in this venerable one. The bodily behavior and the verbal behavior of this venerable one are not those of one affected by greed. And the Dhamma that this venerable one teaches is profound, hard to see and hard to understand, peaceful and sublime, unattainable by mere reasoning, subtle, to be experienced by the wise. This Dhamma cannot easily be taught by one affected by greed.'

18. "When he has investigated him and has seen that he is purified from states based on greed, he next investigates him in regard to states based on hate: 'Are there in this venerable one any states based on hate such that, with his mind obsessed by those states... he might urge others to act in a way that would lead to their harm and suffering for a long time?' As he investigates him, he comes to know: 'There are no such states based on hate in this venerable one. The bodily behavior and the verbal behavior of this venerable one are not those of one affected by hate. And the Dhamma that this venerable one teaches is profound... to be experienced by the wise. This Dhamma cannot easily be taught by one affected by hate.'

19. "When he has investigated him and has seen that he is purified from states based on hate, he next investigates him in regard to states based on delusion: 'Are there in this venerable one any states based on delusion such that, with his mind obsessed by those states... he might urge others to act in a way that would lead to their harm and suffering for a long time?'

BV: What is delusion? ... What is delusion? Anybody?

ST: Ignorance.

BV: Of what?

ST: The Truth.

BV: And what is the Truth?

ST: ??

BV: Delusion is the belief that thoughts and feelings are yours personally. It's when you have a deluded mind, that means you have atta (idea of self). When you have an undeluded mind it means anatta. So that'll help make this a little bit clearer.

As he investigates him, he comes to know: There are no such states based on delusion in this venerable one. The bodily behavior and the verbal behavior of this venerable one are not those of one affected by delusion. And the Dhamma that this venerable one teaches is profound... to be experienced by the wise.

Now what we're talking about here, is the seeing of Dependent Origination. That's what he's really talking about when he says you see... understood by and experienced by the wise. Wisdom, every time it's mentioned in the suttas, is talking about Dependent Origination.

This Dhamma cannot easily be taught by one affected by delusion.'

Now in some traditions, they call these the three poisons. And everybody knows what greed is, or lust, and hatred is, but almost nobody understands what delusion is. You should hear some of the answers I get when I ask people what delusion is. So, try to keep that in mind, that every time you relax, you're letting go of delusion. Because right after you relax, there's a clear space that has very good awareness in it, but there's no self identifying with it, it's just this pure awareness.

ST: So what is clinging?

BV: Clinging are all of the thoughts about whatever your craving is on. It's a feeling, at one of the sense doors, right? In order to see, you have good working eye, color and form; meeting the three is called contact. Now this is directly Dependent Origination. With contact as condition, feeling arises. With feeling as condition, craving arises. With craving as condition, clinging arises. This is your thoughts, your opinions, your imaginations, your story, your concepts. Basically your "thought-y" mind. And when you take an opinion or you take a concept, and you start saying "This is right! This is what I believe!," now you're attaching a lot of clinging onto that. And like it says here, maybe it's right and maybe it's not, it just depends. But when you see something without the clinging, and without the craving, you're seeing it with such a pure mind - you're seeing it with an arahat's mind.

ST: So you don't necessarily have to see each one of those things, because they may not be there.

BV: Well, when you let go of the craving, the clinging doesn't arise, the habitual tendency doesn't arise, and the rest of the Dependent Origination, the birth and the sorrow and lamentation and all that stuff doesn't arise either. So that's one of the reasons why craving is such a major thing that it's talked about in the suttas.

ST: So craving is the identification?

BV: It's the start of the identification process. Now when I'm telling you to look and see what happens in between the feeling and the craving, I'm telling you to look at craving even more closely. Because this is subtle stuff. And it always is the start of "I am that. I like that. I don't like that." When it gets into the clinging, that's when the big "Oh Yeah" and the attachment to the concepts and imaginations and ideas and story about, and taking it personally, and then your habitual tendency - which another monk in San Diego doesn't like that I use "habitual tendency" for bhava, because that's what it is. I had a major discussion with U Silananda about this and we agreed. The habitual tendency is your justification of your clinging, and you're holding onto that view. It's the thing that really grabs onto that view: "I'm right, you're wrong." And when you let go of craving, in its subtlest form, your mind is so pure, none of that other stuff comes into being. This is why craving is considered to be the weak link in Dependent Origination. Because there's no identification unless there is craving. Now, you have this pure awareness that you're able to see things.

ST: They always talk about if you see impermanence, suffering and no-self you will attain enlightenment. What about those?

BV: You see anicca, dukkha, anatta automatically. Because you're seeing, when you see Dependent Origination, you're seeing the arising and passing away of things. And you're seeing the cause and effect of these things. You're seeing that when you let go of the craving, there is no dukkha after that. But as long as there's even the littlest flash of craving, there is dukkha, and that is the identification with it. That is the "I"-dentification with it! And, that also very much clouds your experience.

For example, somebody calls me up on the phone and they tell me something that I don't like to hear and all of a sudden there's anger coming up. And that means that your habitual tendency of the way you look at the world is taking you completely away from the present moment. And it causes all kinds of pain and suffering to arise.

Because I put a stress on smiling, that helps your mind to be light enough to be able to catch these other things, so you stop identifying with them. You know "It's just this feeling, it's a painful feeling." Yeah, ok, so it's painful. So what? It's allowing the feeling to be, without reacting to it.

ST: So if you keep going with the smiling, you're keeping...

BV: You're keeping your mind open and light.

SK: Before this when I first met Bhante I was still working for a couple of CEO's, and he said, yes, you can use the mirror by the telephone... the mirror has to sit by the telephone. You're not allowed to handle any situations that come in on the telephone without the mirror being there. Watch yourself while you are talking in the mirror. Are you smiling? Are you frowning?

I had to sit one up there, you know, it's really funny. I kept forgetting to look at it...

BV: It's hard to be mad when you're smiling!

20. "When he has investigated him and has seen that he is purified from states based on delusion, then he places faith in him; filled with faith he visits him and pays respect to him; having paid respect to him, he gives ear; when he gives ear, he hears the Dhamma; having heard the Dhamma, he memorizes it and examines the meaning of the teachings he has memorized; when he examines their meaning, he gains a reflective acceptance of those teachings; when he has gained a reflective acceptance of those teachings, enthusiasm (zeal) springs up; when enthusiasm has sprung up, he applies his mindfulness; having applied his mindfulness, he scrutinizes; having scrutinized, he strives; resolutely striving, he realizes with the body the supreme truth and sees it by penetrating it with wisdom.

Now you start to get more of a feel for the suttas. The instructions are real simple, and yet very precise, and they go through everything. That's one of the things that just blew my mind when I started getting into them. I started seeing how absolutely precise he was by giving the instructions the way he did, that it works in every situation. And... oh man! That's why I went out for two weeks and wound up staying three months, I couldn't believe it! And I kept having to go back and say, "I wanna see that again."

In this way, Bhāradvāja, there is the discovery of truth; in this way one discovers truth; in this way we describe the discovery of truth. But as yet there is no final arrival at truth."

I wanna do this again just because it's really good...

{repeat} 20. **"When he has investigated him and has seen that he is purified from states based on delusion, then he places faith in him; filled with faith he visits him and pays respect to him; having paid respect to him, he gives ear; when he gives ear, he hears the Dhamma; having heard the Dhamma, he memorizes it and examines the meaning of the teachings he has memorized; when he examines their meaning, he gains a reflective acceptance of those teachings; when he has gained a reflective acceptance of those teachings, enthusiasm springs up; when enthusiasm has sprung up, he applies his mindfulness; having applied his mindfulness,**

That is he starts making the choices. Either, or not.

... he scrutinizes; having scrutinized, he strives; resolutely striving, he realizes with the body the supreme truth...

Now the body is the relaxing of the tension because it's done in the body and in the mind. That's another reason why the instructions in the Ānāpānasati Sutta are amazing, because it's only four sentences, and it tells you exactly you how to tranquilize the bodily formation! That means the subtle tightnesses that arise in body, when you do that, the tightnesses in the mind go away. It's really something! I mean it's way too simple for us folks. We have to have it much more complicated than that! Ha Ha!

and sees it [the process of dependent origination] by penetrating it with wisdom. In this way, Bhāradvāja, there is the discovery of truth; in this way one discovers truth; in this way we describe the discovery of truth. But as yet there is no final arrival at truth."

21. "In that way, Master Gotama, there is the discovery of truth; in that way one discovers truth; in that way we recognize the discovery of truth. But in what way, Master Gotama, is there the final arrival at truth? In what way does one finally arrive at truth? We ask Master Gotama about the final arrival at truth."

Now it's getting good!

"The final arrival at truth, Bhāradvāja, lies in the repetition, development, and cultivation of those same things.

The repetition... the development... and cultivation. The development is the development of the habit of letting go of craving, as soon as any tiny feeling starts to arise. So you can say, that as soon as feeling arises, and you relax right then, craving won't arise.

It's release, relax, and return to your object of meditation, and your object of meditation gets really subtle as if on the breath you start doing that, and you start seeing there's all kinds of other tiny, tiny little feelings that are there. And they keep getting more and more subtle, as you go deeper. Until finally you get to the state of neither perception nor non-perception, because you can't perceive whether there's any tension there or not. There still is, but you can't perceive it, in a regular way. When you get out of that state, then you start reflecting what you saw while you were in that state, and then you can say "Yes there's still this little tightness, so there still needs to be more of the relaxing while I'm in that state."

Now, this is where it gets tricky. Because when people practice one-pointed concentration, the breath just seems to disappear, and they don't see it anymore. But, according to some of the suttas, there is still the five aggregates that are present, even when you go into the arūpa jhānas. That means there's still contact, and there is still breath, causing that contact to arise. And the breath is the reminder to relax. And then it gets real subtle with the different things that start happening as you go deeper; it just gets great!

ST: But it seems like each time, it seems like each time that you release when you relax, that's the spot where it's like another lens comes in and you can see it a little more.

BV: Right, but it's only teeny, tiny at a time.

ST: If you release and you don't relax, and then let the lens focus down and then- you look, you'll start to notice that it's deeper and it's deeper, and the subtle little things like when you're looking at the stuff in nothingness and neither perception nor non-perception, it's so completely subtle, but if you start to go through the different pieces...

BV: That's why the development of the habitual tendency of relaxing...

ST: Right. It's really important.

I have a tendency to get absorbed into the perception or non-perception then it's just like gone and later it's like come back again.

BV: Yeah, that's the way it is, but then you have to reflect on what's happening in there. By the time you get to that state, you should have developed the habit of relaxing often. But you don't see any breath at that time. You don't see, you just see, there are some mental things that happen while you're in there.

ST: But there's this realization that absorption has taken place

BV: But it's really absorption then you are suppressing the arising of other things. It's just the subtler and subtler vibrations of mind when you use the relax step. It's not really being absorbed. Because by that time you should still have that habit of relaxing.

ST: Remember a student that was on retreat got absorbed into that state? Remember how she used to say when she came out she couldn't remember anything. There wasn't anything to remember. It was absorption. But a couple times she did experience, you know where she could walk around afterwards and she could remember a little bit of what was going on, and that's what you mean, the awareness is afterwards, right?

BV: Well, no the awareness is there, but it's hard to tell whether it's there, and there is still a little bit of feeling perception and consciousness there. That's not the state of neither perception and feeling, nor, you know, neither/or with perception and feeling; it's just perception. The feeling and consciousness are still there, and that's the thing that's still vibrating a little bit. Then when you get to the cessation of the perception and feeling and consciousness , that's when everything stops. And that's why you need to have that habit of relaxing. Because every time you relax, the vibration becomes less, and less, and less, and less, until it does finally stops.

ST: And then Dependent Origination arises?

When the perception, feeling and consciousness start arising again, that's when your mindfulness is so incredibly sharp that you see exactly how the links of dependent origination occurs. You see the cause and effect, and you see when this doesn't arise, that won't arise, and you see the cessation. And then, the big WHOOPEE! Great stuff!

In this way, Bhāradvāja, there is the final arrival at truth; in this way one finally arrives at truth; in this way we describe the final arrival at truth."

22. "In that way, Master Gotama, there is the final arrival at truth; in that way one finally arrives at truth; in that way we recognize the final arrival at truth. But what, Master Gotama, is most helpful for the final arrival at truth?

Good question!

We ask Master Gotama about the thing most helpful for the final arrival at truth." - "Striving is most helpful for the final arrival at truth, Bhāradvāja. If one does not strive, one will not finally arrive at truth; but because one strives, one

does finally arrive at truth. That is why striving is most helpful for the final arrival at truth."

This is why it is so important that we uses the 6R's and the relax step all of the time!

23. "But what, Master Gotama, what is most helpful for striving? We ask Master Gotama about the thing most helpful for striving." - "Scrutiny...

I don't like this word. Instead of "scrutiny," I much rather prefer "interest." The more interest you have in the subtlety of how things are working, now you're scrutinizing it, yes you are, but it's the interest, it's the thing that just keeps you going with it, like "Wow, look at that, this is great stuff!" And you have to do this in a balanced way.

Scrutiny is most helpful for striving, Bhāradvāja. If one does not scrutinize, one will not strive; but because one scrutinizes, one strives. That is why scrutiny is most helpful for striving."

24. "But what, Master Gotama, is most helpful for scrutiny? We ask Master Gotama about the thing most helpful for scrutiny." - "Application of mindfulness

The conscious decision to keep doing this. Keep relaxing.

is most helpful for scrutiny, Bhāradvāja. If one does not apply one's mindfulness, one will not scrutinize; but because one applies one's mindfulness, one scrutinizes. That is why application of mindfulness is most helpful for scrutiny."

25. "But what, Master Gotama, is most helpful for application of mindfulness? We ask the Master Gotama about the thing most helpful for application of mindfulness." - "Enthusiasm is most helpful for application of mindfulness, Bhāradvāja. If one does not arouse enthusiasm, one will not apply one's mindfulness; but because one arouses enthusiasm, one applies one's

mindfulness. That is why enthusiasm is most helpful for application of mindfulness."

26. "But what, Master Gotama, is most helpful for enthusiasm? We ask Master Gotama about the thing most helpful for enthusiasm." - "A reflective acceptance of the teachings is most helpful for enthusiasm, Bhāradvāja. If one does not gain a reflective acceptance of the teachings, enthusiasm will not spring up; but because one gains a reflective acceptance of the teachings, enthusiasm springs up. That is why a reflective acceptance of the teachings is most helpful for enthusiasm."

27. "But what, Master Gotama, is most helpful for a reflective acceptance of the teachings? We ask Master Gotama about the thing most helpful for a reflective acceptance of the teachings." - "Examination of the meaning is most helpful for a reflective acceptance of the teachings, Bhāradvāja. If one does not examine their meaning, one will not gain a reflective acceptance of the teachings; but because one examines their meaning, one gains a reflective acceptance of the teachings. That is why examination of the meaning is most helpful for a reflective acceptance of the teachings."

28. "But what, Master Gotama, is most helpful for examination of the meaning? We ask Master Gotama about the thing most helpful for examination of meaning." - "Memorizing the teachings is most helpful for examining the meaning, Bhāradvāja. If one does not memorize a teaching, one will not examine its meaning; but because one memorizes a teaching, one examines its meaning."

29. "But what, Master Gotama, is most helpful for memorizing the teachings? We ask Master Gotama about the thing most helpful for memorizing the teachings." - "Hearing the Dhamma is most helpful for memorizing the teachings, Bhāradvāja. If one does not hear the Dhamma, one will not memorize the teachings; but because one hears the Dhamma, one memorizes the teachings. That is why

hearing the Dhamma is most helpful for memorizing the teachings."

30. "But what, Master Gotama, is most helpful for hearing the Dhamma? We ask Master Gotama about the thing most helpful for hearing the Dhamma." - "Giving ear is most helpful for hearing the Dhamma, Bhāradvāja. If one does not give ear, one will not hear the Dhamma; but because one gives ear, one hears the Dhamma. That is why giving ear is most helpful for hearing the Dhamma."

31. "But what, Master Gotama, is most helpful for giving ear? We ask Master Gotama about the thing most helpful for giving ear." - "Paying respect is most helpful for giving ear, Bhāradvāja. If one does not pay respect, one will not give ear; but because one pays respect, one gives ear. That is why paying respect is most helpful for giving ear."

32. "But what, Master Gotama, is most helpful for paying respect? We ask Master Gotama about the thing most helpful for paying respect." - "Visiting is most helpful for paying respect, Bhāradvāja. If one does not visit [a teacher], one will not pay respect to him; but because one visits [a teacher], one pays respect to him. That is why visiting is most helpful for paying respect."

33. "But what, Master Gotama, is most helpful for visiting? We ask Master Gotama about the thing most helpful for visiting." - "Faith is most helpful for visiting, Bhāradvāja. If faith [in a teacher] does not arise, one will not visit him; but because faith [in a teacher] arises, one visits him. That is why faith is most helpful for visiting."

34. "We asked Master Gotama about the preservation of truth, and Master Gotama answered about the preservation of truth; we approve of and accept that answer, and so we are satisfied. We asked Master Gotama about the discovery of truth, and Master Gotama answered about the discovery of truth; we approve of and accept that answer, and so we are satisfied. We asked Master Gotama about the final

arrival at truth, and Master Gotama answered about the final arrival at truth; we approve of and accept that answer, and so we are satisfied. We asked Master Gotama about the thing most helpful for the final arrival at truth, and Master Gotama answered about the thing most helpful for the final arrival at truth; we approve of and accept that answer, and so we are satisfied. Whatever we asked Master Gotama about, that he has answered us; we approve of and accept that answer, and so we are satisfied. Formerly, Master Gotama, we used to think: 'Who are these bald-pated recluses, these swarthy menial offspring of the Kinsman's feet, that they would understand the Dhamma?' But Master Gotama has indeed inspired in me love for recluses, confidence in recluses, reverence for recluses.

35. "Magnificent, Master Gotama! Magnificent. From today let Master Gotama remember me as a lay follower who has gone to him for refuge for life."

That's a really, it was a major coup, this particular sutta, when he gave it to this young Brahman student, because there were so many other Brahman teachers around at that time, and they all accepted the Buddha's teaching, and they let go of the Brahmanism of a permanent self. A lot of people became awakened with this particular sutta.

I like that sutta a lot. I really do. And it touches on things that, if you don't really have a practice you would never understand the subtleties of what the Buddha was talking about with this particular sutta. You can go to some of the Dhamma teachers, just some of the big teachers in this country that really are renowned for their scholarship, and because they don't have the practice in the same way that the Buddha was describing, they will skip over some of the finer points of what is in the Teachings.

Like what is delusion? And what you gave was a good answer. But it wasn't as precise as it could be, that's why I kept going with that, so that you could see that yes, what you said was true, but you have to go deeper. And then you gave another answer, and you have go deeper still.

And as far as I can see, seeing the characteristics of all existence always, well, it just boils down to one characteristic. And that is, anatta. When you see everything that arises, every one of the links of Dependent Origination as being an impersonal process, it's just a cause and effect thing that's happening, and when you see that in each one of those links, that to me is when you actually get the deep realization that this is the way it is. And with that deep understanding, there's that openness. And Nibbāna occurs because of that, because of that deep understanding.

And each level of the jhāna is another level of your understanding of the process, because you're going more and more subtle all the time, and you're starting to see little tiny things, where before you were seeing these huge movements.

And you got real enthusiastic because you could see those, now you're starting to work with the real fine stuff. And trying to keep your meditation going all of the time. I don't care what you're doing, keep your meditation going, keep relaxing, keep letting go. You have a thought, and the thought might all of a sudden be "It shouldn't be like this" - a critical thought. Now that's anger. That's aversion. That's dislike of the feeling of whatever sense door it was that caused that to arise. And you get a chance to see how really fast that comes, and then all of a sudden you're caught in your habitual tendency. And the faster you can recognize that and let it go, the easier everything becomes. And the more subtleness you start to see when you're able to do that.

Doing the daily activities is a very important part of the practice because that's when your calmness isn't as deep as it could be, and you still get to see some of the old tendencies come up.

Now when I would tell people that I don't want them to take anything seriously, and to smile into everything, there's a definite reason for doing that. Because when you have that smile going into what you're doing in the present moment, you can start to see that happen. And you start to see, "That's painful, I don't wanna do that anymore" and then you start changing the old way of, whenever this feeling arises, then this always happens. And when you're able to do that, there's a freedom, and a happiness that comes that's just remarkable.

Nibbāna is what we want in this lifetime, that's really true, but we have to have a lot of mundane Nibbānas occur before we get the big "Oh Wow!," before the big Nibbāna, the supramundane, occurs. And that means we have to start letting go of more and more subtleties about how mind grabs onto things. And being able to let those go and relax into them.

There's two things that happen when you start doing this. One, you learn how to let go of the control. Like we've all developed for I don't know how many lifetimes, the idea that, with our mind, we can control what happens. And when we can't see , that's when the dissatisfaction comes up. So what you're doing, every time you relax, is you're letting go of the idea that there is any controller at all. And as you do that, more and more, then you start developing this lighter, more alert mind. So the smile, as dumb as it sounds, is a key that really helps. And the lighter you can keep your mind, with the attitudes, the opinions, the concepts, the imaginations, the projections, all of these, you start letting go of those, because they really don't matter, they're only your ideas about what the truth is, and looking at the underlying cause of that; which is always the craving and clinging and perception.

Why do we do what we do?

ST: One of the things that I find interesting is the awareness of where the decision is being made. For example you might be driving in a car, and you might be coming up to an intersection that allows you to take a different route to your destination. And at that intersection there's two choices, and both of them are equally the same, but somehow a decision gets made to take this one or that one. And it's like, why did that happen?

BV: It happened because of past experience. And it's not necessarily just because of past experience in this lifetime. The intuition, that little quiet voice that says stuff, and it's always right, that is from your wholesome nature of past lifetimes, arising right now. And then it comes to the point, and it says "Turn left here." And that's where your decision, if the intuition is strong enough, you'll just follow it without considering it. If it's not, then you'll have the craving and the clinging get into it, and the justifying mind that says "No, I don't wanna turn here, I wanna go there."

ST: I remember my dad was kind of funny, he would never at a fork in a road go left, it was just weird.

BV: That might've happened from ten lifetimes of having something bad happen when he went left.

ST: I distinctly remember my mother getting real mad at him once because she knew that where we were supposed to go was right down there, and he made this weak guess and justification and went the other way. It wasn't like they were bad people at the time or anything, it was just the habit.

It's the point of decision that I find kind of curious, because it doesn't seem conscious. It doesn't even seem intuitive. It's just all of a sudden, "Oh I'm going this way." Where was that decision made? You know?

BV: Subtle stuff!

But it gets incredibly fun to watch. I mean, everything comes into it. You know that I like to do repetitious things, like that picture that I made for you, with those little pieces of string. That repetition gives me the opportunity to watch how my mind is working. And I love that.

But, other people don't like it, they say it's boring, but it's anything but boring to me! It's doing the same movements over and over again, but being able to watch what my mind is doing while I'm doing that. Because that is basically what you're doing when you're sitting. You're watching your breath, you're doing it over and over again, you're not moving your body. It's basically doing the same thing. And you have to learn, when you first start, you have to learn that, yes, boredom is going to come up, and welcome to the real world, and whose boredom is it, and what do you do when you get bored, and how do you distract yourself so that you won't have that? And then when you go through that, doors all of a sudden open up, and everything becomes real interesting.

ST: That's like pulling weeds in the garden. It becomes a very dynamic kind of meditation practice.

BV: It is. It really is. And you have to be careful while you're doing it, or else you'll screw up, and pull the wrong plants, or miss something, or whatever.

One of the things that Bhikkhu Bodhi does in this book is he uses the word "extirpate." So when he goes to pull weeds, he's going to extirpate the weeds.

ST: Liberate the weeds!

BV: Pulling out by the root.

Any question about your practice at all?

ST: I sometimes feel like I'm floundering around, but I think I got some clarity tonight. I'm watching the breath, and relaxing the mind, and it's kind of, almost mantra-like, it's a rote.

BV: But watch the littleness, it gets real interesting. Don't put your mind on automatic while you're doing it. When you do things by rote, you have a tendency to think while you're doing it.

ST: I'm not thinking. But it's just that I'm staying with it, but it's... it doesn't seem like a real depth of investigation.

BV: Well take more interest in it. The more interested you get, the more enthusiasm you get, the deeper you go, that's just, it's such subtle things. You have to really be careful with your energy because if you put too much in, your mind is going to start to get a little restless. That doesn't necessarily mean that you're going to have a lot of thoughts, but the restlessness is a feeling that's a painful feeling, and there is reaction to that. And if you don't put quite enough energy into it, you go into the dullness. You're not going to go into sleepiness so much anymore. But your mind is just going to dull out a little bit. When your mind gets dull, you'll hit the space, where it's just like your mind just blanks. It's just like somebody took the eraser and cleaned off the board. Ok that's because you're not putting enough effort and energy into watching. So take more interest in how that happens. And also you have to be careful of your body energy too. Because that will happen when your body energy starts to go down. When that happens, that's a sign that you need to get up and walk.

Now also watch when we do this in the morning, how your mind doesn't really want to, so it just kind of puts it on automatic. Don't let it. I mean, really do it. There's a reason for doing this. And that's just showing you another set of your clinging and your attachment. "This is boring, I do it everyday, I don't really like doing it, I don't wanna do it... But I'll do it anyway." But that has a lot of aversion in it. So let go of the aversion and things will come alive for you when you're doing this. I mean it's really amazing.

ST: Hallelujah!

BV: Let's share some merit.

May suffering ones be suffering free
And the fear struck fearless be.
May the grieving shed all grief
And may all beings find relief.
May all beings share this merit
That we have thus acquired
For the acquisition of
All kind of happiness.
May beings inhabiting space and earth
Devas and Nagas of mighty power
Share in this merit of ours.
May they long protect
the Buddha's Dispensation.
Sādhu… Sādhu… Sādhu…

MN-148: The Six Sets of Six (Chachakka Sutta)

This is one of the small group of Suttas at the conclusion of which we find large numbers of bhikkhus attaining Arahantship. Now the text looks dry enough and very repetitious, so why didn't they yawn and go to sleep? That shows the difference between the mind of a person who has practiced Dhamma intensively gradually building up his power of understanding and people like ourselves who find it difficult to take much interest in 'dry' material.

Of course, the Buddha spoke this discourse. He spoke it no doubt in measured phrases and with that peculiar beauty that the Pàli of the Suttas has. The bhikkhus who were listening were also seated in meditation posture and checking up on his words in themselves as he went on. And then there is the great force of the many repetitions, to drum the teaching home, to ensure that it was clearly seen by those bhikkhus in their own minds and bodies.

In the first part of the Sutta the process of perception from the six sense bases to the arising of craving is described, step by step. The second part takes the six steps for each sense base and analyzes them to see that there is no lasting entity there called 'self' or 'soul'. How the idea of self comes into being is described in the third part and how it ceases in the fourth. Of great importance is the fifth section on the underlying tendencies and how they arise and how they cease to arise. The conclusion illustrates the Arhant's dispassion.

The Buddha, in this way led those sixty bhikkhus to the highest attainment and we do not doubt that they 'delighted in the Blessed One's words'.[6]

Presented on August 2011 at Dhamma Sukha Meditation Center

(Note: The word "Students" has been put in place of the word "Bhikkhus.")

BV: This particular sutta is probably one of the most powerful suttas in the Majjhima Nikaya. This is called The Six Sets of

---

[6] *Ibid.*

Six, the Chachakka Sutta, number 148. It's translated by Bhikkhu Bodhi and published by Wisdom Publications.

Now what I've done is I've taken a lot of the ditto marks out, and left the repetition in, so there is going to be a lot of repetition with this sutta. If you listen closely, it will help your meditation very much.

1. "THUS HAVE I HEARD. On one occasion the Blessed One was living at Sāvatthi in Jeta's Grove, Anāthanpiṇḍika's Park. There he addressed the students thus: "Students." - "Venerable sir," they replied. The Blessed One said this:

2. "Students, I shall teach you the Dhamma that is good in the beginning, good in the middle, and good in the end, with the right meaning and phrasing; I shall reveal a holy life that is utterly perfect and pure, that is, the six sets of six. Listen and attend closely to what I shall say." - "Yes, venerable sir," the students replied. The Blessed One said this:

(Synopsis)

3. "The six internal bases should be understood. The six external bases should be understood. The six classes of consciousness should be understood. The six classes of contact should be understood. The six classes of feeling should be understood. The six classes of craving should be understood.

(Enumeration)

4. (i) " 'The six internal bases should be understood.' So it was said. And with reference to what was this said? There are the eye-base, the ear-base, the nose-base, the tongue-base, the body-base, and the mind-base. So it was with reference to this that it was said: 'The six internal bases should be understood.' This is the first set of six.

5. (ii) " 'The six external bases should be understood.' So it was said. And with reference to what was this said? There

are the form-base, the sound-base, the odor-base, the flavor-base, the tangible-base, and the mind-object-base. So it was with reference to this that it was said: 'The six external bases should be understood.' This is the second set of six.

6. (iii) " 'The six classes of consciousness should be understood.' So it was said. And with reference to what was this said? Dependent on the eye and forms, eye-consciousness arises; dependent on the ear and sounds, ear-consciousness arises; dependent on the nose and odors, nose-consciousness arises; dependent on tongue and flavors, tongue-consciousness arises; dependent on the body and tangibles, body-consciousness arises; dependent on mind and mind-objects, mind-consciousness arises. So it was with reference to this that it was said: 'The six classes of consciousness should be understood.' This is the third set of six.

7. (iv) " 'The six classes of contact should be understood.' So it was said. And with reference to what was this said? Dependent on the eye and forms, eye-consciousness arises; the meeting of the three is eye-contact. Dependent on the ear and sounds, ear-consciousness arises; the meeting of the three is ear-contact. Dependent on the nose and odors, nose-consciousness arises; the meeting of the three is nose-contact. Dependent on the tongue and flavors, tongue-consciousness arises; the meeting of the three is tongue-contact. Dependent on body and tangibles, body-consciousness arises; the meeting of the three is body-contact. Dependent on mind and mind-objects, mind-consciousness arises; the meeting of the three is mind-contact. So it was with reference to this that it was said: 'The six classes of contact should be understood.' This is the fourth set of six.

8. (v) " 'The six classes of feeling should be understood.' So it was said. And with reference to what was this said? Dependent on the eye and forms, eye-consciousness arises; with the meeting of the three there is eye-contact; with eye-

contact as condition there is eye-feeling. Dependent on the ear and sounds, ear-consciousness arises; with the meeting of the three there is ear-contact; with ear-contact as condition there is ear-feeling. Dependent on the nose and odors, nose-consciousness arises; with the meeting of the three there is nose-contact; with nose-contact as condition there is nose-feeling. Dependent on the tongue and flavors, tongue-consciousness arises; with the meeting of the three there is tongue-contact; with tongue-contact as condition there is tongue-feeling. Dependent on the body and tangibles, body-consciousness arises; with the meeting of the three there is body-contact; with body-contact as condition there is body-feeling. Dependent on the mind and mind-objects, mind-consciousness arises; with the meeting of the three there is mind-contact; with mind-contact as condition there is mind-feeling. So it was with reference to this that it was said: 'The six classes of feeling should be understood.' This is the fifth set of six.

9. (vi) " 'The six classes of craving should be understood.' So it was said. And with reference to what was this said? Dependent on the eye and forms, eye-consciousness arises; the meeting of the three is eye-contact; with eye-contact as condition there is eye-feeling; with eye-feeling as condition there is eye-craving. Dependent on the ear and sounds, ear-consciousness arises; the meeting of the three is ear-contact; with ear-contact as condition there is ear-feeling; with ear-feeling as condition there is ear-craving. Dependent on the nose and odors, nose-consciousness arises; the meeting of the three is nose-contact; with nose-contact as condition there is nose-feeling; with nose-feeling as condition there is nose-craving. Dependent on the tongue and flavors, tongue-consciousness arises; the meeting of the three is tongue-contact; with tongue-contact as condition there is tongue-feeling; with tongue-feeling as condition there is tongue-craving. Dependent on the body and tangibles, body-consciousness arises; the meeting of the three is body-contact; with body-contact as condition there is body-

feeling; with body-feeling as condition there is body-craving. Dependent on mind and mind-objects, mind-consciousness arises; the meeting of the three is mind-contact; with mind-contact as condition there is mind-feeling; with mind-feeling as condition there is mind-craving. So it was with reference to this that it was said: 'The six classes of craving should be understood.' This is the sixth set of six.

(Demonstration of Not-Self)

10. (i) "If anyone says, 'The eye is self,' that is not acceptable. The rise and fall of the eye is seen and understood, and since its rise and fall are discerned, it would follow: 'My self rises and falls.' That is why it is not acceptable for anyone to say, 'The eye is self.' Thus the eye is not self.

"If anyone says, 'Forms are self,' that is not acceptable. The rise and fall of forms are seen and understood, and since their rise and fall are discerned, it would follow: 'My self rises and falls.' That is why it is not acceptable for anyone to say, 'Forms are self.' Thus the eye is not self, forms are not self.

"If anyone says, 'Eye-consciousness is self,' that is not acceptable. The rise and fall of eye-consciousness is seen and understood, and since its rise and fall are discerned, it would follow: 'My self rises and falls.' That is why it is not acceptable for anyone to say, 'Eye-consciousness is self.' Thus eye is not self, forms are not self, eye-consciousness is not self.

"If anyone says, 'Eye-contact is self,' that is not acceptable. The rise and fall of eye-contact is seen and understood, and since its rise and fall are discerned, it would follow: 'My self rises and falls.' That is why it is not acceptable for anyone to say, 'Eye-contact is self.' Thus eye is not self, forms are not self, eye-consciousness is not self, eye-contact is not self.

"If anyone says, 'Eye-feeling is self,'" that is not acceptable. The rise and fall of the eye-feeling is seen and understood, and since its rise and fall are discerned, it would follow: 'My self rises and falls.' That is why it is not acceptable for anyone to say 'Eye-feeling is self'. Thus the eye is not self, forms are not self, eye-consciousness is not self, eye-contact is not self, eye-feeling is not self.

"If anyone says, 'Eye-craving is self,' that is not acceptable. The rise and fall of eye-craving is seen and understood, and since its rise and fall are discerned, it would follow, 'My self rises and falls'. That is why it is not acceptable for anyone to say 'Eye-craving is self'. Thus eye is not self, forms are not self, eye-consciousness is not self, eye-contact is not self, eye-feeling is not self, eye-craving is not self.

11. (ii) "If anyone says, 'The ear is self,' that is not acceptable. The rise and fall of the ear is seen and understood, and since its rise and fall are discerned, it would follow: 'My self rises and falls.' That is why it is not acceptable for anyone to say, 'The ear is self.' Thus the ear is not self.

"If anyone says, 'Sounds are self,' that is not acceptable. The rise and fall of sounds are seen and understood, and since their rise and fall are discerned, it would follow: 'My self rises and falls.' That is why it is not acceptable for anyone to say, 'Sounds are self.' Thus the ear is not self, sounds are not self.

"If anyone says, 'Ear-consciousness is self,' that is not acceptable. The rise and fall of ear-consciousness is seen and understood, and since its rise and fall are discerned, it would follow: 'My self rises and falls.' That is why it is not acceptable for anyone to say, 'Ear-consciousness is self.' Thus the ear is not self, sounds are not self, ear-consciousness is not self.

"If anyone says, 'Ear-contact is self,' that is not acceptable. The rise and fall of ear-contact is seen and understood, and since its rise and fall are discerned, it would follow: 'My self rises and falls.' That is why it is not acceptable for anyone to say, 'Ear-contact is self.' Thus the ear is not self, sounds are not self, ear-consciousness is not self, ear-contact is not self.

"If anyone says, 'Ear-feeling is self,' that is not acceptable. The rise and fall of ear-feeling is seen and understood, and since its rise and fall are discerned, it would follow: 'My self rises and falls.' That is why it is not acceptable for anyone to say, 'Ear-feeling is self'. Thus the ear is not self, sounds are not self, ear-consciousness is not self, ear-contact is not self, ear-feeling is not self.

"If anyone says, 'Ear-craving is self,' that is not acceptable. The rise and fall of ear-craving is seen and understood, and since its rise and fall are discerned, it would follow: 'My self rises and falls'. That is why it is not acceptable for anyone to say, 'Ear-craving is self'. Thus the ear is not self, sounds are not self, ear-consciousness is not self, ear-contact is not self, ear-feeling is not self, ear-craving is not self.

12. (iii) "If anyone says, 'The nose is self,' that is not acceptable. The rise and fall of the nose is seen and understood, and since its rise and fall are discerned, it follows: 'My self rises and falls'. That is why it is not acceptable for anyone to say, 'The nose is self'. Thus the nose is not self.

"If anyone says, 'Odors are self,' that is not acceptable. The rise and fall of odors are seen and understood, and since their rise and fall are discerned, it follows: 'My self rises and falls'. That is why it is not acceptable for any one to say, 'Odors are self'. Thus the nose is not self, odors are not self.

"If anyone says, 'Nose-consciousness is self,' that is not acceptable. The rise and fall of nose-consciousness is seen and understood, and since its rise and fall are discerned, it follows: 'My self rises and falls'. That is why it is not acceptable for any one to say, 'Nose-consciousness is self'.

Thus the nose is not self, odors are not self, nose-consciousness is not self.

"If anyone says, 'Nose-contact is self,' that is not acceptable. The rise and fall of nose-contact is seen and understood, and since its rise and fall are discerned, it follows: 'My self rises and falls'. That is why it is not acceptable for any one to say, 'Nose-contact is self'. Thus the nose is not self, odors are not self, nose-consciousness is not self, nose-contact is not self.

"If anyone says, 'Nose-feeling is self,' that is not acceptable. The rise and fall of nose-feeling is seen and understood, and since its rise and fall are discerned, it follows: 'My self rises and falls'. That is why it is not acceptable for anyone to say, 'Nose-feeling is self'. Thus nose is not self, odors are not self, nose-consciousness is not self, nose-contact is not self, nose-feeling is not self.

"If anyone says, 'Nose-craving is self,' that is not acceptable. The rise and fall of nose-craving is seen and understood, and since its rise and fall are discerned, it follows: 'My self rises and falls'. That is why it is not acceptable for anyone to say, 'Nose-craving is self'. Thus nose is not self, odors are not self, nose-consciousness is not self, nose-contact is not self, nose-feeling is not self, nose-craving is not self.

13. (iv) "If anyone says, 'The tongue is self,' that is not acceptable. The rise and fall of the tongue is seen and understood, and since its rise and fall are discerned, it would follow: 'My self rises and falls.' That is why it is not acceptable for anyone to say, 'The tongue is self.' Thus the tongue is not self.

"If anyone says, 'Flavors are self,' that is not acceptable. The rise and fall of flavors are seen and understood, and since their rise and fall are discerned, it would follow: 'My self rises and falls.' That is why it is not acceptable for anyone to say, 'Flavors are self.' Thus the tongue is not self, flavors are not self.

"If anyone says, 'Tongue-consciousness is self,' that is not acceptable. The rise and fall of tongue-consciousness is seen and understood, and since its rise and fall are discerned, it would follow: 'My self rises and falls.' That is why it is not acceptable for anyone to say, 'Tongue-consciousness is self'. Thus the tongue is not self, flavors are not self, tongue-consciousness is not self.

"If anyone says, 'Tongue-contact is self,' that is not acceptable. The rise and fall of tongue-contact is seen and understood, and since its rise and fall are discerned, it would follow: 'My self rises and falls.' That is why it is not acceptable for anyone to say, 'Tongue-contact is self'. Thus the tongue is not self, flavors are not self, tongue-consciousness is not self, tongue-contact is not self.

"If anyone says, 'Tongue-feeling is self,' that is not acceptable. The rise and fall of tongue-feeling is seen and understood, and since its rise and fall are discerned, it would follow: 'My self rises and falls'. That is why it is not acceptable for anyone to say, 'Tongue-feeling is self'. Thus the tongue is not self, Flavors are not self, tongue-consciousness is not self, tongue-contact is not self, tongue-feeling is not self.

"If anyone says, 'Tongue-craving is self,' that is not acceptable. The rise and fall of tongue-craving is seen and understood, and since its rise and fall are discerned, it would follow: 'My self rises and falls'. That is why it is not acceptable for anyone to say, 'Tongue-craving is self'. Thus the tongue is not self, flavors are not self, tongue-consciousness are not self, tongue-contact is not self, tongue-feeling is not self, tongue-craving is not self.

14. (v) "If anyone says, 'The body is self,' that is not acceptable. The rise and fall of the body is seen and understood, and since its rise and fall are discerned, it would follow: 'My self rises and falls'. That is why it is not acceptable for anyone to say, 'The body is self'. Thus the body is not self.

"If anyone says, 'Tangibles are self,' that is not acceptable. The rise and fall of tangibles are seen and understood, and since their rise and fall are discerned, it would follow: 'My self rises and falls'. That is why it is not acceptable for anyone to say, 'Tangibles are self'. Thus the body is not self, tangibles are not self.

"If anyone says, 'Body-consciousness is self,' that is not acceptable. The rise and fall of body-consciousness is seen and understood, and since its rise and fall are discerned, it would follow: 'My self rises and falls'. That is why it is not acceptable for anyone to say, 'Body-consciousness is self'. Thus the body is not self, tangibles are not self, body-consciousness is not self.

"If anyone says, 'Body-contact is self,' that is not acceptable. The rise and fall of body-contact is seen and understood, and since its rise and fall are discerned, it would follow: 'My self rises and falls'. That is why it is not acceptable for anyone to say, 'Body-contact is self'. Thus the body is not self, tangibles are not self, body-consciousness is not self, body-contact is not self.

"If anyone says, 'Body-feeling is self,' that is not acceptable. The rise and fall of body-feeling is seen and understood, and since its rise and fall are discerned, it would follow: 'My self rises and falls'. That is why it is not acceptable for anyone to say, 'Body-feeling is self'. Thus the body is not self, tangibles are not self, body-consciousness is not self, body-contact is not self, body-feeling is not self.

"If anyone says, 'Body-craving is self,' that is not acceptable. The rise and fall of body craving is seen and understood, and since its rise and fall are discerned, it would follow: 'My self rises and falls'. That is why it is not acceptable for anyone to say, 'Body-craving is self'. Thus the body is not self, tangibles are not self, body-consciousness is not self, body-contact is not self, body-feeling is not self, body-craving is not self.

15. (vi) "If anyone says, 'The mind is self,' that is not acceptable. The rise and fall of mind is seen and understood, and since its rise and fall are discerned, it would follow: 'My self rises and falls'. That is why it is not acceptable for anyone to say, 'The mind is self'. Thus mind is not self.

"If anyone says, 'Mind-objects are self,' that is not acceptable. The rise and fall of mind-objects is seen and understood, and since their rise and fall are discerned, it would follow: 'My self rises and falls'. That is why it is not acceptable for anyone to say, 'Mind-objects are self'. Thus mind is not self, mind-objects are not self.

"If anyone says, 'Mind-consciousness is self,' that is not acceptable. The rise and fall of mind-consciousness is seen and understood, and since its rise and fall are discerned, it would follow: 'My self rises and falls'. That is why it is not acceptable for anyone to say, 'Mind-consciousness is self'. Thus mind is not self, mind-objects are not self, mind-consciousness is not self.

"If anyone says, 'Mind-contact is self,' that is not acceptable. The rise and fall of mind-contact is seen and understood, and since its rise and fall are discerned, it would follow: 'My self rises and falls'. That is why it is not acceptable for anyone to say, 'Mind-contact is self'. Thus mind is not self, mind-objects are not self, mind-consciousness is not self, mind-contact is not self.

"If anyone says, 'Mind-feeling is self,' that is not acceptable. The rise and fall of mind-feeling is seen and understood, and since its rise and fall are discerned, it would follow: 'My self rises and falls'. That is why it is not acceptable for anyone to say, 'Mind-feeling is self'. Thus mind is not self, mind-objects are not self, mind-consciousness is not self, mind-contact is not self, mind-feeling is not self.

"If anyone says, 'Mind-craving is self,' that is not acceptable. The rise and fall of mind-craving is seen and understood, and since its rise and fall are discerned, it would follow: 'My self rises and falls'. That is why it is not acceptable for anyone to say, 'Mind-craving is self'. Thus mind is not self, mind-objects are not self, mind-consciousness is not self, mind-contact is not self, mind-feeling is not self, mind-craving is not self.

(The Origination of Identity)

16. "Now, Students, this is the way leading to the origination of identity. (i) One regards the eye thus: 'This is mine, this I am, this is my self.' One regards forms thus: 'This is mine, this I am, this is my self.' One regards eye-consciousness thus: 'This is mine, this I am, this is my self.' One regards eye-contact thus: 'This is mine, this I am, this is my self.' One regards eye-feeling thus: 'This is mine, this I am, this is my self.' One regards eye-craving thus: 'This is mine, this I am, this is my self.'

17. (ii) "One regards ear thus: 'This is mine, this I am, this is my self.' One regards sounds thus: 'This is mine, this I am, this is my self.' One regards ear-consciousness thus: 'This is mine, this I am, this is my self.' One regards ear-contact thus: 'This is mine, this I am, this is my self.' One regards ear-feeling thus: 'This is mine, this I am, this is my self.' One regards ear-craving thus: 'This is mine, this I am, this is my self.'

18. (iii) "One regards nose thus: 'This is mine, this I am, this is my self.' One regards odors thus: 'This is mine, this I am, this is my self'. One regards nose-consciousness thus: 'This is mine, this I am, this is my self'. One regards nose-contact thus: 'This is mine, this I am, this is my self'. One regards nose-feeling thus: 'This is mine, this I am, this is my self'. One regards nose-craving thus: 'This is mine, this I am, this is myself'.

19. (iv) "One regards tongue thus: 'This is mine, this I am, this is my self'. One regards flavors thus: 'This is mine, this I am, this is my self'. One regards tongue-consciousness thus: 'This is mine, this I am, this is my self'. One regards tongue-contact thus: 'This is mine, this I am, this is my self'. One regards tongue-feeling thus: 'This is mine, this I am, this is my self'. One regards tongue-craving thus: 'This is mine, this I am, this is my self'.

20. (v) "One regards body thus: 'This is mine, this I am, this is my self'. One regards tangibles thus: 'This is mine, this I am, this is my self'. One regards body-consciousness thus: 'This is mine, this I am, this is my self'. One regards body-contact thus: 'This is mine, this I am, this is my self'. One regards body-feeling thus: 'This is mine, this I am, this is my self'. One regards body-craving thus: 'This is mine, this I am, this is my self'.

21. (vi) "One regards mind thus: 'This is mine, this I am, this is my self'. One regards mind-objects thus: 'This is mine, this I am, this is my self'. One regards mind-consciousness thus: 'This is mine, this I am, this is my self'. One regards mind-contact thus: 'This is mine, this I am, this is my self'. One regards mind-feeling thus: 'This is mine, this I am, this is my self'. One regards mind-craving thus: 'This is mine, this I am, this is my self'.

(The Cessation of Identity)

22. "Now, Students, this is the way leading to the cessation of identity. (i) One regards eye thus: 'This is not mine, this I am not, this is not my self'. One regards forms thus: 'This is not mine, this I am not, this is not my self'. One regards eye-consciousness thus: 'This is not mine, this I am not, this is not my self'. One regards eye-contact thus: 'This is not mine, this I am not, this is not my self'. One regards eye-feeling thus: 'This is not mine, this I am not, this is not my self'. One regards eye-craving thus: 'This is not mine, this I am not, this is not my self'.

23. (ii) "One regards ear thus: 'This is not mine, this I am not, this is not my self'. One regards sounds thus: 'This is not mine, this I am not, this is not my self'. One regards ear-consciousness thus: 'This is not mine, this I am not, this is not my self'. One regards ear-contact thus: 'This is not mine, this I am not, this is not my self'. One regards ear-feeling thus: 'This is not mine, this I am not, this is not my self'. One regards ear-craving thus: 'This is not mine, this I am not, this is not my self'.

24. (iii) "One regards nose thus: 'This is not mine, this I am not, this is not my self'. One regards odor thus: 'This is not mine, this I am not, this is not my self'. One regards nose-consciousness thus: 'This is not mine, this I am not, this is not my self'. One regards nose-contact thus: 'This is not mine, this I am not, this is not my self'. One regards nose-feeling thus: 'This is not mine, this I am not, this is not my self'. One regards nose-craving thus: 'This is not mine, this I am not, this is not my self'.

25. (iv) "One regards tongue thus: 'This is not mine, this I am not, this is not my self'. One regards flavors thus: 'This is not mine, this I am not, this is not my self'. One regards tongue-consciousness thus: 'This is not mine, this I am not, this is not my self'. One regards tongue-contact thus: 'This is not mine, this I am not, this is not my self'. One regards tongue-feeling thus: 'This is not mine, this I am not, this is not my self.' One regards tongue-craving thus: 'This is not mine, this I am not, this is not my self'.

26. (v) "One regards body thus: 'This is not mine, this I am not, this is not my self'. One regards tangibles thus: 'This is not mine, this I am not, this is not my self'. One regards body-consciousness thus: 'This is not mine, this I am not, this is not my self'. One regards body-contact thus: 'This is not mine, this I am not, this is not my self'. One regards body-feeling thus: 'This is not mine, this I am not, this is not my self'. One regards body-craving thus: 'This is not mine, this I am not, this is not my self'.

27. (vi) "One regards mind thus: 'This is not mine, this I am not, this is not my self'. One regards mind-objects thus: 'This is not mine, this I am not, this is not my self'. One regards mind-consciousness thus: 'This is not mine, this I am not, this is not my self'. One regards mind-contact thus: 'This is not mine, this I am not, this is not my self'. One regards mind-feeling thus: 'This is not mine, this I am not, this is not my self'. One regards mind-craving thus: 'This is not mine, this I am not, this is not my self'.

(The Underlying Tendencies)

28. (i) "Students, dependent on the eye and forms, eye-consciousness arises; the meeting of the three is eye-contact; with eye-contact as condition there arises [an eye-feeling] felt as pleasant or painful or neither-pleasant-nor-painful. When one is touched by a pleasant eye-feeling, if one delights in it, welcomes it, and remains holding to it, then the underlying tendency to lust lies within one. When one is touched by a painful eye-feeling, if one sorrows, grieves and laments, weeps beating one's breast and becomes distraught, then the underlying tendency to aversion lies within one. When one is touched by neither-pleasant-nor-painful eye-feeling, if one does not understand as it actually is the origination, the disappearance, the gratification, the danger, and the escape in regard to that eye-feeling, then the underlying tendency to ignorance lies within one. Students, that one shall here and now make an end of suffering without abandoning the underlying tendency to lust for pleasant eye-feeling, without abolishing the underlying tendency to aversion towards eye-painful feeling, without extirpating the underlying tendency to ignorance in regard to neither-pleasant-nor-painful eye-feeling, without abandoning ignorance and arousing true knowledge - this is impossible.

(ii) "Students, dependent on the ear and sounds, ear-consciousness arises: the meeting of the three is ear-contact; with ear-contact as condition there arises [an ear-feeling] felt as pleasant or painful or neither-pleasant-nor-painful. When one is touched by a pleasant ear-feeling, if one delights in it, welcomes it, and remains holding to it, then the underlying tendency to lust lies within one. When one is touched by a painful ear-feeling, if one sorrows, grieves and laments, weeps beating one's breast and becomes distraught, then the underlying tendency to aversion lies within one. When one is touched by neither-pleasant-nor-painful ear-feeling, if one does not understand as it actually is the origination, the disappearance, the gratification, the danger, and the escape in regard to that ear-feeling, then the underlying tendency to ignorance lies within one. Students, that one shall here and now make an end of suffering without abandoning the underlying tendency to lust for pleasant ear-feeling, without abolishing the underlying tendency to aversion towards painful ear-feeling, without extirpating the underlying tendency to ignorance in regard to neither-pleasant-nor-painful ear-feeling, without abandoning ignorance and arousing true knowledge - this is impossible.

(iii) "Students, dependent on nose and odors, nose-consciousness arises; the meeting of the three is nose-contact; with nose-contact as condition there arises [a nose-feeling] felt as pleasant or painful or neither-pleasant-nor-painful. When one is touched by a pleasant nose-feeling, if one delights in it, welcomes it, and remains holding to it, then the underlying tendency to lust lies within one. When one is touched by a painful nose-feeling, if one sorrows, grieves and laments, weeps beating one's breast and becomes distraught, then the underlying tendency to aversion lies within one. When one is touched by a neither-pleasant-nor-painful nose-feeling, if one does not understand as it actually is the origination, the disappearance, the gratification, the danger, and the escape in regard to that nose-feeling, then the underlying tendency to ignorance lies within one. Students, that one shall here and now make an end of suffering without abandoning the underlying tendency to lust for pleasant nose-feeling, without abolishing the underlying tendency to aversion towards painful nose-feeling, without extirpating the underlying tendency to ignorance in regard to neither-pleasant-nor-painful nose-feeling, without abandoning ignorance and arousing true knowledge - this is impossible.

(iv) "Students, dependent on tongue and flavors, tongue-consciousness arises; the meeting of the three is tongue-contact; with tongue-contact as condition there arises [a tongue-feeling] felt as pleasant or painful or neither-pleasant-nor-painful. When one is touched by a pleasant tongue-feeling, if one delights in it, welcomes it, and remains holding to it, then the underlying tendency to lust lies within one. When one is touched by a painful tongue-feeling, if one sorrows, grieves and laments, weeps beating one's breast and becomes distraught, then the underlying tendency to aversion lies within one. When one is touched by a neither-pleasant-nor-painful tongue-feeling, if one does not understand as it actually is the origination, the disappearance, the gratification, the danger, and the escape in regard to that tongue-feeling, then the underlying tendency to ignorance lies within one. Students, that one shall here and now make an end of suffering without abandoning the underlying tendency to lust for pleasant tongue-feeling, without abolishing the underlying tendency to aversion towards painful tongue-feeling, without extirpating the underlying tendency to ignorance in regard to neither-pleasant-nor-painful tongue-feeling, without abandoning ignorance and arousing true knowledge - this is impossible.

(v) "Students, dependent on body and tangibles, body-consciousness arises; the meeting of the three is body-contact; with body-contact as condition there arises [a body-feeling] felt as pleasant or painful or neither-pleasant-nor-painful. When one is touched by a pleasant body-feeling, if one delights in it, welcomes it, and remains holding to it, then the underlying tendency to lust lies within one. When one is touched by a painful body-feeling, if one sorrows, grieves and laments, weeps beating one's breast and becomes distraught, then the underlying tendency to aversion lies within one. When one is touched by a neither-pleasant-nor-painful body-feeling, if one does not understand as it actually is the origination, the disappearance, the gratification, the danger, and the escape in regard to that body-feeling, then the underlying tendency to ignorance lies within one. Students, that one shall here and now make an end of suffering without abandoning the underlying tendency to lust for pleasant body-feeling, without abolishing the underlying tendency to aversion towards painful body-feeling, without extirpating, the underlying tendency to ignorance in regard to neither-pleasant-nor-painful body-feeling, without abandoning ignorance and arousing true knowledge - this is impossible.

(vi) "Students, dependent on mind and mind-objects, mind-consciousness arises; the meeting of the three is mind-contact; with mind-contact as condition there arises [a mind-feeling] felt as pleasant or painful or neither-pleasant-nor-painful. When one is touched by a pleasant mind-feeling, if one delights in it, welcomes it, and remains holding to it, then the underlying tendency to lust lies within one. When one is touched by a painful mind-feeling, if one sorrows, grieves and laments, weeps beating one's breast and becomes distraught, then the underlying tendency to aversion lies within one. When one is touched by a neither-pleasant-nor-painful mind-feeling, if one does not understand as it actually is the origination, the disappearance, the gratification, the danger, and the escape in regard to that mind-feeling, then the underlying tendency to ignorance lies within one. Students, that one should here and now make an end of suffering without abandoning the underlying tendency to lust for pleasant mind-feeling, without abolishing the underlying tendency to aversion towards painful mind-feeling, without extirpating the underlying tendency to ignorance in regard to neither-pleasant-nor-painful mind-feeling, without abandoning ignorance and arousing true knowledge - this is impossible.

(The Abandonment of the Underlying Tendencies)

34. (i) "Students, dependent on the eye and forms, eye-consciousness arises; the meeting of the three is eye-contact; with eye-contact as condition there arises [an eye-feeling] felt as pleasant or painful or neither-pleasant-nor-painful. When one is touched by a pleasant eye-feeling, if one does not delight in it, welcome it, and remains holding to it, then the underlying tendency to lust does not lie within one. When one is touched by a painful eye-feeling, if one does not sorrow, grieve and lament, does not weep beating one's breast and become distraught, then the underlying tendency to aversion does not lie within one. When one is touched by a neither-pleasant-nor-painful eye-feeling, if one understands as it actually is the origination, the disappearance, the gratification, the danger, and the escape in regard to that eye-feeling, then the underlying tendency to ignorance does not lie within one. Students, that one shall here and now make an end of suffering by abandoning the underlying tendency to lust for pleasant eye-feeling, by abolishing the underlying tendency to aversion towards painful eye-feeling, by extirpating the underlying tendency to ignorance in regard to neither-pleasant-nor-painful eye-feeling, by abandoning ignorance and arousing true knowledge - this is possible.

35. (ii) "Students, dependent on the ear and sounds, ear-consciousness arises; the meeting of the three is ear-contact; with ear-contact as condition there arises [an ear-feeling] felt as pleasant or painful or neither-pleasant-nor-painful. When one is touched by a pleasant ear-feeling, if one does not delight in it, welcome it, and remain holding to it, then the underlying tendency to lust does not lie within one. When one is touched by a painful ear-feeling, if one does

not sorrow, grieve and lament, does not weep beating one's breast and become distraught, then the underlying tendency to aversion does not lie within one. When one is touched by a neither-pleasant-nor-painful ear-feeling, if one understands as it actually is the origination, the disappearance, the gratification, the danger, and the escape in regard to that ear-feeling, then the underlying tendency to ignorance does not lie within one. Students, that one shall here and now make an end to suffering by abandoning the underlying tendency to lust for pleasant ear-feeling, by abolishing the underlying tendency to aversion towards painful ear-feeling, by extirpating the underlying tendency to ignorance in regard to neither-pleasant-nor-painful ear-feeling, by abandoning ignorance and arousing true knowledge - this is possible.

36. (iii) "Students, dependent on the nose and odors, nose-consciousness arise: the meeting of the three is nose-contact; with nose-contact as condition there arises [a nose-feeling] felt as pleasant or painful or neither-pleasant-nor-painful. When one is touched by a pleasant nose-feeling, if one does not delight in it, welcome it, and remain holding to it, then the underlying tendency to lust does not lie within one. When one is touched by a painful nose-feeling, if one does not sorrow, grieve and lament, does not weep beating one's breast and become distraught, then the underlying tendency to aversion does not lie within one. When one is touched by a neither-pleasant-nor-painful nose-feeling, if one understands as it actually is the origination, the disappearance, the gratification, the danger, and the escape in regard to that nose-feeling, then the underlying tendency to ignorance does not lie within one. Students, that one shall here and now make an end of suffering by abandoning the underlying tendency to lust for pleasant nose-feeling, by abolishing the underlying tendency to aversion towards painful nose-feeling, by extirpating the underlying tendency in regard to neither-pleasant-nor-

painful nose-feeling, by abandoning ignorance and arousing true knowledge - that is possible.

37. (iv) "Students, dependent on the tongue and flavors, tongue-consciousness arises; the meeting of the three is tongue-contact; with tongue-contact as condition there arises [a tongue-feeling] felt as pleasant or painful or neither-pleasant-nor-painful. When one is touched by a pleasant tongue-feeling, if one does not delight in it, welcome it, and remain holding to it, then the underlying tendency to lust does not lie within one. When one is touched by a painful tongue-feeling, if one does not sorrow, grieve and lament, does not weep beating one's breast and become distraught, then the underlying tendency to aversion does not lie within one. When one is touched by a neither-pleasant-nor-painful tongue-feeling, if one understands as it actually is the origination, the disappearance, the gratification, the danger, and the escape in regard to that tongue-feeling, then the underlying tendency to ignorance does not lie within one. Students, that one shall here and now make an end of suffering by abandoning the underlying tendency to lust for pleasant tongue-feeling, by abolishing the underlying tendency to aversion towards painful tongue-feeling, by extirpating the underlying tendency to ignorance in regard to neither-pleasant-nor-painful tongue-feeling, by abandoning ignorance and arousing true knowledge - this is possible.

38. (v) "Students, dependent on body and tangibles, body-consciousness arises; the meeting of the three is body-contact; with body-contact as condition there arises [a body-feeling] felt as pleasant or painful or neither-pleasant-nor-painful. When one is touched by a pleasant body-feeling, if one does not delight in it, welcome it, and remain holding to it, then the underlying tendency to lust does not lie within one. When one is touched by a painful body-feeling, if one does not sorrow, grieve and lament, does not weep beating one's breast and becomes distraught, then the

underlying tendency to aversion does not lie within one. When one is touched by a neither-pleasant-nor-painful body-feeling, if one understands as it actually is the origination, the disappearance, the gratification, the danger, and the escape in regard to that body-feeling, then the underlying tendency to ignorance does not lie within one. Students, that one shall here and now make an end of suffering by abandoning the underlying tendency to lust for pleasant body-feeling, by abolishing the underlying tendency to aversion towards painful body-feeling, by extirpating the underlying tendency to ignorance in regard to neither-pleasant-nor-painful body-feeling, by abandoning ignorance and arousing true knowledge - this is possible.

39. (vi) "Students, dependent on mind and mind-objects, mind-consciousness arises; the meeting of the three is mind-contact; with mind-contact as condition there arises [a mind-feeling] felt as pleasant or painful or neither-pleasant-nor-painful. When one is touched by a pleasant mind-feeling, if one does not delight in it, welcome it, and remain holding to it, then the underlying tendency to lust does not lie within one. When one is touched by a painful mind-feeling, if one does not sorrow, grieve and lament, does not weep beating one's breast and become distraught, then the underlying tendency to aversion does not lie within one. When one is touched by a neither-pleasant-nor-painful mind-feeling, if one understands it as it actually is the origination, the disappearance, the gratification, the danger, and the escape in regard to that mind-feeling, then the underlying tendency to ignorance does not lie within one. Students, that one shall here and now make an end of suffering by abandoning the underlying tendency to lust for pleasant mind-feeling, by abolishing the underlying tendency to aversion for painful mind-feeling, by extirpating the underlying tendency to ignorance in regard to neither-pleasant-nor-painful mind-feeling, by

abandoning ignorance and arousing true knowledge - this is possible.

(Liberation)

40. (i) "Seeing thus, Students, a well-taught noble disciple becomes disenchanted with eye, disenchanted with forms, disenchanted with eye-consciousness, disenchanted with eye-contact, disenchanted with eye-feeling, disenchanted with eye-craving.

(ii) "He becomes disenchanted with the ear, disenchanted with sounds, disenchanted with ear-consciousness, disenchanted with ear-contact, disenchanted with ear-feeling, disenchanted with ear-craving.

(iii) "He becomes disenchanted with nose, disenchanted with odors, disenchanted with nose-consciousness, disenchanted with nose-contact, disenchanted with nose-feeling, disenchanted with nose-craving.

(iv) "He becomes disenchanted with tongue, disenchanted with flavors, disenchanted with tongue-consciousness, disenchanted with tongue-contact, disenchanted with tongue-feeling, disenchanted with tongue-craving.

(v) "He becomes disenchanted with body, disenchanted with tangibles, disenchanted with body-consciousness, disenchanted with body-contact, disenchanted with body-feeling, disenchanted with body-craving.

(vi) "He becomes disenchanted with mind, disenchanted with mind-objects, disenchanted with mind-consciousness, disenchanted with mind-contact, disenchanted with mind-feeling, disenchanted with mind-craving.

41. "Being disenchanted, he becomes dispassionate. Through dispassion [his mind] is liberated. When it is liberated, there comes the knowledge: 'It is liberated.' He understands: 'Birth is destroyed, the holy life has been lived, what had to be done has been done, there is no more coming to any state of being.' "

That is what the Blessed One said. The Students were satisfied and delighted in the Blessed One's words. Now while this discourse was being spoken, through not clinging the minds of sixty Students were liberated from the taints.

May suffering ones be suffering free
And the fear struck fearless be.
May the grieving shed all grief
And may all beings find relief.
May all beings share this merit
That we have thus acquired
For the acquisition of
All kind of happiness.
May beings inhabiting space and earth
Devas and Nagas of mighty power
Share in this merit of ours.
May they long protect
the Buddha's Dispensation.
Sādhu… Sādhu… Sādhu…

MN-21: The Simile of the Saw (Kakacūpama Sutta)

A Sutta on patience and forbearance full of interesting and memorable similes and stories. Each one of them should be considered carefully so that their full meaning is appreciated, especially with regard to one's own conduct. The story of Mistress Vedehikà and her maid Kàli is both amusing and instructive. Are we, like her, patient only when the going is good? Are we kind and gentle so long as we get no rough words from anyone, or while we are quite prosperous with nothing lacking? It is unexpected roughness of speech and hardships which are trials of our Dhamma-strength and will show us how deep Dhamma has permeated into our minds. Four similes (the great earth, drawing pictures on space, warming up the Ganges with a torch . and making a cured catskin bag crackle) follow which show what one's reaction should be to the five kinds of speech--'We shall abide with a mind of loving-kindness extending to that person, and we shall abide with an abundant, exalted, measureless mind of loving-kindness...' In each of these similes some impossibility is pictured, and it will be just as impossible for some with a measureless mind of loving-kindness, measureless as the great earth, space or the Ganges water, to become impatient or the great earth, space or the Ganges water, to become impatient or angry. People who come to annoy such a person would only 'reap weariness and disappointment'. Finally there is the famous simile of the saw and certainly if one can 'keep one's cool' when being dismembered, as the Bodhisatta did in his birth as the Preacher of Patience, one has reached the heights of patience founded on loving-kindness. This is the refrain which runs all through this Sutta: ' Now this is how you should train herein: "Our minds will remain unaffected and we shall utter no bad words, and we shall abide compassionate for welfare with a mind of loving-kindness and no inner hate".'[7]

Presented on 12th March 2010 at Dhamma Dena Vipassanā Center, Joshua Tree, California

BV: Here is the "Simile of the Saw."

1. THUS HAVE I HEARD. On one occasion the Blessed One was living at Sāvatthi in Jeta's Grove, Anāthapiṇḍika's Park.

---

[7] *Ibid.*

2. Now on that occasion the venerable Moliya Phagguna was associating over-much with nuns. He was associating so much with nuns that if any monk spoke dispraise of those nuns in his presence, he would become angry and displeased and would rebuke him; and if any monk spoke dispraise of the venerable Moliya Phagguna in those nuns' presence, they would become angry and displeased and would rebuke him. So much was the venerable Moliya Phagguna associating with nuns.

3. Then a certain monk went to the Blessed One, and after paying homage to him, he sat down at one side and told the Blessed One what was taking place.

4. Then the Blessed One addressed a certain monk thus: "Come, monk, tell the monk Moliya Phagguna in my name that the Teacher calls him." - "Yes, venerable sir," he replied, and he went to the venerable Moliya Phagguna and told him: "The Teacher calls you, friend Phagguna." - "Yes, friend," he replied, and he went to the Blessed One, and after paying homage to him, sat down at one side. The Blessed One asked him:

5. "Phagguna, is it true that you are associating over-much with nuns, that you are associating so much with nuns that if any monk speaks dispraise of those nuns in your presence, you become angry and displeased and rebuke him; and if any monk speaks dispraise of you in those nuns' presence, they become angry and displeased and rebuke him? Are you associating so much with nuns, as it seems?" - "Yes, venerable sir." - "Phagguna, are you not a clansman who has gone forth out of faith from the home life into homelessness?" - "Yes, venerable sir."

6. "Phagguna, it is not proper for you, a clansman gone forth out of faith from the home life into homelessness, to associate over-much with nuns. Therefore, if anyone speaks dispraise of those nuns in your presence, you should abandon any desires and any thoughts based on the household life. And herein you should train thus: 'My mind

will be unaffected, and I shall utter no evil words; I shall abide compassionate for his welfare, with a mind of loving-kindness, without inner hate.' That is how you should train, Phagguna.

"If anyone gives those nuns a blow with his hand, with a clod, with a stick, or with a knife in your presence, you should abandon any desires and any thoughts based on the household life. And herein you should train thus: 'My mind will be unaffected, and I shall utter no evil words; I shall abide compassionate for his welfare, with a mind of loving-kindness, without inner hate.' That is how you should train. If anyone speaks dispraise in your presence, you should abandon any desires and any thoughts based on the household life.

Now, what we're talking about is showing anger. That doesn't mean that if somebody is coming after a nun, that you would, as a monk, allow that to happen and go and step in front of them. It means that you won't start talking to the offenders with harsh language, with anger, or with hatred. One of the jobs of the monks is to see someone who is breaking a precept and stand in front of them so they'll stop. Ok? It doesn't mean you resort to violence, it just means you get in the way, so that they can change their mind, and you always try to get in the way with a mind of loving-kindness.

And herein you should train thus: 'My mind will be unaffected, and I shall utter no evil words; I shall abide compassionate for his welfare, with a mind of loving-kindness, without inner hate.' That is how you should train.

If anyone should give you a blow with his hand, with a clod, with a stick, or with a knife, you should abandon any desires and any thoughts based on the household life. And herein you should train thus: 'My mind will be unaffected, and I shall utter no evil words; I shall abide compassionate for his welfare, with a mind of loving-kindness, without inner hate.' That is how you should train, Phagguna."

7. Then the Blessed One addressed the monks thus: "Monks, there was an occasion when the monks satisfied my mind. Here I addressed the monks thus: 'Monks, I eat at a single session. By so doing, I am free from illness and affliction, and I enjoy health, strength, and a comfortable abiding. Come, Monks, eat at a single session.

A single session here means from sunup until high noon. Now, you'll notice when you take the precepts and I give you the precept not to eat after the noonday meal, that if you're still eating after twelve o'clock, you can continue eating, or if you're meditating and you don't start eating 'til after twelve o'clock you can still take your meal. I'm doing this for you so that you can, if your meditation is good and you don't want to stop, you can still get something to eat. We, monks, on the other hand have to eat before high noon.

Now, an interesting thing, I had a real adventure when I went to Australia, I went on the longest day of the year in the northern hemisphere, to the shortest day of the year in the southern hemisphere, and it was winter, and I came from Malaysia where it's eighty-five and beautiful all the time. I was so unprepared that I didn't even have a pair of socks. So I'm walking around and it's cold and it's raining and my feet are frozen to the bone, and I started thinking you know "My kingdom for a pair of socks" it was so cold. So I just kind of let that go and I went to a monastery and I sat in there for a little while, and the monk looks at my feet which were blue at the time, and he said, "Do you need a pair of socks?" - I said "It would be wonderful." So he gave me a pair of socks, and two days later somebody gave me two pair of socks, and a week later somebody gave me six pair of socks, and I can't turn the socks off to this day! I get socks like you can't believe. The last time we travelled somebody gave me twenty-four pair of socks! What in the world am I going to do with twenty-four pair of socks? And they were big enough to fit me. I have big feet, so I can't give them to somebody that's small. So they come up over here.

Anyway, the reason I went to Australia was because I wanted to practice meditation with a certain Thai monk that was traveling in Australia. And I developed a habit of only eating one meal a day. Now, we went through some real cold weather where the frost would be on the ground until about ten-thirty or eleven o'clock in the morning, and I never caught a cold. I was healthy the whole time. And then it got to be springtime, I spent three months in a forest in Australia, it got be springtime and I started coming out and hanging out with monks, they were eating breakfast, and I started taking a little bit here and a little bit there and before long I was eating breakfast. I Immediately caught a cold. So I cut out the breakfast and the cold went away, and that's why I eat one meal a day because if you fill your stomach up too much you get dull or sleepy, every time you eat a meal, it winds up taking about three hours. Preparing the food, eating the food, cleaning up after the food, digesting the food.

So by not eating three times a day, and not eating even two times a day, I have a lot more time to do the things that I want to do. So that's one of the reasons that the Buddha, he said "You know you're walking around sometimes at night, you go to these people's house for a meal, and you come home." But they didn't have flashlights then, so they walked without any light and sometimes they were falling in cesspools, and sometimes they'd run into a cow that was sleeping on the ground, that's a dangerous thing. And sometimes they would walk by somebody that had walked outside and it would scare them, they think you were some kind of ghost or something, so the Buddha said, "Don't eat in the evening." And the monks kind of grumbled at that. And then the Buddha said, "Don't eat in the afternoon, only eat in the morning." So what the Buddha is talking about here when he was very pleased or satisfied with his mind was when he told the monks

I eat at a single session. By so doing, I am free from illness and affliction, and I enjoy lightness, strength, and a

comfortable abiding. Come, Monks, eat at a single session. By so doing, you will be free from illness and affliction, and you will enjoy lightness, strength, and a comfortable abiding.' And I had no need to keep on instructing those monks; I had only to arouse mindfulness in them. Suppose there were a chariot on even ground at the crossroads, harnessed to thoroughbreds, waiting with goad lying ready, so that a skilled trainer, a charioteer of horses to be tamed, might mount it, and taking the reins in his left hand and the goad in his right hand, might drive out and back by any road whenever he likes. So too, I had no need to keep on instructing those monks; I had only to arouse mindfulness in them.

8. "Therefore, Monks, abandon what is unwholesome and devote yourselves to wholesome states,

What have I been talking about this whole retreat? Ok. Carry this with you. It's not just for being here, and then forget about it. Practicing meditation is an active way of life. You practice your generosity.

ST: Bhante, I'll just take a moment and tell you. I did the retreat last June, you said "take it with you," so I did. So first thing I did, I realized that I was talking to drivers on the road, and they weren't good things I was saying! So I said I shall talk to drivers just to start, but then that was like, you know, Recognize. And so then I decided "Oh, I'm going to wish them well on their journey," so I did. And my driving is a pleasure and I don't speed as much. And I'm a speeder, so that kind of time, and I don't talk to other drivers, and it's been the greatest practice of the 6R's. I think Los Angeles would completely change everywhere. And I let people go, and people signal "thank you;" you see it in the rear-view mirror. It's gratifying. So that's generosity, there you go!

BV: Yes, it is.

Being in Germany, you think of Germans as being hard, super-organized, and rather harsh, and they are the politest drivers. I mean, they're driving down the road, and it's kind of a narrow road, they pull off the road even if they get stuck, they'll pull off the road and let this other person pass. It's wonderful to watch the way they drive... until they get on the autobahn... Then things change a little bit.

So you practice your generosity with your speech, you practice generosity with your action. You letting other drivers in, is one way of doing that. You practice generosity with your inner mind. You think of people in kindly ways, wishing them well. Now, this particular sutta, the reason that I'm thinking that to do this whole sutta tonight is because this sutta is the way you practice life. Doesn't matter what somebody else says, it doesn't matter what somebody else does, you radiate loving-kindness to them, be gentle, you be kind, be helpful in whatever way you can be. Saying things to the clerks that are running the cash register in busy stores, saying things that are kind to them, that help them to smile gives them a brief moment of relief. And then they're kind to the next person.

At one time I was traveling all over the country when I first got back from Asia, I was going all over by bus, which everybody here goes "Bus, oh, how can you do that?," but it was high luxury to me. I was used to buses in Asia where everybody rides on the side that the door's on, so that the bus is tilting like this

ST: Why did they do that?

BV: Because there's so many people on the bus, they want to be able to get off when the bus stops. They're hanging on all over the place.

Being kind to people, letting them have your seat if they look like they're having problems, whatever, is really a nice thing. But I travelled all around the United States. I went to the Northeast, I went all the way down to Florida, I came all the way back, and I had to do my laundry one day. And I hate those little boxes that cost a buck, you know. So I went to a store and I bought a fairly big box of soap, but I didn't need a box. So I used the soap I wanted and a lady came in and she had just piles of clothes. And I said, "I bought this because it's cheaper than buying three little things, but there's a lot left over. How about if I give that to you?" - "Well, you can't do that." - "Yeah, I can. Go ahead and use it, please." So she used it and there was still some left. Another lady came in with a load of clothes; this lady gave the soap to that other lady. Yeah! It was wonderful to see how people can be kind if you practice a kind act to them first. That's what this practice is for.

Why do I want you to smile all the time? So you can give it away. And what are you doing when you do that? You're letting go of unwholesome states and developing wholesome states. You're practicing the 6R's. So you carry this with you as much as you can remember, but you can't criticize yourself when you forget. Ok? That's an unwholesome state too. So you forgive yourself for making a mistake and then start over again. That's what this practice attempts to show you.

For that is how you will come to growth, increase, and fulfillment in this Dhamma and Discipline.

So the whole of the Buddha's practice is practicing universal law of your generosity, your kindness, and your practice of keeping your precepts. Then when you sit in meditation, your meditation is good. You break your precepts, you can look forward to having not-so-good meditation.

Suppose there were a big sāla-tree grove near a village or town, and it was choked with castor-oil weeds, and some man would appear desiring its good, welfare, and protection. He would cut down and throw out the crooked saplings that robbed the sap, and he would clean up the interior of the grove and tend the straight well-formed saplings, so that the sāla-tree grove later on would come to growth, increase, and fulfillment. So too, Monks, abandon what is unwholesome and devote yourselves to wholesome

states, for that is how you will come to growth, increase, and fulfillment in this Dhamma and Discipline.

Harmonious Noble Eightfold Path

So the more you dwell on wholesome things, the more you practice wholesome speech, the more you practice wholesome actions, the more successful you become. We'll get back to this in just a moment. When I told you at the start of the retreat I was going to tell you about the Eightfold Path, and I never did it. So now's the time.

Everybody know the Eightfold Path? Right View, Right Thought [not Right Intention], Right Speech, Right Action, Right Livelihood, Right Effort, Right Mindfulness, Right Concentration. But I don't like those interpretations of those words. So for Right View; I changed that a little bit. I don't like that word "right." You use the word, "right" because if something is "right," then something is "wrong," and that turns the world into black and white, and it doesn't give you any room to adjust. Either it's "right" or it's "wrong." So instead of using the word "Right," I use the word "Harmonious."

Harmonious Perspective

So View is good, Understanding is good, but I like the word "Perspective." So when you practice Harmonious Perspective, you're practicing how to see everything that arises as part of an impersonal process. Your perspective is, when it's in harmony, your perspective is always seeing things as they actually are. Right? Seeing things as they actually are means being able to change your view on what arises in your mind at the time. By that I mean anger, dissatisfaction, fear, anxiety, sadness, boredom. Whatever arises, when you take it personally, your mind is not in harmony at that time. Your mind is fighting with what's arising in the present moment, and you get caught up in trying to think your feeling. The more you try to think a feeling away, the bigger and more intense that feeling becomes. So Harmonious Perspective means being able to change that view from the personal perspective [atta] to the impersonal perspective [anatta]. Now, you've been hearing me talk for a week. What is the fastest way to change your perspective? Ha ha!

Now, it's weird. It's a weird thing, and when I first realized that, I was a layman. I was living in Hawaii and This guy that was building the house and I decided to help him. I wasn't getting paid to do it, I just wanted to help, and hang out with this guy a little while. And before long he started thinking that he was my boss. And one day he said something and it really got me angry, and I walked away, and I'm walking and the heels of my feet are driving into the ground, and thinking that "You dumb so and so!" "He thinks he's my boss," and as soon as I said that to myself, I started laughing. I got "he thinks he's my boss" and as soon as I did that the anger went from "I'm mad and I don't like it" changed to "Well, there's this anger. Now, I can keep this anger if I want, but who wants to walk around angry? Let it go." Then I relaxed.

Every time you laugh with yourself about how crazy your mind is: "Welcome to the human race, we're all crazy." Every time you laugh with yourself, it changes your view, it changes your perspective of the world. And I chuckled for a little while and I saw how clear my mind was, how uplifted it was. And then I started doing it with all kinds of mental states that arose, and it happened every time.

When you laugh with yourself about how crazy you are and people say "Oh, that's really hard to do." And when they say that it makes me laugh, and they get mad at me for laughing, but I keep laughing and before long they're laughing too. And then no problem; I've been told on more than one occasion "this is serious." Isn't that funny? So how does your mind feel when you laugh? You're alert, you're bright, you're not attached to anything. That's Harmonious Perspective.

That's taking that unwholesome "I am that, and I'm going to make it the way I want it to be" to "Well, it's only that." Now, I can hold onto this and I can play around with it a little bit I suppose, but who wants to be mad? Let it go. And as soon as that happens, what happens in your mind? Your mind is all of a sudden back in the present moment, your mind is uplifted, and you're ready for whatever else arises. But if you get caught by an emotional state, and you don't laugh, you make yourself more and more miserable, you make yourself suffer. You're in control, you must remember that.

One of the things about Buddhism that I particularly admire is it makes everybody be responsible for themselves. I've been at meditation centers where everybody blames: "Oh, it's their fault," it's "Oh, I couldn't do it because of this." And I started calling that monastery "Blame Central." So you're not taking responsibility for your own actions and your own mind here. Come on! You can't blame your suffering on anyone else. Your suffering is yours, and I can't take your suffering away, but you can certainly take your own away. Right? By letting go of the unwholesome. Why is it unwholesome? Because "I am that." It's the false belief in a self: "I have this opinion, I have this concept, I have this idea, and boy I'm going to bend it to the end." That's how wars start, isn't it? You want to affect the world around you in a positive way? Smile, laugh, be happy. Don't blame anything else or anyone else for your problems. "It's his fault, he didn't do what he was going to say." Oops, who has their own anger, who's making themselves suffer? Who's causing problems for themselves that spreads out and makes it problems for other people because they're putting up with your negative mental state.

One time, and I was a layman again, it did happen, I was a layman for a lot of years afterward. Munindra-ji was a little Indian man that came to visit us in San Jose. And he used to talk about loving-kindness and how you can change the world, change everybody's view of the world by practicing loving-kindness. I didn't believe it. So I decided I was going to test this. So I went into a huge shopping mall.

There must have been thousands of people there. And I sat down on a bench and I had a sour face, and I kept it like that, looking really sad and dejected, miserable. And I looked at people around me and they had sour faces. They weren't smiling and happy, they were catching what I was doing. So I thought "Ok, we know that negative thoughts don't work. Change the world in a positive way, so let's try smiling." So as I was sitting on the bench, I decided to close my eyes, just started smiling and happy feeling and I started feeling "eyes" on me. You know when somebody looks at the back of your head, you feel them looking at you. So I thought, "I wonder what's happening." So I opened up my eyes, there were ten or twelve people standing around me looking at me smiling. And I thought "Oh, that worked"! I got up and left.

The more you smile the more you take the effort to wish people love and happiness and well-being and clear mind. The more you affect the world around you in a positive way, the more you're practicing Harmonious Perspective.

Harmonious Imaging

The next part of the Eightfold Path, they call it Right Thought, and I really don't like that definition, those words very much because it doesn't really describe what the next fold of the Eightfold Path is. So I call it Harmonious Imaging. And that sounds like, almost like imagination, but it's not. What kind of image do you hold in your mind? Do you hold an image of being happy? Do you hold an image of being prosperous? I know a lot of people talk about "wanting to be rich," but what kind of image do they hold in their mind? Being poor! Image yourself as being prosperous. Use that image and the universe will come running to you.

Now, a lot of people right now are out of work, twenty percent in some places in California. Well, you can get into

MN 21: The Simile of the Saw

that image of depression, or not. It's your choice. You hold an image of kindness. You hold an image of sending loving and kind thoughts to other people. And what did this sutta just say? It said when you let go of the unwholesome, and you stay with the wholesome, you become prosperous! The outside circumstances don't have anything to do with your prosperity. You have to do with your own prosperity.

The thing with Loving-Kindness Meditation that's really amazing; in the sutta in the Aṅguttara Nikāya, the Buddha talked about making merit. And he said, "You make an immeasurable amount of merit if you offer food to the saṅgha. You make a huge amount of merit by doing that. And you have to offer in the right way. It's not just throw it down on the table, like people that come and offer food for me. I tell them they have to use two hands and it has to be done with respect. Why? Because I'm helping you so that you make more merit. What kind of an image are you holding? When you offer food to saṅgha members, are you holding an image of happiness, then you're doing it right.

The next part is you make even more merit when you take the refuge in the Buddha, Dhamma and Saṅgha; more merit than feeding the monks. Isn't that amazing? You make more merit still when you take and keep the five precepts, without breaking them in your daily activities. Now, that's pretty impressive. When you take and keep the five precepts, what does that do if you're in business? People know you're not going to lie to them, you're not going to try take advantage from them, you're not going to steal from them. What kind of reputation do you have? Do you have a reputation of picking up the phone and somebody says something you don't like so you curse them out. Or do you have a little mirror on your desk that you can look and see whether you're smiling or not before the phone rings and be smiling and wishing them happiness while you're talking with them. What kind of an image are you holding? Uplifting, happy. You make more merit still by one thought moment of loving-kindness. How much merit have you made while you're here? Huh? Yeah?

ST: How do you explain merit?

BV: It has to do with karma. The merit you gain by doing good, uplifting, wholesome things, you gain merit by doing that. And when you gain merit, you're letting go of the unwholesome and you're developing the wholesome, and that's how you become more and more prosperous. Not only in this lifetime, but whenever. It always comes back to you. If you do things with an unwholesome mind, then you get demerit. That's the way karma works; it's action. Some people say that karma is intention; intention is part of it. You have to have good intentions to do good action, but if you only have the good intention and you don't have the action behind it, you don't get such good results from it. And you make the most merit by seeing and recognizing how Dependent Origination actually does work. This all comes back. The more you have this uplifted mind, what kind of images are you holding? Happy, uplifted images.

There's one lady around Ironton (Missouri) that is continually saying "I can't afford it, I don't have any money," and all she and her husband talk about is getting money, and they hold an image of poverty. They can do that if they want, but it's not as much fun as it is being around people that hold the idea of prosperity. When people hold an idea of prosperity, or an image of prosperity about themselves, they also do it for other people around them. So this just leads to more good, uplifting imaging.

The newspapers right now are trying to make everyone afraid, and they're being somewhat successful with it. So what do I suggest? Don't read the newspapers. Don't look at the news on TV. "Well I gotta find out what's happening." I'll tell you a secret, you don't. "Well, I have to be educated." Well anything that is major, that happened, you'll hear about it from somebody else. You don't have to read it in the newspaper. And most of the stuff you read in the newspaper, you have this idea that it's really important to know, and actually it isn't. The Queen Mum died. "Ok, how does that change my life?" Not at all. Russia fell, "How does that change my life?" How did I find out about it? Somebody told me two years after it happened. And how did that affect my life, my personal life? It didn't. "Well all this news is important to know." No, not really. How much more time would you have if you didn't read the newspapers, except for the funnies; let's not get over-carried away with it. Heh. The only thing that's really interesting in the newspapers, to be honest, is the weather and the funnies.

And people ask me about television, I tell them "Note, there's a real good thing, it's called a brick." Put it through the TV and look at how much more time you have to do things that are really worth doing. Especially now, since they went to digital. I mean, this is really amazing, the mind control things that are happening on the television. We have a TV at our Centre, we don't have any TV reception. And we have a radio at our Centre, and we don't have any radio reception. Ha.

When I go into town with somebody, when they're going into Wal-Mart, I get my news from the Enquiring Mind. All of the important stuff is there. I look at the front page, that's all I do! Ha Ha! But you get to see who's sick right now and who's suffering, whatever. But how much more time would you have if you didn't indulge in all of these things? It doesn't really affect your prosperity. Your prosperity is affected by your own mind, and your own image. The more you become in harmony with a positive image of yourself and other people around you, the more prosperous everyone becomes. It's a universal law. That's the way it works. When you image yourself being successful on the spiritual path then you will be.

Harmonious Communication

The next part of the Eightfold Path is called Right Speech and I don't like that so much, so I call it Harmonious

Communication. Who do you communicate with more than anybody else in the world? Yourself. How kind are you to yourself? Or how critical are you of yourself? If you're critical of yourself, who is developing an un-harmonious image? Who is developing a mind that is unwholesome by being critical?

Now, you heard me say a couple days ago you go through the day and you do fifty things that are absolutely brilliant. Everybody is happy around you, you're happy yourself, and you do one thing that might not be so good, at least in your own mind. It might not be bad to anybody else, but in your own mind. What do you wind up thinking about, over and over again? Are you practicing Harmonious Perspective at that time? Are you practicing Harmonious Imaging at that time? Are you practicing Harmonious Communication with yourself at that time? The more you can be kind to yourself, not critical, and forgive yourself for not being perfect.

I haven't met too many people that are yet, perfect, so. And your mindfulness improves. Your observation power of what you're doing with yourself, and to yourself, becomes easier to recognize. But this all takes practice. Ok? It takes practice. It's not an easy thing, we got a lot of old habits and we like to think about how we screwed up this or that. We didn't do it right, and how we should criticize ourselves for it. But when you see you're doing that, forgive yourself for not being perfect. Welcome to the real world. And make a determination not to do that again.

Harmonious Movement

The next part is called Right Action, I admit that I do change stuff around, and I call it Harmonious Movement.

Now, what is Harmonious Movement, especially when you're sitting? It's doing things at the right speed. It's doing it with the right amount of energy. You're not jerking your mind around, trying to make things better than they are, putting too much energy into things, causes yourself to get restless. Harmonious Movement in daily life means watching what you're doing while you're doing.

Harmonious Lifestyle

Now, the next part of the Eightfold Path I've really come to enjoy, and that's Right Livelihood. And the standard definition of Right Livelihood is: don't kill anything, don't sell any poisons, don't sell any guns, don't take slaves, things like that. Now, think about the Eightfold Path, the first time anybody heard it in this Buddha era, was in the first discourse that the Buddha gave. And he gave this discourse to five ascetics that were practicing purifying themselves. How much sense does that make? Not to sell poisons; they wouldn't do that. Not to sell weapons; they wouldn't do that. Not to take on slaves; well that doesn't make sense. I call it Harmonious Lifestyle. What kind of lifestyle are you leading? Is it a lifestyle that leads to happiness for you and others around you, or pain for you and others around you?

Now, there was a lady in Malaysia, she was absolutely great. She came to me one day and she said, "I'm having these terrible dreams. They're nightmares!" And I said, "Oh, why?" She said, "I don't know. It always happens right after I go to a horror movie show." So I said, "Well, don't do that anymore." And she said, "But I like it." And I said, "Then don't bother me about your nightmares! Leave me alone."

In the suttas, in one sutta in particular, in the Middle Length Sayings, it says that Right Speech, Right Action, and Right Livelihood, are part of morality. So when you're meditating you're automatically practicing your morality, so you don't need to pay attention to these three things. So they're effectively saying that the Eightfold Path is actually a lie, it's a Fivefold Path. And then you have people practicing straight Vipassanā and they'll tell you that the last one, the Right Concentration, where the definition is absolutely: the first jhāna, second jhāna, third jhāna, fourth jhāna. It doesn't really mean that and it can mean 'momentary concentration' [khanika samadhi]. So they're effectively picking that one away, so now they have a Fourfold Path.

But when the Buddha gave the discourse, the first time on the Eightfold Path, he was talking to monks about their practice, and how they can practice this. So there's no taking out, and I found out later that ever since the Buddha died, the scholars have divided the Eightfold Path into the Fivefold Path, and the three you don't need, and the practitioners are saying "No, no, no, no, no, no, you can't do that." And monks have been fighting about this for over two thousand years. And it will probably go on until the end of the Buddha Sāsana. But because I'm a practicing monk, I like to give you the whole Eightfold Path.

Practice Right Lifestyle, what does that mean? Keeping your mind uplifted, and doing things that help other people to have an uplifted mind. Saying things that are uplifting, saying things to other people that are uplifting. With your actions during the day, doing things that don't harm anybody else, or any other animal. In other words, live a very clear, aware life.

Some people like to read books that aren't necessarily good, and they can cause all kinds of confusion and that sort of thing. Sometimes some people like to get on the internet and look at things that aren't necessarily good to look at. What are they doing with their mind at that time? Is that Right Livelihood, spending your time looking at things that aren't necessarily good for you to be getting involved in?

Harmonious Practice

So the next part of the Eightfold Path, they call it Right Effort, and I can go along with Right Effort, but I still change it, and I call it Harmonious Practice, or four parts. Recognizing the unwholesome, letting go of the unwholesome and relaxing, bringing up the wholesome, smile, and come back to your object of meditation, and stay with that wholesome state. It's Right Effort, also this can be called the 6R's.

Harmonious Attention

The next part of the Eightfold Path, they call it Right Mindfulness, and mindfulness itself is a word that has a lot of confusion around it. Sister Khema showed me an article in the newspaper where there was four or five different teachers discussing what the definition of mindfulness was, and one person came out and said "Mindfulness is remembering to remember to remember!" What in the world are they talking about? So the sharper your observation power is in how mind's attention moves from one thing to another, the more clear Dependent Origination becomes, and so seeing it.

Now, a lot of people question me about whether I'm really teaching anything about insight, and the answer is "absolutely." While you're in the jhāna, I'm showing you what insight is all the time. I'm not showing you, you're showing yourself. The insights you get are recognizing how mind's attention moves, and you see these little links sometimes that are there, and you go "Oh, wow!" I actually wanted to call this meditation "Oh Wow," but I got vetoed on that one. So I want to make a magazine called "Oh, Wow," and have people write in and say "You know, I saw this in my meditation. I really had an 'Oh, wow!'"

The function of mindfulness is to remember, to remember what? To remember to observe how mind's attention moves. And what does it do when your mindfulness becomes good? It makes you look more and more closely to all of these little tiny things that arise and pass away, and how they do it. There's one student here that almost every time I see them I ask them if they'd "Have you 6R'ed that?," "Oh, there you go again." Ok, look more closely. That's the whole point of the 6R's, so you can look more closely with the clear mind, the bright mind, with an alert mind, with an uplifted mind, with a very clear Harmonious Perspective of how everything works.

Harmonious Collectedness

The last part of the Eightfold Path is Right Concentration, and "concentration" is a four-letter word, almost. So I call it Harmonious Collectedness. What's the definition of collectedness? Collectedness is a mind that's calm, very composed, very alert, and still. And that's what happens when you get into the jhānas, you go to different degrees of these things. The word Jhana has been misinterpreted for a very long time and there is some confusion about his word. There are actually two different types of jhana currently used in the world today. Jhana in the Buddha's teachings means a level or stage of understanding! Understanding what? Each different level of understanding is showing us ever more deeply how dependent origination actually occurs. This is called an Aware Jhana, it still has Full Awareness and Mindfulness in it.

The absorption jhana is the other kind of jhana practice that is most popular today. When a meditator practices this one-pointed jhana their mind becomes so deeply concentrated that it stays only on the object of meditation. Absorption concentration is done like this: The meditator puts their attention on an object of meditation for example, on the in-breath and the out breath. When a distraction occurs the instructions say to immediately let go of that distraction and come back to the breath. When mind begins to stay just on the sensation of the breath eventually there will arise some mental sign that in Pali is called a nimmita. This is like a shiny disk then the meditator is the let go of the breath and just stay with that mental disc. When mind becomes more concentrated the meditator will lose feeling in their body and the force of the concentration will stop all distractions from arising. This is when mind is truly absorbed. This state of concentration is called jhana, but it is not the same kind of jhana that the Buddha taught and practiced. This was what the Bodhisatta practiced when he was looking for Nibbana. He rejected this form of meditation because he saw that there was something not quite right with this form of jhana.

The kind of meditation that the Buddha taught and practiced is similar to the absorption concentration and it goes like this: instead of focusing exclusively on just the breath, the Buddha added one extra step into the meditation practice and this one extra step doesn't allow mind's attention to get deeply absorbed. This one extra step is the relax step. Why is it so important to use this relax step in meditation? First before telling you this I want to ask you a question. What is craving and how are we supposed to recognize it?

St: It is grasping!

BV: what does that mean?

ST: It is a kind of wanting and then holding on to something.

BV: No, that is not quite it. Craving is the "I want it" or the "I don't want it" mind. Craving always manifest as a tension or tightness in our mind and body.

When we use the relax step in our meditation practice we are letting go of craving and this is how we experience the Third Noble Truth! So you see every time we use the relax step we are purifying our mind. When a meditator relaxes, they will notice that mind becomes exceptionally clear and bright. Why is that? Because there is no craving in our mind or body.

So when the Buddha added this one extra step into the meditation he was showing us how to let go of craving. The Buddha did teach a form of aware jhana but this form has no craving in it. Plus, this type of aware jhana practice allows the meditator to know, see, and experience the Noble 8-Fold Path directly. The absorption type of jhana still has craving in it, but it is not seen or recognized.

This is a brief description of the differences between the 2 forms of jhana. Because the absorption jhana doesn't let go of craving practicing it can never lead the meditator to the experience of nibbana.

So that's the Eightfold Path.

End of Harmonious Noble Eightfold Path

When you're practicing the 6R's, you're practicing the entire Eightfold Path at that time. When you smile, you're practicing the entire Eightfold Path at that time. When you laugh, you're practicing the entire Eightfold Path at that time. See how simple it is?

Now, the whole point of talking about the Eightfold Path is to realize that the Buddha's path, the Middle Path, the way that he teaches, is to learn how to let go of the unwholesome identification with whatever arises, and bring up the harmonious perspective, the impersonal observation of all thoughts, all feeling, all sensation. Everything that happens in the world to you is an impersonal process. Doesn't have any concepts in it, doesn't have any opinions in it. Do you see things in an impersonal way; you're seeing things very clearly as being a process. Now, what good is that? When you see things as being part of a process, you've let go of suffering; you've let go of craving. And your mind becomes very content, at ease, and life starts to become fun.

Any time you're serious, guess who's there; "I am." Guess who's causing themselves suffering; "I am." Guess who tries to control; "I do." Because you're taking all of your thoughts and your feelings personally, and you're grabbing onto them with that craving, and the clinging is your opinions and your ideas and your concepts, and that big identification with all of those things. So when you start to see things in an impersonal way, your mind doesn't have any hindrances in it, and when it doesn't have any hindrances in it then guess who's not identifying with thoughts and feelings. Any time you have repeat thoughts, guess who's there; "I am." Who needs to 6R all this stuff, "I do."

9. "Formerly, Monks, in this same Sāvatthi there was a housewife named Vedehikā. And a good report about Mistress Vedehikā had spread thus: 'Mistress Vedehikā is gentle, Mistress Vedehikā is meek, Mistress Vedehikā is peaceful.' Now Mistress Vedehikā had a maid named Kāli, who was clever, nimble, and neat in her work. The maid Kāli thought: 'A good report about my lady has spread thus: "Mistress Vedehikā is gentle, Mistress Vedehikā is meek, Mistress Vedehikā is peaceful." How is it now, while she does not show anger, is it nevertheless actually present in her or is it absent? Or else is it just because my work is neat that my lady shows no anger though it is actually present in her? Suppose I test my lady.'

"So the maid Kāli got up late. Then Mistress Vedehikā said: 'Hey, Kāli!' - 'What is it, madam?' - 'What is the matter that you get up so late?' - 'Nothing is the matter, madam.' - 'Nothing is the matter, you wicked girl, yet you get up so late!' and she was angry and displeased, and she scowled. Then the maid Kāli thought: 'The fact is that while my lady does not show anger, it is actually present in her, not absent; and it is just because my work is neat that my lady shows no anger though it is actually present in her, not absent. Suppose I test my lady a little more.'

"So the maid Kāli got up later in the day. Then Mistress Vedehikā said: 'Hey, Kāli!' - 'What is it, madam?' - 'What is the matter that you get up later in the day?' - 'Nothing is the matter, madam.' - 'Nothing is the matter, you wicked girl, yet you get up later in the day!' and she was angry and displeased, and she spoke words of displeasure. Then the maid Kāli thought: 'The fact is that while my lady does not show anger, it is actually present in her, not absent; and it is just because my work is neat that my lady shows no anger though it is actually present in her, not absent. Suppose I test my lady a little more.'

"So the maid Kāli got up still later in the day. Then Mistress Vedehikā said: 'Hey, Kāli!' - 'What is it, madam?' - 'What is the matter that you get up still later in the day?' - 'Nothing is the matter, madam.' - 'Nothing is the matter, you wicked girl, yet you get up still later in the day!' and she was angry and displeased, and she took a rolling-pin, gave her a blow on the head, and cut her head.

"Then the maid Kāli, with blood running from her cut head, denounced her mistress to the neighbors: 'See, ladies, the gentle lady's work! See, ladies, the meek lady's work! See, ladies, the peaceful lady's work! How can she become angry and displeased with her only maid for getting up late? How can she take a rolling-pin, give her a blow on the head, and cut her head?' Then later on a bad report about Mistress Vedehikā spread thus: 'Mistress Vedehikā is rough, Mistress Vedehikā is violent, Mistress Vedehikā is merciless.'

10. "So too, Monks, some monk is extremely gentle, extremely meek, extremely peaceful, so long as disagreeable courses of speech do not touch him. But it is when disagreeable courses of speech touch him that it can be understood whether that monk is really kind, gentle, and peaceful. I do not call a monk easy to admonish who is easy to admonish and makes himself easy to admonish only for the sake of getting robes, alms food, a resting place, and medicinal requisites.

These are the four requisites. So a monk is not supposed to be kind and gentle just to try to get these things, with that kind of mind.

Why is that? Because that monk is not easy to admonish nor makes himself easy to admonish when he gets no robes, alms food, resting place, and medicinal requisites. But when a monk is easy to admonish and makes himself easy to admonish because he honors, respects, and reveres the Dhamma, him I call easy to admonish. Therefore, Monks, you should train thus: 'We shall be easy to admonish and make ourselves easy to admonish because we honor, respect, and revere the Dhamma.'

Do you understand the word "admonish?"

Discipline.

That is how you should train, Monks.

11. "Monks, there are these five courses of speech that others may use when they address you: their speech may be timely or untimely, true or untrue, gentle or harsh, connected with good or with harm, spoken with a mind of loving-kindness or with inner hate. When others address you, their speech may be timely or untimely; when others address you, their speech may be true or untrue; when others address you, their speech may be gentle or harsh; when others address you, their speech may be connected with good or with harm; when others address you, their speech may be spoken with a mind of loving-kindness or with inner hate. Herein, Monks, you should train thus: 'Our minds will remain unaffected, and we shall utter no evil words; we shall abide compassionate for their welfare, with a mind of loving-kindness, without inner hate. We shall abide pervading that person with a mind imbued with loving-kindness, and starting with him, we shall abide pervading the all-encompassing world with a mind imbued with loving-kindness, abundant, exalted, immeasurable, without hostility and without ill will.' That is how you should train, Monks.

Ok, that's what you're learning now. It doesn't matter what somebody else's opinion is. It doesn't matter if they give it to you, they give you information in a timely or untimely way. It doesn't matter if they give you hatred. It doesn't matter if they give you criticism. You radiate loving-kindness to that person. And remember that that's just the first part of the practice. Then you start radiating loving-kindness to all beings around you and the whole world.

Now, because of the nature of the way that I teach there is a lot of criticism that comes my way because I'm not teaching in the normal way. Yeah, that's what I do. Somebody in

Germany, they took one part of one thing that I said and they blew it up into some kind of major thing, and they were very critical of what I said. And somebody in Germany read it and they sent it to me and they said, "Oh, you gotta repeat, you gotta come back and you have to tell this person what's really true, and what's not true. You should rebuke what he said." And I said, "No, I don't care. I don't care what they say at all."

And there was another article that was written and it criticized me for saying that there's two different kinds of Nibbāna; mundane and supra-mundane, and they criticize me for it. I felt like writing back to them and say, "Criticize me some more." So many people came to our website it was unbelievable; Germany. There's no need to respond to that sort of thing, there's no need to respond to negative criticisms. Love the person and use that as the reminder to practice your Loving-Kindness Meditation to all beings. Keep your mind on loving-kindness as often as you possibly can during the day.

You will be well thought of, you will be prosperous. Now, prosperous doesn't necessarily mean have anything to do with material wealth. But other people say to you that, because you're kind, because you're helpful, because you can do things that will make life easier for other people, prosperity comes to you; that's being prosperous. Worry about not having material things? No thanks.

This year, I'm not really traveling all that much. I'm only going to be traveling twelve thousand miles to Vietnam, and it was about six thousand miles to Germany. So that's twenty-four thousand and twelve thousand, so that's... I'm only traveling thirty-six thousand miles and I don't have a dime. I don't have any money. Any money I get goes in the kitty to help build the monastery. I don't need any money, and I travel all around the world. How do I do that? By helping other people. By showing other people that I really appreciate them, and I wish them well by teaching Dhamma.

ST: Right. It's warm. It's more than warm.

BV: It's a lot warmer than where I live obviously, outside no. I have a wood burning stove in my kuti. We call it a kuti, it's actually a fairly big hut. And I don't like cold weather. I'm sorry, I just don't like it. I spent twelve years in Asia, I was in heaven because it was warm. So I build up the stove in the morning, get it up to about eighty degrees, and I'm fine. You know, I'm sitting around with a light robe on and, no problem. Everybody that comes in, they come in then "Oh, it's warm in here." And they keep their jackets on and they stood; before long they say "You know, it's really hot in here."

But I also, I have a loft. Now, it got cold, I mean it got down to three degrees, it was really cold. I go up to my loft, the fire goes out in the stove, but it stayed so nice and toasty up there, I had to kick blankets off. And then I'd come in, in the morning and say "You know, this is really nice and warm up there." It's too warm, I had to take some of the blankets off and everybody is giving me a very dirty look because they're all freezing. You know, they're wearing full-on clothes, four or five shirts, and a coat, and gloves, and they're cold.

So I get cold but I am prosperous because I hold positive thoughts. I don't get cold often. It's usually pretty warm when I need it to be.

12. "Monks, suppose a man came with a hoe and a basket and said: 'I shall make this great earth to be without earth.' He would dig here and there, strew the soil here and there, spit here and there, and urinate here and there, saying: 'Be without earth, be without earth!' What do you think, Monks? Could that man make this great earth to be without earth?" - "No, venerable sir." - "Why is that? Because this great earth is deep and immeasurable; it is not easy to make it be without earth. Eventually the man would reap only weariness and disappointment."

13. "So too, Monks, there are these five courses of speech that others may use when they address you: their speech may be timely or untimely, true or untrue, gentle or harsh, connected with good or with harm, spoken with a mind of loving-kindness or with inner hate. When others address you, their speech may be timely or untimely; when others address you, their speech may be true or untrue; when others address you, their speech may be gentle or harsh; when others address you, their speech may be connected, with good or with harm; when others address you, their speech may be spoken with a mind of loving-kindness or with inner hate.

Herein, Monks, you should train thus: 'Our minds will remain unaffected, and we shall utter no evil words; we shall abide compassionate for their welfare, with a mind of loving-kindness, without inner hate. We shall abide pervading that person with a mind imbued with loving-kindness, and starting with him, we shall abide pervading the all-encompassing world with a mind similar to the earth, abundant, exalted, immeasurable, without hostility and without ill will.' That is how you should train, Monks.

14. "Monks, suppose a man came with crimson, turmeric, indigo, or carmine and said: I shall draw pictures and make pictures appear on empty space.' What do you think, Monks? Could that man draw pictures and make pictures appear on empty space?" - "No, venerable sir." - "Why is that? Because empty space is formless and non-manifested; it is not easy to draw pictures there or make pictures appear there. Eventually the man would reap only weariness and disappointment."

15. "So too, Monks, there are these five courses of speech that others may use when they address you: their speech may be timely or untimely, true or untrue, gentle or harsh, connected with good or with harm, spoken with a mind of loving-kindness or with inner hate. When others address you, their speech may be timely or untimely; when others

address you, their speech may be true or untrue; when others address you, their speech may be gentle or harsh; when others address you, their speech may be connected, with good or with harm; when others address you, their speech may be spoken with a mind of loving-kindness or with inner hate. Herein, Monks, you should train thus: 'Our minds will remain unaffected, and we shall utter no evil words; we shall abide compassionate for their welfare, with a mind of loving-kindness, without inner hate. We shall abide pervading that person with a mind imbued with loving-kindness, and starting with him, we shall abide pervading the all-encompassing world with a mind similar to empty space, abundant, exalted, immeasurable, without hostility and without ill will.' That is how you should train, Monks.

16. "Monks, suppose a man came with a blazing grass-torch and said: 'I shall heat up and burn away the river Ganges with this blazing grass-torch.' What do you think, monks? Could that man heat up and burn away the river Ganges with that blazing grass-torch?" - "No, venerable sir." - "Why is that? Because the river Ganges is deep and immense; it is not easy to heat it up or burn it away with a blazing grass-torch. Eventually the man would reap only weariness and disappointment.

17. "So too, Monks, there are these five courses of speech that others may use when they address you: their speech may be timely or untimely, ...

As you notice there's a lot of repeating in this one. He wanted it to sink in really deeply. Hold the mind that is attentive and let it sink in and you'll gain benefit from this. If you judge it, "I've already heard this, I don't need to hear it more than once," what kind of an uplifted mind are you holding at that time? What kind of a wholesome mind are you holding at that time? Be attentive.

Their speech may be timely or untimely, true or untrue, gentle or harsh, connected with good or with harm, spoken

with a mind of loving-kindness or with inner hate. When others address you, their speech may be timely or untimely; when others address you, their speech may be true or untrue; when others address you, their speech may be gentle or harsh; when others address you, their speech may be connected, with good or with harm; when others address you, their speech may be spoken with a mind of loving-kindness or with inner hate. Herein, Monks, you should train thus: 'Our minds will remain unaffected, and we shall utter no evil words; we shall abide compassionate for their welfare, with a mind of loving-kindness, without inner hate. We shall abide pervading that person with a mind imbued with loving-kindness, and starting with him, we shall abide pervading the all-encompassing world with a mind similar to the river Ganges, abundant, exalted, immeasurable, without hostility and without ill will.' That is how you should train, Monks.

18. "Monks, suppose there were a catkin bag that was rubbed, well rubbed, thoroughly well rubbed, soft, silky, rid of rustling, rid of crackling, and a man came with a stick or a potsherd and said: 'There is this catkin bag that is rubbed, well rubbed, thoroughly well rubbed, soft, silky, rid of rustling, rid of crackling. I shall make it rustle and crackle.' What do you think, Monks? Could that man make it rustle or crackle with the stick or the potsherd?" - "No, venerable sir." - "Why is that? Because that catkin bag being rubbed, well rubbed, thoroughly well rubbed, soft, silky, rid of rustling, rid of crackling, it is not easy to make it rustle or crackle with the stick or the potsherd. Eventually the man would reap only weariness and disappointment."

19. "So too, Monks, there are these five courses of speech that others may use when they address you: their speech may be timely or untimely, true or untrue, gentle or harsh, connected with good or with harm, spoken with a mind of loving-kindness or with inner hate. When others address you, their speech may be timely or untimely; when others

address you, their speech may be true or untrue; when others address you, their speech may be gentle or harsh; when others address you, their speech may be connected with good or with harm; when others address you, their speech may be spoken with a mind of loving-kindness or with inner hate. Herein, Monks, you should train thus: 'Our minds will remain unaffected, and we shall utter no evil words; we shall abide compassionate for their welfare, with a mind of loving-kindness, without inner hate. We shall abide pervading that person with a mind imbued with loving-kindness; and starting with him, we shall abide pervading the all-encompassing world with a mind similar to a catkin bag, abundant, exalted, immeasurable, without hostility and without ill will.' That is how you should train, Monks.

20. "Monks, even if bandits were to sever you savagely limb by limb with a two-handled saw, he who gave rise to a mind of hate towards them would not be carrying out my teaching. Herein, Monks, you should train thus: 'Our minds will remain unaffected, and we shall utter no evil words; we shall abide compassionate for their welfare, with a mind of loving-kindness, without inner hate. We shall abide pervading them with a mind imbued with loving-kindness; and starting with them, we shall abide pervading the all-encompassing world with a mind imbued with loving-kindness, abundant, exalted, immeasurable, without hostility and without ill will.' That is how you should train, Monks.

21. "Monks, if you keep this advice on the simile of the saw constantly in mind, do you see any course of speech, trivial or gross, that you could not endure?" - "No, venerable sir." - "Therefore, Monks, you should keep this advice on the simile of the saw constantly in mind. That will lead to your welfare and happiness for a long time."

That is what the Blessed One said. The monks were satisfied and delighted in the Blessed One's words.

Great advice! Absolutely brilliant because it keeps your mind focused on loving-kindness all the time. Now, what do you think about when you go from your house to your car? Ho hum, think about this, think about that. Why don't you 6R those thoughts and radiate some loving-kindness? When you have to wait in line at the grocery store, what are you doing with your mind? Looking at your watch, "I gotta get going, this is taking so long." Well, you know what everybody else's mind is doing, so why don't you take the time to radiate loving-kindness at that time?

There's a lot of little keys, a lot of little things that you do in the day that if you make the determination that: "Every time I'm going to do this action, every time I open up this drawer, every time I open up a door, that that's going to be the reminder for me to practice loving-kindness to all beings, and radiate that happy feeling." What do you wind up doing with your mind most of the day?

Remember that the Buddha said, "What you think and ponder on, that's the inclination of your mind." The more you think smiling happy thoughts, the more your mind will tend to have smiling happy thoughts. So what to do? When you get out of here, the retreat's not done. This is only the first part of the retreat. The real retreat's out there. The one that's going to test you in all kinds of ways. Remember this sutta.

May suffering ones be suffering free
And the fear struck fearless be.
May the grieving shed all grief
And may all beings find relief.
May all beings share this merit
That we have thus acquired
For the acquisition of
All kind of happiness.
May beings inhabiting space and earth
Devas and Nagas of mighty power
Share in this merit of ours.
May they long protect
the Buddha's Dispensation.
Sādhu… Sādhu… Sādhu…

About the Author

Most Venerable Bhante Vimalaraṁsi Mahāthera was born in New York and grew up in Chicago and California. He did his first Insight meditation retreat in California at the age of 28, and subsequently became a Buddhist monk in 1986 because of his keen interest in meditation. He went on to Burma in 1988 to practice intensive meditation at the famous meditation center Mahasi Yeiktha in Rangoon. Bhante then traveled to Malaysia and practiced Loving-Kindness Meditation extensively for 6 months.

In 1990, Bhante went back to Burma for more Vipassanā meditation, for 14 to 16 hours a day, at Chanmyay Yeiktha in Rangoon. He practiced for 2 years, sometimes sitting in meditation for as long as 7 to 8 hours a sitting. After two years of intensive meditation and experiencing what was said to be the final result, he became very disillusioned with the straight Vipassanā method and left Burma to continue his search.

He went to Malaysia again and began teaching Loving-Kindness Meditation. In 1995, Bhante was invited to live and teach at Brickfields, the largest Theravādan monastery in Malaysia directed by K. Sri Dhammanada. There, K. Sri was so impressed by Bhante's knowledge that he had him take over some of his talk and teaching schedule at the temple.

Bhante subsequently met with a venerable Sri Lankan monk who told him that he was teaching meditation correctly, but to stop referencing the Vissudhi Magga and just use the Suttas.

Thus, Bhante then began to study the sutta texts more thoroughly and to practice meditation according to these texts. After a three month self-retreat, he came back to Malaysia and wrote a book on the Mindfulness of Breathing called "The Ānāpānasati Sutta: A Practical Guide to Mindfulness of Breathing and Tranquil Wisdom Meditation." This book has been revised and has now been published as "The Breath of Love."

Bhante Vimalaraṁsi came back to the USA in 1998, and he has been teaching meditation throughout the country since then. In 2003 he co-founded the United International Buddha-Dhamma Society, UIBDS. UIBDS supports the Dhamma Sukha Meditation Center located near Annapolis, Missouri, USA, where he teaches meditation from May through October each year. The balance of the year is spent traveling around the world giving retreats and talks. He is the USA representative to the World Buddhist Council of Kobe Japan and was installed in 2007.

If you would like to, you can go to Bhante's website for more information and listen to more of his talks. You may see videos of his talks on youtube.com as well as at dhammasukha.org.

Index of Suttas

Suttas are taken from the Majjhima Nikāya, Translation by Bhikkhu Bodhi, © 1995, 2001, 2005 Wisdom Publications:

- MN-20: The Removal of Distracting Thoughts (Vitakkasanthāna Sutta), page 211
- MN-10: The Foundations of Mindfulness (Satipaṭṭhāna Sutta), page 145
- MN-111: One By One As They Occurred (Anupada Sutta), page 899
- MN-38: The Greater Discourse on the Destruction of Craving (Mahātanhāsankhaya Sutta), page 349
- MN-135: The Shorter Exposition of Action (Cūḷakammavibhanga Sutta), page 1053
- MN-95: With Cankī (Cankī Sutta), page 775
- MN-148: The Six Sets of Six (Chachakka Sutta), page 1129
- MN-21: The Simile of the Saw (Kakacūpama Sutta), page 217

Glossary – Frequent Substitutions

As Bhante reads through the text he substitutes some terms with what he believes to be a better representation of the Pāli and the original meaning intended by the Buddha.

In English text:

Re-translated as:

Applied and
    sustained thought
Bhikkhu
Concentration
Contemplate
Eight Fold Path
Enlightenment
Pleasure
Rapture
Volition
Zeal

Thinking and
    examining thought
Monk (Bhante prefers)
Collectedness
Observe
Harmonious Path
Awakening
Happiness
Joy
Formation
Enthusiasm

Made in the USA
Charleston, SC
12 December 2012